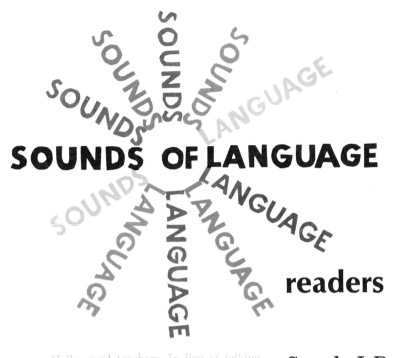

SOUNDS OF LANGUAGE

readers

Hello, good teachers. In lieu of talking with you face-to-face, we are relying on man's miraculous invention, print. These annotations, like this reader, are an invitation for all of us to rejoice in the act of language and how it influences man's becoming.

The SOUNDS OF LANGUAGE program is designed to enhance a child's use of language as a speaker, a listener, a writer and a reader, and to give you teachers both the opportunities and the skills for bringing dimensions into the teaching of reading that conventional programs have precluded.

Our essay at the back of this book and the page-by-page annotations are not prescriptive. Nor are they ritual. They offer you up-to-date information about language, about human growth and about classroom organization. They offer a view of the classroom as a launching pad to human greatness, both yours and the children's.

This book is affectionately dedicated to my friend
M. JERRY WEISS
whose humanness and linguistic insight
have enriched teacher education

TEACHER'S EDITION

The pupil texts are a collection of stories, poems, songs, essays, pictures and paintings that celebrate the human yen for beauty, excitement, drama, well-being, and pleasure. Once you have a rich familiarity with yours and the children's materials in the SOUNDS OF LANGUAGE program, you will have become, we believe, another link in mankind's attempt to stay the chaos of an increasingly hostile world environment.

We believe you will also discover that, without becoming a slave to a teacher's guide, you can fashion day-by-day language encounters that help children claim their human heritage as successful readers.

SOUNDS OF MYSTERY

The very title of this book conjures up the notion of storytelling.

BY BILL MARTIN JR.
IN COLLABOR-ATION WITH PEGGY BROGAN

Holt, Rinehart and Winston, Inc., New York, Toronto, London, Sydney

Acknowledgments

The Author and Holt, Rinehart and Winston, Inc., thank the following authors, publishers, agents and parties whose help and permissions to reprint materials have made this book possible. If any errors in acknowledgments have occurred, the errors were inadvertent and will be corrected in subsequent editions as they are realized.

Aaron Ashley, Inc., New York, for the painting "The Smoke Signal," on page 166.

Abelard-Schuman Ltd., New York, for "Pussy-Willows," reprinted from *Runny Days, Sunny Days,* by Aileen Fisher, by permission of Abelard-Schuman Ltd. All rights reserved. Copyright © 1958 by Aileen Fisher.

Addison-Wesley, Inc., for "Beans, Beans, Beans," from *Hooray for Chocolate,* by Lucia and James L. Hymes, Jr. Copyright © 1960 by the authors. Permission granted by the publisher, Addison-Wesley, Inc.

Atheneum House, Inc., for "Alligator on the Escalator," from *Catch a Little Rhyme.* Copyright © 1966 by Eve Merriam. Used by permission of Atheneum Publishers.

Atheneum House, Inc., for *Teevee,* by Eve Merriam from *Catch a Little Rhyme.* Copyright © 1966. Used by permission of Atheneum Publishers.

Burke and Van Heusen, Inc., for "Swinging on a Star" by Johnny Burke. © 1944 by Burke and Van Heusen, Inc.

Thomas W. Crowell Co., for "Did You Feed My Cow?"

John Day Company, Inc., for "Stop-Go" by Dorothy Baruch. Reprinted from *I Like Automobiles,* by Dorothy Baruch. Copyright © 1931 by Dorothy Baruch. Used by permission of Bertha Klauser, International Literary Agency, Inc.

Doubleday & Company, Inc., Publishers, for "archy, the cockroach, speaks" from *the lives and times of archy and mehitabel,* by Don Marquis. Copyright © 1927 by Doubleday & Company, Inc. Reprinted by permission of the publisher.

Dover Publications, Inc., for "Devilish Mary" from *American Folk Tales & Songs* by Richard Chase. Dover Publications, Inc., New York, 1956. Reprinted through permission of the publisher.

Gerald Duckworth & Co., Ltd., for "Overheard on a Saltmarsh," from *Collected Poems,* by Harold Monro, published by Gerald Duckworth & Co., Ltd. Courtesy Mrs. Alida Monro.

Harvey Dunn Collection at South Dakota State College, for the three paintings by Harvey Dunn on pages 232-233.

E. P. Dutton, Inc., for "Blue," from *Poems of Earth and Space,* by Claudia Lewis. Copyright © 1967 by Claudia Lewis. Reprinted by permission.

E. P. Dutton & Co., Inc. for "Giant Thunder," from the book, *The Blackbird in the Lilac,* by James Reeves. Published 1959 by E. P. Dutton & Co., Inc., and reprinted with their permission.

E. P. Dutton, Inc., for "Spring Rain." Copyright 1941 by Marchette Chute. From the book, *Around and About,* by Marchette Chute. Copyright © 1957 by E. P. Dutton & Co., Inc., and reprinted with their permission.

Lothrop, Lee & Shepard Co., Inc., for "White Snow, Bright Snow." Copyright © 1947 by Lothrop, Lee and Shepard Company, Inc., and used with their permission.

The Macmillan Company, for "A Bat Is Born," from *The Bat Poet,* by Randall Jarrell and illustrated by Maurice Sendak. Copyright © 1963, 1964 by The Macmillan Company. Reprinted by permission of the publisher.

Lothrop, Lee & Shepard Co., for the painting on pages 350-351 from the book *Coyote Cry.*

Helen Irish May, for permission to use her poem, "The Robin."

Esther MacBain Meeks, 2911 Oak Street, Terre Haute, Indiana, for her short story, "The Web of Winter."

Mary Britton Miller, for the poem "Foal."

Natural History Magazine, The Journal of the American Museum of Natural History, New York, for the paintings by Basil Ede, accompanying the picture story herein, "Birds in a Gallery," from the December, 1967 issue of *Natural History.*

Hugh Noyes, for the poem, "Daddy Fell into the Pond" by Alfred Noyes, on page 90. Used by permission.

Oxford University Press, Inc., London, Publishers, for "Giant Thunder," from the book, *The Blackbird in the Lilac,* by James Reeves.

Laurence Pollinger, Ltd., Authors' Agents, London, for the selection "But Toads Don't Bite," from "The Pomegranate Tree" from the book, *My Name Is Aram,* by William Saroyan, published by Faber and Faber, Ltd.

Laurence Pollinger, Ltd., Authors' Agents, London, for "The Last Word of a Bluebird," from *Complete Poems of Robert Frost,* published by Jonathan Cape Ltd. Proprietors: Holt, Rinehart and Winston, Inc.

Laurence Pollinger Ltd., Authors' Agents, London, for "October," from *Complete Poems of Robert Frost,* published by Jonathan Cape Ltd. Proprietors: Holt, Rinehart and Winston, Inc.

Rand McNally & Company, for "The Conjure Wives," from *Happy Holidays,* by Francis Wicke. Copyright © 1921.

Charles Scribner's Sons, for "Night Wind," from *Poems of Childhood,* by Eugene Field, published by Charles Scribner's Sons.

Shel Silverstein, for "Boa Constrictor," Copyright © 1966 by Shel Silverstein.

The Society of Authors, Representative for The Literary Trustees of Walter de la Mare, for "All but Blind," by Walter de la Mare.

St. Regis Paper Company for "Trees Alone Do Not Make a Forest," adapted from copyrighted corporate advertising material of the St. Regis Paper Company with their kind permission.

Williamson Music, Inc., New York, and Williamson Music Ltd., London, for "My Favorite Things," from *The Sound of Music.* Copyright © 1959 by Richard Rodgers and Oscar Hammerstein II. Used by permission of the publisher.

Acknowledgment is made to Judy Kopecky, Paul Waldman, Allen Moss and Lex Caiola who prepared the front matter.

Acknowledgment is also made to Betty Jean Martin for permission to use the character, Noodles the Ghost, in this edition of *Sounds of Mystery.*

And no acknowledgment list would be complete without special thanks and appreciation to Lydia Vita, Mel Rohr and Victor Hernandez for their skilled preparation of this book for delivery to the printer.

TABLE OF CONTENTS
PART I
FIGURING OUT HOW READING WORKS

In introducing *Sounds of Mystery,* invite the children to respond to the cover, endsheet, title page, and Table of Contents—with no preconceived notions about what they should discover. As they come upon the Table of Contents and find titles that intrigue them, encourage them to look back in the book to see what those selections actually look like. This is the best possible kind of readiness for reading a new book. And if the class should find a selection that they want to read immediately, permit them to do so. The next time they come upon it in the natural progression of the program, they will greet it like an "old friend" to be read with new insight and interest.

The Table of Contents reveals both the literary range of the selections and the plan of organization that molds them into a reading program. Part I of the book gives children new insights into the whole and pleasurable act of reading. Part II invites children to respond to reading in a variety of ways that enlighten and brighten the original reading encounter. It is this latter aspect of reading that is so often overlooked in programs that focus primarily on narrow comprehension and skillbuilding requirements. Children who have come to dislike reading most likely have been trapped in the rigidities of reading instruction that centers on arbitrary skills and drills at the expense of the more pleasurable and insightful dimensions of reading. Reading in our culture can and should be a natural response to life, and it is the main purpose of this program to help children acquire the kind of reading habits that support their self-respect and eagerness to be human.

The titles in red are introductory essays that organize the selections that follow around some important aspect of reading. While it is important for you to know the overall organization of the book, don't expect the children to get it before they've lived through the actual reading experiences. It's after they

PART II
RESPONDING TO READING

have read and experienced a unitized portion of the book that they can begin to sense the larger organization of the program. And after they have completed the book, they can reread the Table of Contents as a truly comprehensive symbolic structure of the concept of reading they have internalized. Their eventual understanding of how *Sounds of Mystery* is organized enlivens and heightens their growing awareness of language and how it works.

PART I

Children who come to know and love Noodles will be pleased to know that this friendly ghost has grown into a rogue who badgers Bill Martin while helping him make linguistic insights available. Read the dialogue as *dialogue*. Let it be fun, all the while you and the children discuss the implications for unlocking print. Don't be surprised if the children want to write to Bill Martin or Noodles to argue about points he is making, because Noodles invites this kind of reader-author participation. The children's letters will be answered. Moreover, the children will recognize that Noodles has great affection for Bill Martin just as they have for you even when they disagree. This is the healthiest climate we can provide for learning.

This first dialogue simply sets the stage for the subsequent meetings of Noodles and Bill Martin, and invites children to become personally involved in both the organization of the book and the methodology.

Bill: Hello, boys and girls.
         This is your friend, Bill Martin.

Noodles: Oodeley, oodeley.

Bill: And Noodles is here.
         Noodles where are you?
         I can't see you.

Noodles: That's because I'm a ghost.

Bill: Where are you, Noodles?

Noodles: I'm hiding.

Bill: Noodles, now stop this foolishness.
         These boys and girls
         are waiting to meet you.

Noodles: I already did meet them.

Bill: Then come say hello to your friends.

Noodles: Tell me one thing.
         Are you going to talk a lot again
         and go on and on
         until I'm so tired I can't stand it?

Bill: Oh, Noodles, I never talk that much.

Noodles: You don't think so because
         you don't have to listen to you, Bill Martin.

Bill: Then I promise, I'll not talk too much.

Noodles: All right, then. Here I come . . .

APPEAR
APPEAR
APPEAR
APPEAR
APPEAR
APPEAR

Here I am.
Hello, boys and girls.
Hello, Bill Martin.

Bill: Good morning, Noodles.
Isn't it exciting to be starting a new book?

Noodles: Yes, and this is my favorite book
because it's spooky
and I'm a ghost.

Bill: *Sounds of Mystery.*

Noodles: Bill, you're talking too much.

Bill: Am I, boys and girls?

Noodles: They can't answer you.

Bill: Why not.

Noodles: Because I asked them not to but
you're talking too much.

Bill: Oh, Noodles.

Noodles: I think I'll go now.

Bill:	But could I ask you one question, Noodles? Just one.
Noodles:	Well, maybe, just one.
Bill:	Will you tell the boys and girls what this little rendezvous is all about?
Noodles:	This little what?
Bill:	This little meeting we're having.
Noodles:	I don't know. I suppose because it's school.
Bill:	No, Noodles, it's becau . . .
Noodles:	Goodbye, Bill. Goodbye.
Bill:	Please help me, Noodles. Please.
Noodles:	Pretty please with sugar on it?
Bill:	Yes, pretty please with sugar on it.
Noodles:	All right, Bill Martin. Boys and girls, we're here right now to invite you to *Sounds of Mystery*, where everything squeaks and haunts and blows and blusters and laughs and sings and dances and coos and prods and pries and pushes and pulls . . . and talks too much.
Bill:	This book will help you know what you already know

about reading
but perhaps didn't know
that you knew.

Noodles: Say, that really is my big problem.
I know everything
but just can't remember it.

Bill: *Sounds of Mystery*
is divided into two parts.
Part I which we've just begun
is "Figuring Out How Reading Works."
Part II is "Responding to What You Read."

Noodles: Hey, Bill Martin,
that sounds pretty dull.
I think I'll go now.
But before I go
just so you won't sit here
and talk talk talk, Bill Martin,
I'm going to turn you into a blot.

Bill: Oh, no, Noodles. Not right now.

Noodles: Hokus pokus diddeley dokus ...
Bill Martin you're changing into a blot.

Bill: Oh, no, No - o - o - o - - - - -

Noodles: There! Bill Martin is now a blot!
We've got to take care of
one another, right, boys and girls?
So goodbye.
Oodeley, oodeley.

These antics of Noodles come alive on cassette recordings that accompany this program. So do the language learnings and the love of literature that Bill Martin engenders. The recordings feature Noodles, Bill, and the masterful guitarist, Al Caiola whom you've probably heard frequently on radio and TV.

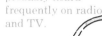

On A Wonderful Day Like Today

I defy any cloud to appear in the sky,

Dare any raindrop to plop in my eye

On a wonderful day like today.

On a wonderful morning like this.

When the sun is as big as a yellow balloon,

Even the sparrows are singing in tune

On a wonderful morning like this.

On a morning like this I could kiss ev'rybody

I'm so full of love and goodwill.

Let me say furthermore

I'd adore ev'rybody to come and dine.

The pleasure's mine, and I will pay the bill.

May I take this occasion to say

That the whole human race should

  go down on its knees,

Show that we're grateful for mornings like these,

For the world's in a wonderful way,

On A Wonderful Day Like Today

The lilt and rhythm of songs are simply an exaggeration of the lilt and rhythm of poetry and prose. Throughout this book you'll find songs both for your enjoyment and for triggering discussion about the melodies of language. Why not get a recording of this song for the children to learn? Then they can compare the sung melodies with the spoken melodies.

a song by Leslie Bricusse and Anthony Newley

painting by R. Palou Rubi

PEANUTS

featuring "Good ol' Charlie Brown"

by SCHULZ

Isn't it interesting that children tend to read comics with all the naturality of spoken language? Stilted word-by-word reading is recognized as inappropriate. Not only that, the children expect the reading to be successful. *Sounds of Language* deliberately inculcates these attitudes in other types of reading.

As you read this spooky story aloud, imagine you're telling it while sitting by a campfire and mysterious shadows flit in and out of the trees. But be careful, lest you scare yourself.

THE SHINNY BONE

A story told by Dupris Knight about 1882
Handlettered by Ray Barber

Once there was a woman who went out to pick beans,
and she found a Shinny Bone.
She took the Shinny Bone home with her,
and that night when she went to bed,
the wind began to moan and groan.
Away off in the distance
she seemed to hear a voice crying,

**"WHO'S GOT MY SHIN-N-N-NY BO-O-O-N-E?
WHO'S GOT MY SHIN-N-N-NY BO-O-O-N-E?"**

The wind rose and began to screech
around the house,
and the woman covered her head with the quilts.
The voice seemed to come nearer:

"WHO'S GOT MY SHIN-N-N-NY BO-O-O-N-E?"

The woman scrooched down,
'way down under the covers,
and 'bout that time
the wind 'peared to hit the house,
SWOOOOOOOOOOOSH,
and the old house creaked and cracked
like somethin' was tryin' to get in.

20

The voice had come nearer, almost at the door now,
and it said,

"WHERE'S MY SHIN-N-NY BO-O-O-N-E ?
WHO'S GOT MY SHIN-N-NY BO-O-O-N-E ?"

The woman scrooched further down under the covers
and pulled them tight around her head.
The wind growled around the house
like some big animal
and r-r-rumbled over the chimbley.

All at once she heard the door
cr-r-rack open
and Somethin' slipped in
and began to creep over the floor.
The floor would cre-e-eak,
cre-e-eak at every step
that Thing took toward her bed.
The woman could almost feel it
bending over her head over the bed.
Then in an awful voice it said,

" WHERE'S MY SHIN-N-NY BO-O-O-N-E ?
WHO'S GOT MY SHIN-N-NY BO-O-O-N-E ?"

"YOU GOT IT !"

Picture reading
is the most universally
used reading skill.
Throughout SOUNDS
OF LANGUAGE,
pictures are used to
invite storytelling and
discussion. There are
no *right* answers. Your
role is to appreciate a
child's ideas, his use of

A Picture
for Storytelling
by Richard Erdoes

a choice word or
well-turned phrase,
supporting his ego in its
quest for language and
language skills.

The ELECTRIC PaiNT

A Freddy Freon Story
by Jerry Warner, illustrations by Peter Lippman

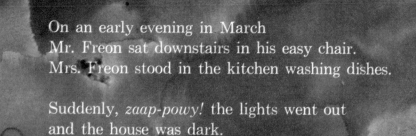

On an early evening in March
Mr. Freon sat downstairs in his easy chair.
Mrs. Freon stood in the kitchen washing dishes.

Suddenly, *zaap-powy!* the lights went out
and the house was dark.

"Not another power failure!" sighed Mr. Freon.
"Yes, dear," said his wife.
"Freddy is inventing again."

Upstairs in the electric room Freddy lit a candle.

"The only trouble with electricity
is that it goes off sometimes!" he muttered.
Freddy sat thinking.
The candle flickered.
Suddenly Freddy's eyes brightened,
and cogs and gears inside his head began to burn
and Freddy Freon hatched another idea—
this time to make a pot of electric paint.
"Wake up, Spiro!" exclaimed Freddy.
He looked at the rooster,
snoring lightly atop his turntable.

"If I can invent a pot of electric paint
that will make things glow brightly,
why rooms and buildings and schools and clubhouses
painted with the stuff
will be lit up all the time.
Nobody will need light bulbs
or get electric bills from the power company!"

Spiro stared a blank look at Freddy.
The rooster did not understand English.
He had no idea at all what Freddy was babbling about,
but he knew for sure that Freddy
was up to building another of his electric marvels,
and Spiro cringed at the very thought.

The next morning Freddy set madly to work in the electric room.
Bottles and cans and buckets littered the floor.
Freddy hummed as he poured
three quarts of battery juice into a large bucket.
He added a dab of ground-up magnets.
He dumped in a jar of pickled electric eels
that he'd bought at a Turkish delicatessen.
In went a packet of flash powder
and a pound of glowworms.

Freddy whistled a merry tune
as he mixed all the ingredients well.

The electric paint was thick as cold maple syrup and the color of sunny-side-up fried egg yolks.

Freddy lugged the bucket of electric paint downstairs
to the kitchen where Mrs. Freon was still washing dishes.

"What's in the bucket, Freddydear?" asked Mrs. Freon.
She always insisted his name was "Freddydear,"
but that was a mother's creation.

"One gallon of electric paint," replied Freddy.
"How many electrics will one gallon cover?"
said Mrs. Freon.

"It doesn't cover electrics, Mom,
  it makes things glow," said Freddy
  who removed a big can of baked beans from the cupboard.
  Freddy carefully painted the big can of baked beans
  with a coat of the electric paint.

"When the paint dries,
  that big can of baked beans will glow like a lightbulb!"
  said Freddy proudly.

The big can of baked beans sat on the drainboard.
  Freddy watched as the paint dried.
  But the can did not glow,
  or even flicker.
  It didn't light up or shine.
  It didn't even change colors....
  BUT...

The word *BUT* followed by the elipse is an obvious literary signal that the course
of events is going to change abruptly. Children not only recognize this literary
strategy — they use it naturally both in conversation and in writing. Just notice how
many times the next week you observe children's use of this technique. That's
the time to react appreciatively to their linguistic and literary know-how by
reminding them that Jerry Warner used the same technique in the Freddy story.
This will help children verbalize their intuitive insights about the ways
authors tell their stories and hang a plot together. See page 24 TE for a discussion
of figuring out how stories and poems work.

......the big can of baked beans
slowly rose into the air.

A big bug jumped into the frying pan.
The big can floated across the living room.
Freddy watched with wide-eyed enchantment
as the can drifted out an open window
and floated up and over the elm trees
on Normal Street just like a balloon.
It rose higher and higher into the air
and disappeared in the light blue sky.

Transforming Sentences: When children replace words in a sentence with
words of their own choosing, they learn much about the way language works
and they tend to claim the sentence pattern for their own personal use.
Throughout this book we shall mark sentences for worthwhile transforming.
This is a basic activity in the *Sounds of Language* program. Soon you
and the children will become aware of the possibilities for transforming any
sentence that suits your fancy. For discussion of ways to help children
transform sentences, see page 75 TE.

"Tonight's supper just flew out the window,"
   Freddy said.

"Well, for gracious sakes!" exclaimed Mrs. Freon.

"The electric paint didn't make a light bulb
   out of a big can of baked beans," said Freddy,
"but it freed it from gravity!"

"It's charming paint, Freddydear,
   but don't get any on yourself," said Mrs. Freon
   who did not understand the fabulous possibilities
   for the pot of electric paint.

   Freddy filled an empty aspirin bottle
   with a sample of the electric paint.
"I must show this to Mr. Merryweather,"
   he said, as he hurried off
to Normal Elementary School that morning.

In the early afternoon
Freddy sat in Mr. Merryweather's science class.
Mr. Merryweather stood at the blackboard
talking about the wild flowers of Tasmania.
Freddy raised his hand.

"Yes, Freddy, what is it?" asked Mr. Merryweather.

Freddy pulled the tiny bottle of electric paint from his pocket.
"I have something to show the class!" said Freddy,
and he proudly held the bottle of electric paint
high for all to see.

"It's a bottle of electric paint," said Freddy.
"Anything painted with this will be free from gravity
and will fly through the air like a bird!"

"How many birds have you painted with it?"
scoffed Mr. Merryweather.
The children giggled.

"It really makes things fly!" Freddy insisted.

The children guffawed.

"Come on, Freddy," said Mr. Merryweather.
"We all know that it is impossible to make something fly
merely by sloshing it with a dab of paint!"

"Well, it made baked beans fly!" said Freddy.

More guffaws from the class.

Mr. Merryweather took the bottle of paint from Freddy.
"HO! HO! HO! Here!" he cried,
"I'll paint a dab on my laboratory apron
and I'll fly out the window! HAW! HAW! HAW!"

The children laughed hysterically.
Some rolled on the floor
holding their stomachs.

"Don't put that on yourself!" cried Freddy.
"Please Mr. Merryweather!
 Don't do it!"

Mr. Merryweather dabbed a spot of electric paint on his apron.

"See?" said Mr. Merryweather.
"See Freddy? I'm not flying around like a bird!
 Now you return to your seat."

Peter Lippman's illustrations for this story should be, at some point, studied by the children and discussed irrespective of the text. His techniques, his humor and his obvious joy in the story are deserving of attention. Often, as in this case, the art and the story can be read separately, yet they innately reinforce one another to create a memorable whole.

"Mr. Merryweather! You must remove your apron
before that paint dries!" pleaded Freddy.

"Freddy! That's enough nonsense!" said Mr. Merryweather.

"Yessir," said Freddy, "but be ready to grab at something
when you start to float away!"

Mr. Merryweather returned to the blackboard
and continued his talk on the wild flowers of Tasmania.

The electric paint dried slightly
and Mr. Merryweather's shoes rose an inch off the floor.

Children naturally use decorative type in expressing themselves. Here it has
been used professionally to add to the story impact. By encouraging children to
play with type cut from a magazine and pasted in at selected places in their
stories, or to hand letter selected phrases or speeches in flamboyant colors, you'll
be freeing not only their imaginations but also their writing skills.

Soon the electric paint dried completely
and Mr. Merryweather drifted upward
and his head smashed into a light fixture on the ceiling.

He raced from his desk
and he grabbed onto Mr. Merryweather's legs.

"HELLLLLLP!" shrieked Mr. Merryweather
who thrashed about,
flailing his arms and legs in a panic.

"I CAN'T HOLD ONTO YOUR LEGS
WITH YOU THRASHING ABOUT SO!" cried Freddy.

Mr. Merryweather drifted toward the open window.
"I TAKE IT BACK FREDDY!" cried Mr. Merryweather,
"YOUR ELECTRIC PAINT REALLY WORKS!
NOW THE JOKE IS OVER,
GET ME DOWN!"

"I can't help you if you don't stop thrashing about so!"
cried Freddy.

The children sat stunned in their seats,
their mouths open wide.

Mr. Merryweather bellowed...

CALL THE POLICE! CALL ANYBODY!

Mr. Merryweather's head and shoulders
drifted out of the open window.

Freddy gripped the struggling science teacher's feet
until Mr. Merryweather's shoes popped off

41

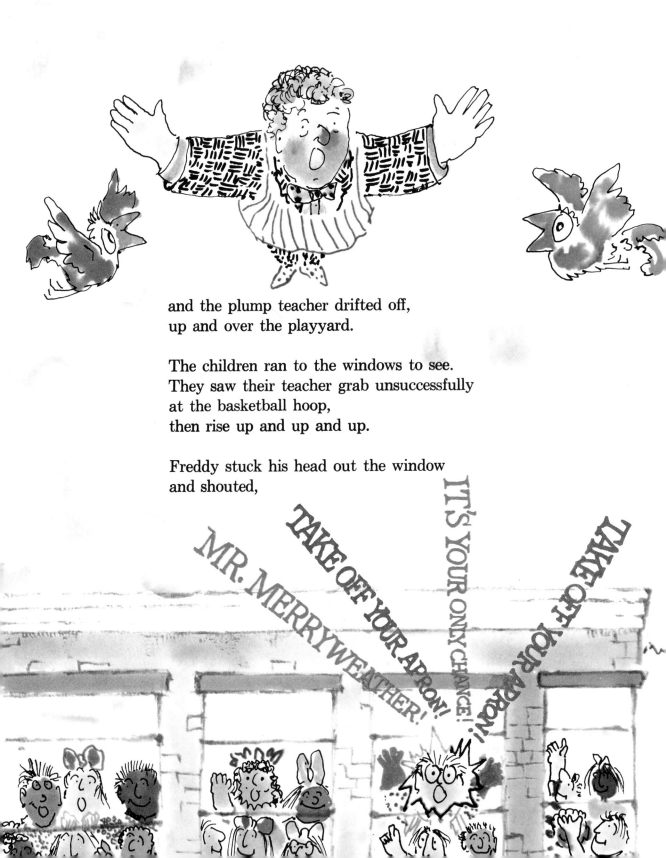

and the plump teacher drifted off,
up and over the playyard.

The children ran to the windows to see.
They saw their teacher grab unsuccessfully
at the basketball hoop,
then rise up and up and up.

Freddy stuck his head out the window
and shouted,

MR. MERRYWEATHER!

TAKE OFF YOUR APRON!

IT'S YOUR ONLY CHANCE!

TAKE OFF YOUR APRON!

The airborne science teacher yanked off his apron and grabbed at the flagpole. The apron floated high into the sky and disappeared.

As you encounter innovative
arrangements of type in this book,
you may be surprised at how confidently
your children are willing
to attack such pages. We adults
have grown accustomed to school books
where the same size and style of type
move relentlessly from left to right,
page after page,
and it is easy to forget that today's children
are encountering imaginative
and flamboyant uses of type
on T.V., in magazine advertising and even
on their cereal boxes. How appropriate
that school books too can call upon
imaginative and intriguing page design
in an effort to bring new dimensions
to the children's linguistic learnings
and to convince today's young readers
that there is much that is alive and
gripping between the covers
of a book.

The phone in the classroom rang.
Freddy answered it.

"Hello, who's this?" said Mr. Winkle, the principal.

"Freddy Freon, sir," replied Freddy.

"Well, put Mr. Merryweather on," said Mr. Winkle.

"I can't," said Freddy.

"Why not?" demanded Mr. Winkle.

"Because he's stuck on top of the flagpole."

"I knew he'd flip sooner or later," roared Mr. Winkle.

"Mr. Winkle, you'd better call a fire truck with a long ladder," said Freddy.

"Thank you and goodby," said Mr. Winkle.

Mr. Winkle sat at his desk thinking.
"Miss Jenkins!" he called to his secretary,
"Mr. Merryweather is stuck atop the flagpole.
Should we call a fire truck
or leave him up there?"

"Is Freddy Freon in his class?" asked Miss Jenkins.

"Yes," replied Mr. Winkle.

"Then I'd call a fire truck for the poor man,"
said Miss Jenkins.

See p. 16 TE.

Parts of this story fall naturally into flowing dialogues and invite acting out. You can ask for volunteers to take the roles, reading aloud as many times as necessary to establish the vocal models and to give turns to all children who want to participate. As children hear the language falling into sentence patterns and melodies, they deposit these patterns in their linguistic storehouses for a lifetime of usage in reading, writing, speaking and thinking. Rather than concentrate, as the schools have for decades, on basic sight words, concentration on sentence models would give more linguistic mileage.

In a few minutes,
a huge red fire truck with a long ladder
pulled up alongside the flagpole in the playyard.
Up went the ladder
and a fireman climbed to the top of the pole
to pry Mr. Merryweather off the golden bulb.

The fireman took Mr. Merryweather
to the Shady Oaks Rest Home to recover.
And Freddy went home to continue
his experiments.

The Automobile Industry

A Look at the Statistics[1]

It seems to many people
that the automobile
is the pulse of American life.
Today, Americans own
about 86 million automobiles.
Eighty-two per cent
of the Americans
who take transportation to work
go in an automobile.
Ninety-four million Americans
have passed tests
to get driver's licenses.

More than 12 million Americans
work in the auto industry
or in businesses
that are closely connected
to the manufacturing of cars.
This means that 1
out of every 7 people who work
are helping to produce
and service cars.
This also means
that 1 out of 6
of the 800,000 businesses
in this country
produce services and materials
for cars.

The auto industry buys
22 per cent of all steel
produced in the United States.
It buys 60 per cent of the rubber,
90 per cent of the gasoline
and lead,
57 per cent of the malleable[2] iron
35 per cent of the zinc,
75 per cent of the plate glass.

In one year
the auto industry uses
enough plastic vinyl
to cover 12 million
living room sofas,
which would be 1 sofa
for every 5 households
in the United States.
The modern automobile
has 7 miles of wiring in it.
More than half of the radios
in this country
are "on the road."

Automobiles in the future
may run on electricity
rather than gasoline,
and there may even be
electronically-controlled highways
to guide driverless cars
to their destinations.

[1]facts expressed in numbers

[2]iron that can be molded

This brief essay is so heavily laden with concepts that you probably will do well to read it aloud to the children while they follow it in their books. This gives them a chance to input the information through both their ears and their eyes. The main concern is that they develop some sensitivity to this type of expression.

Buick

1915

These pictures will evoke a lot of interesting language from boys particularly, many of whom are interested in automotive design. Won't some of your boys be surprised to find that they can read complicated words when they occur in a personally interesting context? Incidentally, the use of the spoked wheel for the *O* in the word *automotive* was another way of acknowledging Goodyear Rubber Company, who provided us with this fascinating sequence of pictures. A similar display of airplane designs might be a worthwhile companion project.

58 consecutive years of automotive design

A picture story of progress

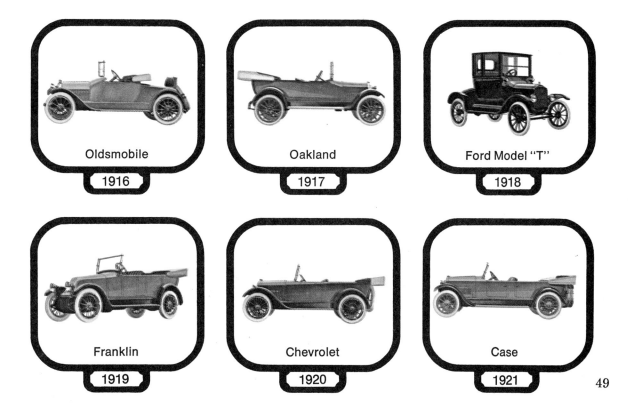

Oldsmobile	Oakland	Ford Model "T"
1916	1917	1918

Franklin	Chevrolet	Case
1919	1920	1921

49

Mercer

1922

Stearns

1923

Chandler

1924

Locomobile

1925

Kissel

1926

Jordan

1927

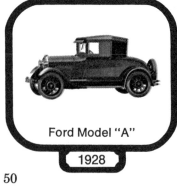

Ford Model "A"

1928

Plymouth

1929

Cord

1930

Durant
1931

Essex
1932

Dodge
1933

Chrysler Airflow
1934

Cadillac
1935

Terraplane
1936

LaSalle
1937

Ford
1938

Packard
1939

Mercury
1940

Plymouth
1941

51

Lincoln
1942

Military Amphibian
1943

Willys Jeep
1944

Staff Car (Ford)
1945

DeSoto
1946

Kaiser
1947

Dodge
1948

Ford
1949

Pontiac
1950

Nash Rambler
1951

Plymouth
1952

Mercury
1953

Learning to
drive and to control a car
is one of our society's major problems.
What do you think should be done
to make highway traffic safer?

Chrysler

1954

Chevrolet

1955

Dodge

1956

Thunderbird

1957

DeSoto

1958

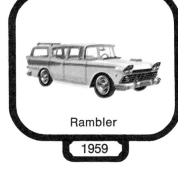

Rambler

1959

Valiant

1960

Willys

1961

Falcon

1962

Dodge

1963

53

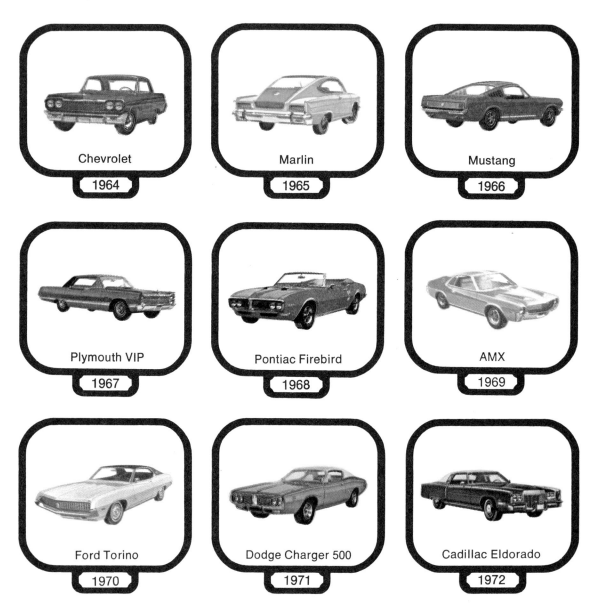

Chevrolet **1964**	Marlin **1965**	Mustang **1966**
Plymouth VIP **1967**	Pontiac Firebird **1968**	AMX **1969**
Ford Torino **1970**	Dodge Charger 500 **1971**	Cadillac Eldorado **1972**

Drawings by Ted Lodigensky

Now may be a productive time to invite children
to start or add to their lists of favorite words.
The names of cars, planes, football teams,
rocks, horses, etc., have strong appeal
for many intermediate grade children.
See pages 92 TE and 99 TE for a discussion of
vocabulary building techniques and of figuring
out how words work.

Do the children have a hunch why there is so much blank space on this page? Does it occur
to them that there will be new designs added to this page each time we reprint the book?

The way the poet positioned the words in "Stop-Go"
is an integral part of the poem itself.
The traffic light colors which we have added to the o's
are simply an extension of the poet's design.
Children enjoy reading experiences of this kind
and they also enjoy writing their own *concrete* poems:
poems which are written to look like pictures.
For example, you may be surprised
how imaginative and original children can be

Stop-Go

A POEM BY DOROTHY W. BARUCH

Automobiles

In

   a

     row

Wait to go

While the signal says:

          STOP

Bells ring

Tingaling!

Red light's gone!

Green light's on!

Horns blow!

And the row

Starts

    to

        GO

if you draw the design of a new moon on the board
and ask them if they'd like to write a poem in that shape.
Once they get the idea of *concrete* poems,
there'll be no end to their inventiveness.

The Web of Winter

A story by Esther MacBain Meeks,
water color illustration by Willi Baum

This quietly moving story has all the tenderness of a boy's love for a wild creature. It is told against a background of a family's love for one another and for life itself. The story is so simple that you may not at first sense its impact, but we're guessing that after you have read it, you'll never forget "The Web of Winter."

Bill stood by the marsh
watching small flocks
of birds
looking for food.
The birds darted
among the dry reeds
and barren branches,
pecking at shriveled berries
and pods
to get at their hidden seeds.
Bill wondered
how the birds kept warm
in the stinging cold.
At last he ran out
on the ice and slid,
making great long tracks.
He alternately ran and slid
across the marsh
until he came
to the *turn-around*—
an empty barrel
frozen into the ice.
He sat down on the barrel
to fasten his boot.
His breath came out
on the cold air
in thin white puffs.

The wind
grew suddenly quiet.
That's when Bill
first heard the sound.
It was so faint
that he was not sure
he had heard it.
The sound came again,
high and thin.
"Quick..."
Bill listened.

Here's a hint
of the problem
to come.

It came again.
"Quick...quick."
Could it be the ice
breaking under his weight?
He looked carefully.
No, the ice was hard
and firm.
"Quick...quick."
What could the sound be?
Bill knew the call
of the winter birds—
the whistle of a cardinal,
the chatter of a blue jay,
the *cheep* of a sparrow.
It wasn't a bird he knew,
and it didn't sound
like the cry of an animal.
"Quick...quick."
The sound floated again
over the marsh.
Bill rose to follow it.

Knowing now that Bill will look
for the source of the cry,
the reader is prepared for much of the language
that he will be reading.

Picking his way
among the weeds
and tall grasses,
he came to the edge
of the marsh.
He pushed the reeds aside
and listened.
All was silent.
He bent his head,
waiting for the sound
to come again.
"Quick ... quick."

"I'm coming," he answered,
making his way
through the brush.
Every few steps he stopped,
waiting for the voice
to guide him.
But the voice
did not come again.
The sun set behind the willows.
It grew late and dark.
Bill waited
as long as he could.

Notice how compelling
the problem has become.
We can predict that Bill
will be the person
who solves it.

See the marked sentence above and page 88 TE.
Sentences with introductory phrases of this kind

can usually be rearranged by placing the phrase
later in the sentence or even at the end. When

Finally he had to leave.
It was suppertime
and his mother
expected him home.

The next day, after school,
Bill returned to the marsh
for skating.
He carried
his skates and a broom
on his sled
and pulled them out

to the center of the marsh
where the ice
could be cleared
for skating.
He sat down
on the sled
to put on his skates.
Then he took the broom
and swept the snow
off the ice,
leaving the surface
smooth for skating.

children achieve this kind of versatility with a sentence's movable parts, they don't bog down on the

first few words in a sentence in their independent
reading, knowing they can come back and pick up
these words later.

59

The great motion Willi Baum communicates
in these paintings intrigues children
who invariably put motion into
their paintings. They also
are intrigued by the "disjointed"
wholeness of his figures.
They might like to experiment
with paintings of their own,
using this technique.

He found an old tomato can and batted it before him
as he skated around, using the broom as a hockey stick.
Then he dropped the broom and raced around and around
the turn-around barrel. His quick turns on the ice
made a deep grating sound and threw up a cloud
of white dust behind him. He practiced
all sorts of turns and skated with abandon—
forward, backward, stopping, starting,
turning, gliding, fast, slow.
He was skating near the turn-around barrel
when he heard the sound again.

"Quick . . . quick."
It came the same as yesterday. Bill cocked
his head and listened.

"Quick . . ."
The sound wasn't far away. Bill skated quietly
toward it.

"Quick . . . quick."
Now he heard quite clearly. The snow
was thicker at the edge of the marsh
and was too rough for skating. He had to walk
on his skates, leaving short thin tracks behind him.
Then suddenly, the same as the day before,
the sound stopped.

Bill stood still. He listened and watched.
After a bit, he kneeled down and called softly,
"Quick . . . quick . . ."

He waited for an answer. None came.

He called again, "Quick."

There was no reply. He listened a long time
and stood up to go. That is when he found it.
In a tangle of dry weeds, he saw a duck
huddled in the snow. It was sitting so still
it looked like a decoy.

"Hello," Bill said, bending down.

The bird trembled and fluttered its wings.
It was a young duck.

"It's too cold here for you, Quick-quick.
Why haven't you flown away?"

The duck beat its wings frantically.
The snow flew, but the bird could not. It was
caught in the ice. Bill knew that birds often rested
in icy water, but he had never heard
of anything like this. The water had frozen firmly
around the duck's feet.

Bill gently took the bird in his hands.
He tried to lift, but the ice held the duck
as tightly as it held the turn-around barrel.

"Don't worry," Bill said. "I'll get you out."

It was easier said than done. The duck
was not only trapped, it was cold and hungry.
Bill broke off some grasses and piled them
in front of the bird where it could get
at the seeds. But Quick-quick
refused the food.

"Maybe he's too weak to eat," Bill thought.

The duck cried a low pitiful sound.
Bill feared the duck was nearly dead.
There was no time to run two miles home for help.
He himself must act—and quickly.

"Here," he said, loosening his scarf
and wrapping it around the duck. "This will warm
you a little."

The wind whipped the scarf out of his hands,
but he grabbed it and wrapped it around
the captive bird.   The reader is pondering this situation right along with Bill,
                        thus rallying appropriate problem-solving language from his
Now what to do?   linguistic storehouse which will help him decode the print.

Bill ran for his sled. He had seen men
make wind shelters when they were ice-fishing,
so he propped the sled up to shelter the duck
while he tried to free it.

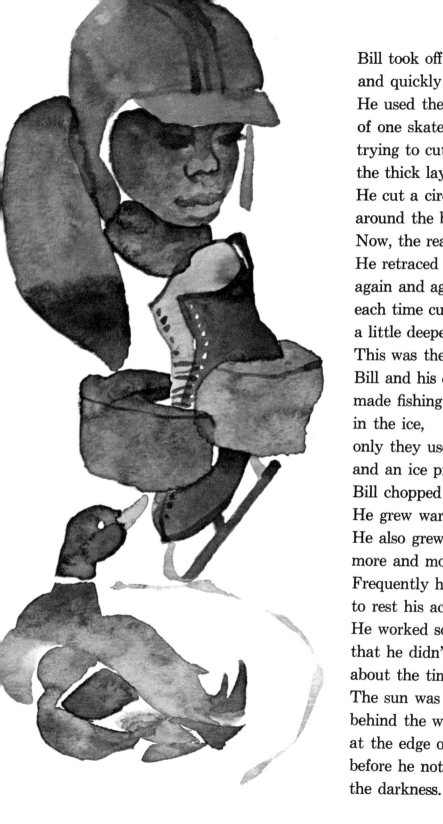

Bill took off his skates
and quickly put on his boots,
He used the blade
of one skate as a knife,
trying to cut through
the thick layer of ice.
He cut a circle
around the bird.
Now, the real work began.
He retraced the marks
again and again,
each time cutting
a little deeper in the ice.
This was the way
Bill and his dad
made fishing holes
in the ice,
only they used a hatchet
and an ice pick.
Bill chopped at the ice.
He grew warmer and warmer.
He also grew
more and more tired.
Frequently he had to stop
to rest his aching arms.
He worked so hard
that he didn't think
about the time.
The sun was low
behind the willow trees
at the edge of the marsh
before he noticed
the darkness.

Notice, from here
on through the
story, how the
time of day occasions
specific action by
the various members
of the family.

63

Someone called. "Bill! Hey, Bill!
Are you down there?" It was his sister.

"Here I am, Thelma! Over here!"

Thelma came toward him through the
tall weeds.

"A duck's caught here in the ice,"
Bill shouted. "I'm cutting him free."

"Where have you been? Mom's worried silly,"
Thelma said.

"I've been here," Bill said. "I can't leave
or this duck will die."

Thelma saw the bird now and how Bill was trying
to free it. "It's dangerous to cut holes in the ice,"
she said. "You should *never never* do it
when you're alone."

"I know," Bill answered. "But it's shallow here
and near the shore. Besides, there wasn't time
to get help."

"Where's the other skate?"
Thelma asked.
Without waiting
for an answer,
she found it
and started to work,
using the tip of the blade
like an ice pick.
She chopped at the ice
with the skate
and gouged out
good-sized chunks.
"Good work, Thelma,"
Bill said.
"We'll have this duck
free in no time."
They chopped and chopped,
but it was hard going,
and very slow.
Soon another voice
came out of the dusk.
"Thelma! Bill!"
Mother had come
to look for them.
"We can't come,"
Thelma called back.
"Bill found a duck
frozen onto the ice.
We are trying
to rescue it."
"Found what?"
Mother called.

If Bill held an after-school job for which he was paid a salary, would he, after finding the
trapped duck, have ignored the reporting in time, just as he did when it was time to report
in to his mother at dark? Would you?

Mother scolded as she came across the ice. Then she saw the bird huddled under the scarf, and her attitude changed. "It's dangerous to cut holes in the ice, and you should *never never* do it without a grownup along."

"Yeah, Mom," Bill said. "You sound just like Thelma. She said the same thing. But there wasn't time."

"Well, I can help, too. Hand me the broom." Mother said. She began sweeping the ice chips away from the crack where Bill and Thelma were chopping.

| The | Patsy
She
men
parrot

Mother | yelled
whistled
danced
fainted

scolded | until
after
while
when

as | we
they
it
he

she | fell
jumped
landed
flew

came | down
around
over
into

across | her
that
some
our

the | doghouse
snakepit
boudoir
pudding

ice. |

A truck came bumping along the shore road, its headlights shining through the weeds. It was Father. He pulled the truck to a stop.

His voice rang out in the dark. "Bill! . . . Thelma! . . . Mother!"

"Over here," Mother answered.

Father got out of the truck and came to see what was doing. When he saw them chopping, he scolded, "Why didn't you call me? It's dangerous to cut holes in the ice. You should *never* do it without a man around."

"Here we go again," Bill said without looking up.

Father looked at the duck,
then at the circle.
"I'll get my tools," he said.
Father went back
to the truck
and returned with a hammer
and a jack handle.
Soon the ice chips were flying.
The duck pulled
its head back in alarm.
Now it was very dark
and hard to see.
"That's enough," Bill said
as he tested the ice
and felt it give.
Father tapped along the circle
with the hammer.
The tapping opened the crack.
The ice cake,
still holding the bird,
broke loose.
Bill and Father
carefully lifted
the small island of ice
and carried it,
bird and all,
to the truck.
Bill laid his hand
on the bird's breast
and felt its heart fluttering.
"He's still alive," he said.

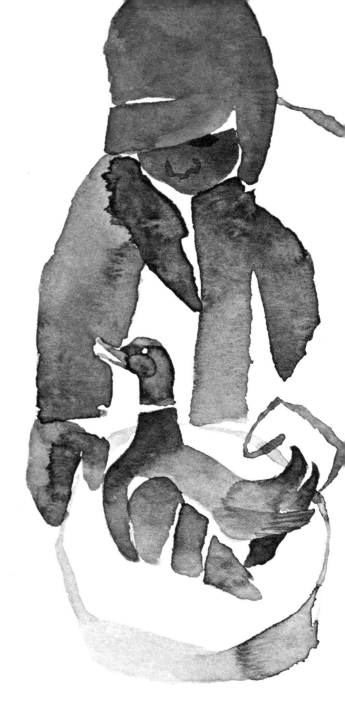

Now the
solution
begins to
unfold.

Quick-quick,
his feet still frozen
in the cake of ice,
was loaded into the truck.
Bill and Thelma sat beside him
on the trip home.
The duck was placed
in the bathtub,
and Bill drew warm water
to hurry the thawing of the ice.
"Quick . . . quick . . ."
Quick-quick seemed
to know that
he had been saved.
His voice was faint,
but, at least Bill knew
he was still alive.
Bill hung over the edge
of the bathtub,
encouraging the duck
with kind talk
and offers of food.
By morning
he was paddling around
in the bathtub
as if he enjoyed
his new home.
"Quick, quick, quack!
Quick, quick, quack!"
He fluttered his wings
and splashed water
over the floor.

The problem is solved.
Now we can expect the
author to bring the
story to a quick
and comfortable
close.

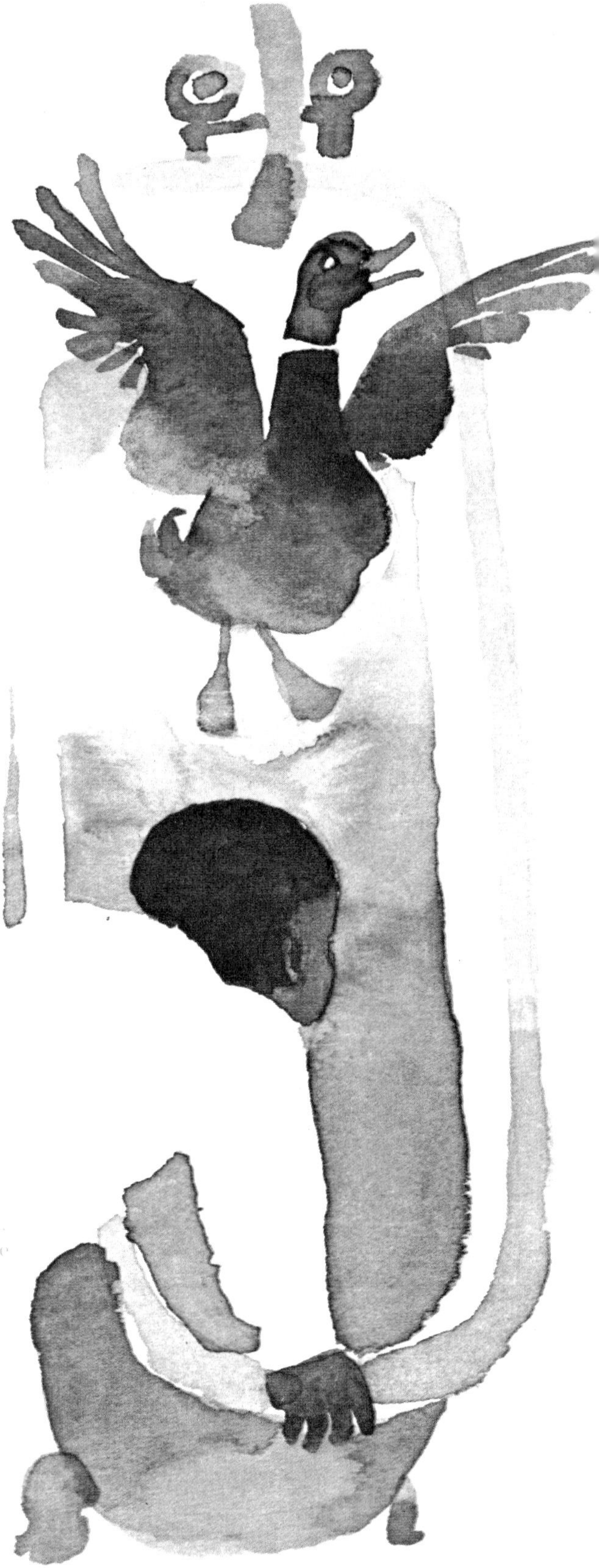

71

The next week, after he was strong enough to go on his way,
Bill and Thelma took him back to the marsh and set him free.
Out he flew over the ice and, without turning back,
disappeared over the woods and over the hill.
Now, in fall and spring when the birds fly overhead,
Bill still watches the ducks that come to the marsh.
He listens for Quick-quick, knowing that the bird
may never remember him, but he will never forget
the bird and his *quick...quick...* and *quick, quick, quack!*

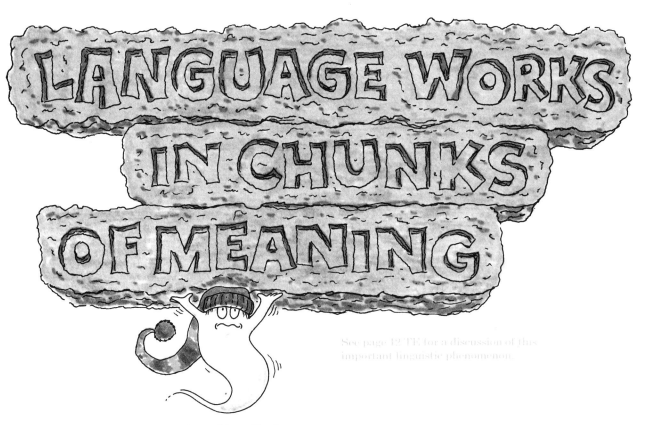

LANGUAGE WORKS IN CHUNKS OF MEANING

Bill: Noodles!
Put those chunks of language
back in your head
where they belong!

Noodles: I don't think I want to, Bill Martin.
Ghosts carry their language
on top of their heads
—or anywhere they want.
That's because we're magic.

Bill: Magic or not, Noodles,
language begins in the head
and always works in chunks.

Noodles: Chunks of what?

Bill: Chunks of meaning.
Listen to me talk, Noodles,
and hear how my words cluster.

Noodles: Clusters? You talking about peanut clusters?

Bill: Well, something like that, Noodles.
Just as peanuts are held together
by sticky chocolate
words also are held together
by the *sound of sense.*

Noodles: I think I like sticky chocolate better.

Bill: Alright, Noodles, let's test your *sound of sense.*

Noodles: There you go, Bill Martin,
talking like a school teacher.
Tests! Tests! Tests!
I like sticky chocolate better.

Bill: Then use your sticky chocolate, Noodles,
to cluster these words together
so they sound like talking:

*(Bill reads these words in monotone
with a pause between each word.
It does not sound like language.
It sounds like a long list of spelling words.)*

Once	was	rode	house	of	was	and
upon	a	a	after	himself	scared	so
a	silly	mouse	dark	in	to	was
time	ghost	through	and,	the	death	his
there	who	the	catching	mirror,		horse.
			a			
			glimpse			

Noodles: I'm glad you don't talk like that very often Bill Martin.
That sounds crazy.

Bill: You're getting the point, Noodles!
Language doesn't work like that.
What does your ear tell you to do
with those words?

Noodles: Well, my little ear tells me
to put "Once upon a time" together,
like a little song. (sings)

Once upon a time . . .
Once upon a time . . .

Bill: Keep going, Noodles,
your "sticky chocolate" is working.

Noodles: Give me that list of words, Bill Martin.
I'll stick 'em together the way they really belong:

Once upon a time . . .
there was a silly ghost . . .

Hey, I'm changing that chunk right now because it's not true . . .

Once upon a time . . .
there was a cool ghost . . .
who rode a mouse . . .
through the house . . .

No, he didn't just "ride a mouse." He rode it

wildly through the house . . .
after dark,
and,
catching a glimpse of himself in the mirror,
said,
"Oh, what a gallant rider!
What a gallant steed!"

Bill: Noodles, I think you changed some of those words.

Noodles: Just a minute, Bill.
Who's putting these peanut clusters together, me or you?

Bill: Well, I can see you are, Noodles,
and I can also see that you know
how to cluster words
into the *sound of sense*.

Noodles:	Yeah, Bill Martin.
	I know how to do lots of things
	—like getting out of here right now.
	Goodbye, Bill Martin, goodbye.
Bill:	Wait a minute Noodles.
	I want you to help me
	put this book together.
	Here are two stories,
	"Toads Don't Bite,"
	and *"The Three Little Pigs and the Ogre."*
	Let's see you put them
	into chunks of meaning
	so that each chunk has the *sound of sense.*
Noodles:	Hokus, pokus,
	diddeley dokus!
	Presto Chango,
	Me go mego!
Bill:	Noodles, finish the job before you leave.
Noodles:	I already finished, Bill Martin.
	Turn the page
	and you'll find *"Toads Don't Bite,"*
	printed in chunks of meaning.
Bill:	What about *"The Three Little Pigs and the Ogre?"*
Noodles:	Oh, gracious, I'm too tired.
	Carrying all those chunks around just wore me out.
	"The Three Little Pigs and the Ogre"
	will have to be done by somebody else, not me!
	Goodbye, Bill Martin.
	Oodeley, oodeley!

This humorous story can be read aloud by the children. It's a memorable character sketch, written as a dialogue—without the use of quotation marks. You and the children will find it fun figuring out or contemplating why you can follow the conversation without the traditional visual clues usually provided by quotation marks. This is an excerpt from William Saroyan's *My Name Is Aram*.

BUT TOADS DON'T BITE

A dialogue by William Saroyan, pictures by John Burningham

Reducing Sentences. See page 86 TE. Most sentences can be trimmed of a word or two, or perhaps a chunk of meaning, without destroying the basic meaning of the sentence. Sentences can also be reduced in a way that does destroy the meaning. The following are fine examples of sentences that cannot be reduced by even one chunk of meaning or word without having the overall meaning altered. Ask the children to consider each chunk of meaning in relation to the whole sentence, evaluating what happens if the chunk is removed.

My uncle and I got out of the ⌈Ford⌉ roadster

⌈in the middle of his land⌉

and began to walk ⌈over the dry earth.⌉

This land is my land, he said.

He walked slowly, ⌈kicking into the dry soil.⌉

Good teachers, notice the second line from the bottom. Do you suppose Woody Guthrie had read this story and had stored this line in his linguistic warehouse, later retrieving it subconsciously to use as the thrust for a song that has become part of our musical and patriotic inheritance? That's the way it is with our linguistic doings.

A HORNED TOAD SCRAMBLED

The uncle in this story
"comes off" as a memorable character.
What do you feel you know about him
after reading the story?
How does the author
reveal the main character to you?
Read some of the lines
that point out his personality.

over the earth
at my uncle's feet.
My uncle
clutched my shoulder
and came to a pious halt.
What is that animal?
  he said.
That little tiny lizard?
  I said.
That mouse with horns.
What is it?
  my uncle said.
I don't know for sure.
We call them horny toads,
  I said.
The horned toad
came to a halt
about three feet away
and turned its head.

My uncle looked down
at the small animal.
Is it poison?
  he said.
To eat?
Or if it bites you?
  I said.
Either way,
  my uncle said.
I don't think
it's good to eat.
I think it's harmless.
I've caught many of them.
They grow sad in captivity,
but never bite.

Shall I catch this one?
  I said.
Please do,
  my uncle said.
I sneaked up
on the horned toad,
then sprang on it
while my uncle looked on.
Careful!
Are you sure it isn't poison?
  he said.
I've caught many of them,
  I said.
I took the horned toad
to my uncle.
He tried not to seem afraid.
A lovely little thing,
isn't it?
  he said.
His voice was unsteady.

Would you like to hold it?
  I said.
No, you hold it.
I have never before been so close
to such a thing as this.
I see it has eyes.
I suppose it can see us,
  my uncle said.
I suppose it can.
It's looking up at you now,
  I said.
My uncle looked the horned toad
straight in the eye.
The horned toad looked my uncle
straight in the eye.
For fully half a minute
they looked one another
straight in the eye
and then the horned toad
turned its head aside
and looked down at the ground.
My uncle sighed with relief.

They never travel
in great numbers.
You hardly ever see
more than one at a time,
  I said.
A big one
could probably bite
a man to death,
  my uncle said.
They don't grow big.
This is as big as they grow,
  I said.
They seem to have an awful eye
for such small creatures.
Are you sure they don't mind
being picked up?
  my uncle said.

A THOUSAND
OF THEM
COULD KILL A MAN
I SUPPOSE,

he said.

One limitation of bookmaking
is that some pictures have to cross
the center of the book (the gutter).
It will be interesting to know
the children's reactions to this circumstance.

82

I suppose they forget
all about it the minute
you put them down,
   I said.
Do you really think so?
   my uncle said.
I don't think
they have very good memories,
   I said.
My uncle straightened up,
breathing deeply.
   He said,
Put the little creature down.
Let us not be cruel
to the innocent creations
of Almighty God.
If it is not poison
and grows no larger
than a mouse
and does not travel
in great numbers
and has no memory
to speak of,
let the timid little thing
return to the earth.
Let us be gentle
toward
these small things
which live
on the earth
with us.

Isn't it amusing
that after the
uncle was assured
that he had noth-
ing to fear from
the toad, he be-
came so benevo-
lent? Is this a
human trait?

Here's a beautiful sentence
to transform and to store
in your linguistic treasury.

Yes, sir,
  I said.
I placed the horned toad
on the ground.
Gently now.
Let no harm come
to this strange dweller
on my land,
  my uncle said.
The horned toad
scrambled away.
These little things
have been living on soil
of this kind for centuries,
  I said.

Centuries?
Are you sure?
  my uncle said.
I'm not sure,
but I imagine they have.
They're still here, anyway,
  I said.
My uncle looked around
at his land,
at the cactus
and brush growing out of it,
at the sky overhead.

What have they been eating
all this time?
  he shouted.
I don't know,
  I said.
What would you say
they've been eating?
  he said.
Insects, I guess.
Insects?
What sort of insects?
  my uncle shouted.
Little bugs, most likely,
  I said.
I don't know their names.
I can find out tomorrow at school.

Research
Project

85

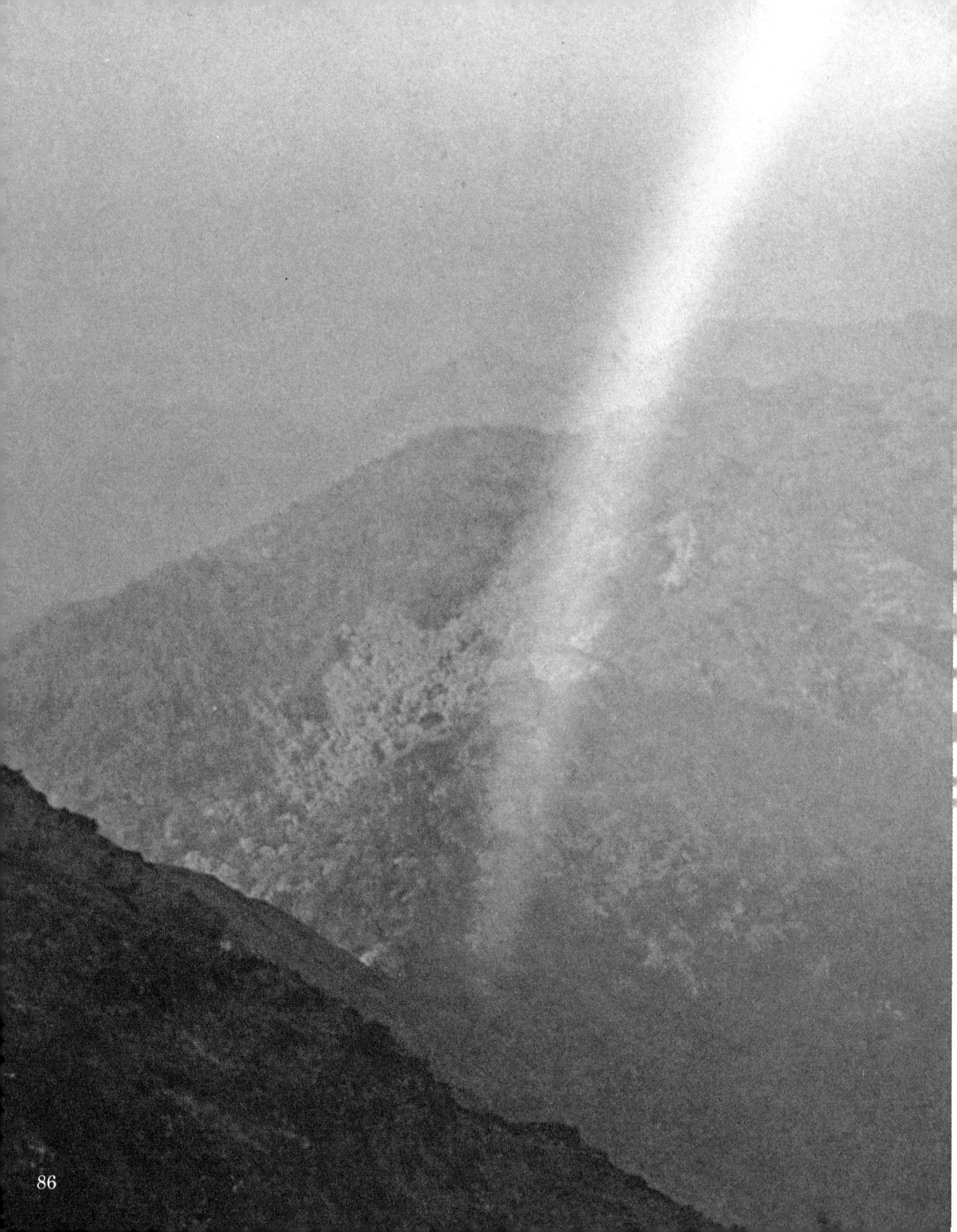

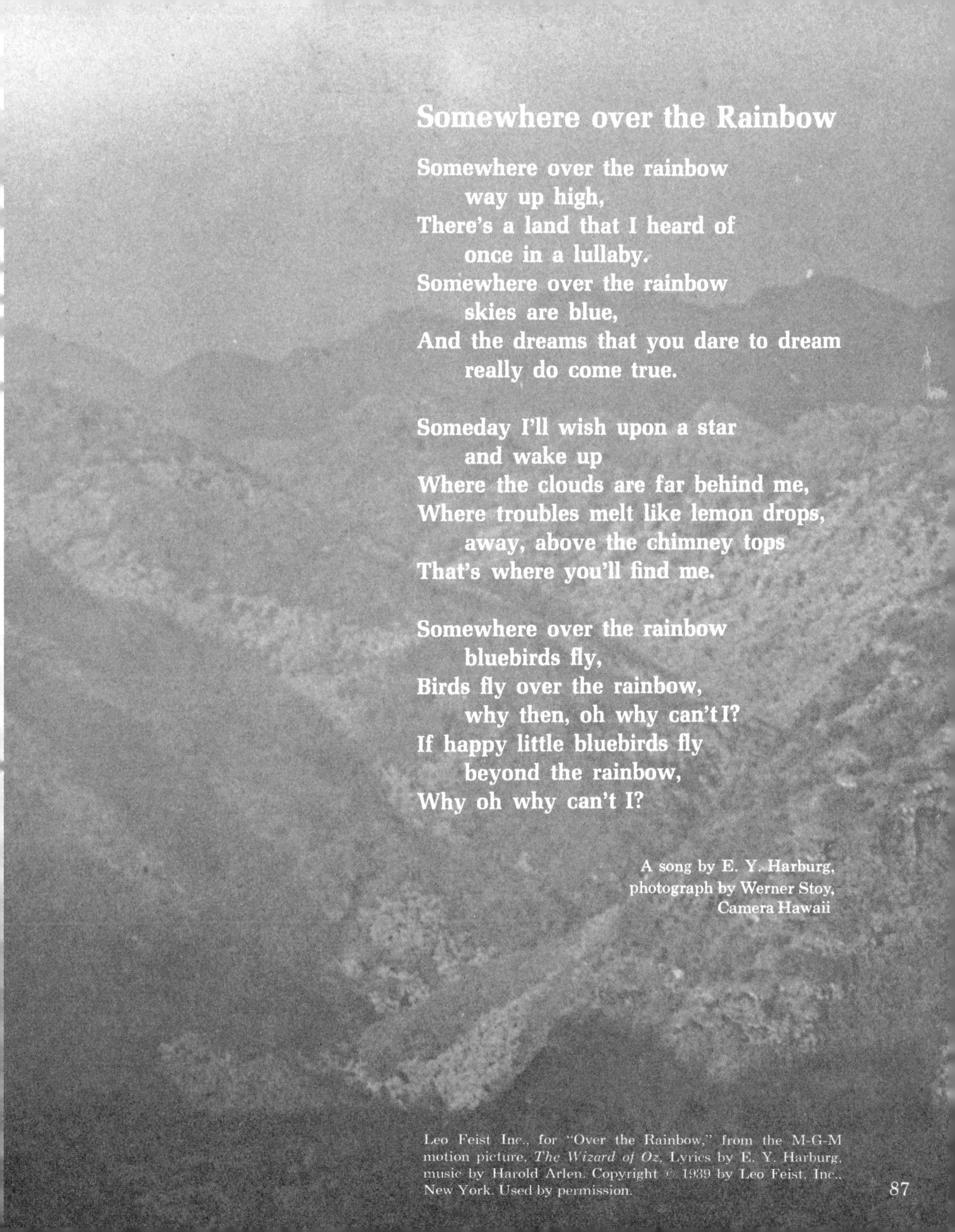

Somewhere over the Rainbow

Somewhere over the rainbow
    way up high,
There's a land that I heard of
    once in a lullaby.
Somewhere over the rainbow
    skies are blue,
And the dreams that you dare to dream
    really do come true.

Someday I'll wish upon a star
    and wake up
Where the clouds are far behind me,
Where troubles melt like lemon drops,
    away, above the chimney tops
That's where you'll find me.

Somewhere over the rainbow
    bluebirds fly,
Birds fly over the rainbow,
    why then, oh why can't I?
If happy little bluebirds fly
    beyond the rainbow,
Why oh why can't I?

A song by E. Y. Harburg,
photograph by Werner Stoy,
Camera Hawaii

We are the children of this soil
Mountains, plains and river flow
Riders of white horses
Brothers of birds, beavers, bears
Honey bees and buffalo –
Caretakers of the forest
Healers of the sick and soul
Beaters of drum
Tenders of grain
Singers of song
Survivors of sorrow
Beseechers of Gods –
For rain and
   a better tomorrow.

This is a beautiful poem for choral reading.
By doing it in unison, children who are less skilled than others
will pick up the cadences and pronunciations with the ear
and use that listening experience to validate what their eyes are seeing.

POEM "CHILDREN OF THIS SOIL" AND PAINTING BY YEFFE KIMBALL,
HANDLETTERING BY JAY ELLS

Daddy Fell into the Pond

Solo 1:
High voices:
Low voices:
Solo 2:
Teacher:
All:
Everyone grumbled. The sky was gray.
We had nothing to do and nothing to say.
We were nearing the end of a dismal day,
And there seemed to be nothing beyond,
                    THEN
            Daddy fell into the pond!

Girls:

Boys:
And everyone's face grew merry and bright,
And Timothy danced for sheer delight.
"Give me the camera, quick, oh quick!
He's crawling out of the duckweed." *Click!*

Girls:

Boys:
Teacher:
Then the gardener suddenly slapped his knee,
And doubled up, shaking silently,
And the ducks all quacked as if they were daft
And it sounded as if the old drake laughed.

All:
O, there wasn't a thing that didn't respond
                    WHEN
            Daddy fell into the pond!

A POEM BY ALFRED NOYES

Story and pictures by Howard P. Pyle

The Three Little Pigs *and the* OGRE

HERE were three nice, fat little pigs. The first was small, the second was smaller, and the third was the smallest of all. And these three little pigs thought of going out into the woods to gather acorns.

"There's a great ogre who lives over yonder in the woods," says the barnyard cock.

"And he will eat you up, body and bones," says the speckled hen.

"And there will be an end of you," says the black drake.

"If folks only knew what was good for them, they would stay at home and make the best of what they had there," says the old gray goose who laid eggs under the barn and who had never gone out into the world or had had a peep of it beyond the garden gate.

But no; the little pigs would go out into the world, whether or no. So out into the woods they went.

Episode 1

They hunted for acorns here and they hunted for acorns there, and by and by whom should the smallest of all the little pigs meet but the great, wicked ogre himself.

Sentences can also be reduced by eliminating describing words. Do you like the result? Do you think the author would?

"Aha!" says the great, wicked ogre, "it is a nice plump little pig that I have been wanting for my supper this many a day past. So you may just come along with me now."

"Oh, Master Ogre," squeaked the smallest of the little pigs in the smallest of voices—"oh, Master Ogre, don't eat me! There's a bigger pig back of me, and he will be along presently."

So the ogre let the smallest of the little pigs go, for he would rather have a larger pig if he could get it.

Episode 2

By and by came the second little pig. "Aha!" says the great, wicked ogre, "I have been wanting just such a little pig as you for my supper for this many a day past. So you may just come along with me now."

Oh, Master Ogre," says the middle-sized pig, in his middle-sized voice, "don't take me for your supper; there's a bigger pig than I am coming along presently. Just wait for him."

Well, the ogre was satisfied to do that; so he waited, and
Episode 3
by and by, sure enough, came the largest of the little pigs.

"And now," says the great, wicked ogre, "I will wait no longer, for you are just the pig I want for my supper."

But the largest of the little pigs had his wits about him, I can tell you. "Oh, very well," says he; "if I am the shoe that fits, there is no use in hunting for another; only, have you a roasted apple to put in my mouth when I am cooked? For no one ever heard of a little pig brought on the table without a roast apple in its mouth."

No; the ogre had no roasted apple.

The largest little pig's reference to the roasted apple shows Howard Pyle's sense of humor and the sophistication of the story. Obviously no hungry ogre would accept this as a reason for letting his dinner walk off, but in the sense of fun of the story, we know it's going to happen and we accept it.

Dear, dear! that was a great pity. If he would wait for a little while, the largest of the little pigs would run home and fetch one, and then things would be as they should.

Yes, the ogre was satisfied with that. So off ran the little pig, and the ogre sat down on a stone and waited for him.

Well, he waited and he waited and he waited and he waited, but not a tip of a hair of the little pig did he see that day, as you can guess without my telling you.

"And now," says the cock and the speckled hen and the black drake and the old gray goose who laid her eggs under the barn and had never been out into the world beyond the garden gate—"and now perhaps you will run out into the world and among ogres no more."

But no; that was not what the smallest of the three little pigs thought.

Episode 4

So out into the woods he went, and there he found all of the acorns that he wanted. But, on his way home, whom should he meet but the great, wicked ogre.

"Aha!" says the ogre, "and is that you?"

Isn't this an interesting technique to indicate conversation without the use of quotation marks?

Oh, yes, it was nobody else; but had the ogre come across three fellows tramping about in the woods down yonder?

No, the ogre had met nobody in the woods that day.

"Dear, dear," says the smallest little pig, "but that is a pity, for those three fellows were three wicked robbers, and they have just hidden a mealbag full of money in that hole up in the tree yonder."

You can guess how the ogre pricked up his ears at this.

"Just wait," said he to the smallest little pig, "and I will be down again in a minute." So he laid his jacket to one side and up the tree he climbed to find that bag of money.

"Do you find the hole?" says the smallest of the little pigs.

Yes; the ogre had found the hole.

"And do you find the money?" says the smallest of the little pigs.

No; the ogre could find no money.

"Then good-by," says the smallest of the little pigs, and off he trotted home, leaving the ogre to climb down the tree again as he chose.

Are you and the children continuing your search for sentences to transform, rearrange, reduce, and expand?

"And now, at least, you will go out into the woods no more," says the cock, the speckled hen, the black drake, and the gray goose.

Oh, well, there was no telling what the middle-sized little pig would do, for he also had a taste for acorns.

So out into the woods the middle-sized little pig went, and there he had all the acorns that he wanted.

But by and by the ogre came along. "Aha!" says he. "Now I have you for sure and certain."

But the middle-sized little pig just stood and looked at a great rock just in front of him, with all of his might and main. "Sh-h-h-h-h-h!" says he, "I am not to be talked to or bothered now!"

Hoity-toity! And why was the middle-sized pig not to be talked to? That was what the ogre should like to know.

Oh, the middle-sized little pig was looking at what was going on under the great rock yonder, for he could see the little folk brewing more beer than thirty-seven men could drink.

So! Why, the ogre would like to see that for himself.

"Very well," says the middle-sized little pig, "there is nothing easier than to learn that trick! Just take a handful of leaves from yonder bush and rub them over your eyes, and then shut them tight and count fifty."

Well, the ogre would have a try at that. So he gathered a handful of the leaves and rubbed them over his eyes, just as the middle-sized pig had said.

"And now are you ready?" said the middle-sized little pig. Yes; the ogre was ready.

The humor gets more and more ridiculous.

"Then shut your eyes and count," said the middle-sized little pig.

So the ogre shut them as tightly as he could and began to count, "One, two, three, four, five," and so on; and while he was counting, why, the little pig was running away home again.

By and by the ogre bawled out *"Fifty!!!"* and opened his eyes, for he was done. Then he saw not more, but less, than he had seen before, for the little pig was not there.

And now it was the largest of the three little pigs who began to talk about going out into the woods to look for acorns.

"You had better stay at home and take things as they come. The crock that goes often to the well gets broken at last"; that was what the cock, the speckled hen, the black drake, and the gray goose said.

Do you know anyone who always is fore-casting doom?

But no; the little pig wanted to go out into the woods, and into the woods the little pig would go, ogre or no ogre.

After he had eaten all of the acorns that he wanted, he began to think of going home again, but just then the ogre came stumping along. "Aha!" says he, "we have met again, have we?"

Episode 6

"Yes," said the largest of the three little pigs, "we have. And I want to say that I could find no roast apple at home, and so I did not come back again."

Yes, yes, that was all very fine; but they should have a settling of old scores now. The largest of the three little pigs might just come along and be made into sausages.

Come, come! the ogre must not be too testy. If it were sausages that the ogre was after, maybe the pig could help him. Over home at the farm yonder was a storehouse filled with more sausages and good things than two men could count.

Well, the ogre and the largest of the three little pigs went off together. By and by they came to the storehouse. There was a window *just* large enough for the ogre to squeeze through without a button to spare in the size.

Then, dear, dear! how the ogre did stuff himself with the sausages and puddings and other good things.

By and by the little pig bawled out as loud as he could, *"Have you had enough yet?"*

"Hush-sh-sh-sh-sh-sh-sh!" says the ogre, "don't talk so loud, or you'll be rousing the folks and having them about our ears like a hive of bees."

"No," bawled the little pig, louder than before, "but tell me, *have* you had enough yet?"

"Yes, yes," says the ogre, "I have had almost enough, only be still about it!"

"Very well!" bawled the little pig, as loud as he could, "if you have had enough, and if you have eaten all of the sausages and all of the puddings you can stuff, it is about time that you were going, for here comes the farmer and two of his men."

When the ogre heard them coming, he felt sure that it was time that he was getting away home again, and so he tried to get out of the same window that he had gotten in a little while before. But he had stuffed himself with so much of the good

Isn't the word *bawled* beautifully descriptive?

Why do you suppose the author italicized the word *just?* Notice the other uses of italics on the page. What special meaning does it indicate to you? How does italic type used in this manner help you hear what you are reading?

things that he had swelled like everything, and there he stuck in the storehouse window like a cork in a bottle and could budge neither one way nor the other; and that was a pretty pickle to be in.

"Oho!" says the farmer, "you were after my sausages and my puddings, were you? Then you will come no more."

And that was so; for when the farmer and his men were done with the ogre he never went into the woods again, for he could not.

The problem is solved. The story is over.

As for the three little pigs, they trotted away into the woods every day of their lives, for there was nobody nowadays to stop them from gathering all the acorns that they wanted.

Designs similar to the triangular design at the end of this story were used many years ago to signal to the reader that the story was over.

99

October

O hushed October
morning mild,
Thy leaves have ripened
to the fall;
Tomorrow's wind,
if it be wild,
Should waste them all.
The crows
above the forest call;
Tomorrow they may form
and go.
O hushed October
morning mild,
Begin the hours
of this day slow.

**AN EXCERPT FROM THE POEM
BY ROBERT FROST,
PAINTING BY STANLEY MALTZMAN**

The children will find that this poem
and painting can evoke meanings far
beyond those that are literally conveyed. Even if words are not forthcom-
ing to express the feelings and ideas
that they're experiencing, you can tell,
just by watching their faces, the basis
and the depth of their involvements.

USING YOUR EARS IN READING

Noodles:	Oodeley, oodeley, little ear, Are you readin' what you hear?
Bill:	Good morning, Noodles.
Noodles:	Don't bother me, Bill Martin. I'm reading... With my ears.
Bill:	Everybody reads partly with his ears.
Noodles:	My ears are busy, Bill Martin. They're reading.
Bill:	Reading what?
Noodles:	Words! Words! Words! This is a mess!
Bill:	I don't see any words on that page, Noodles.
Noodles:	The words are invisible...just for ghosts...like me. So just listen:

Words, Words

A POEM BY ILO ORLEANS

Many words
That sound alike
Mean different things —
 Like these:
Tail and tale,
And pail and pale
And sees and seize
 And seas.

And deer and dear,
And hear and here,
And two and to
 And too,
And pear and pair,
And fare and fair,
And dew and due
 And do.

Many words
That sound alike
Mean different things
 I know;
Like son and sun,
And one and won,
And sew and sow
 And so.

Noodles: I can tell you one thing, Bill Martin,
our language is crazy.
Look at these *words.*
How can anybody read this mess?
Wer-dz! Wer-dz! Wer-dz!
Oh, little ear,
you are my teacher, my dear teacher.
Without you, dear ear, my eye would
be in a slug of trouble.

Bill: No doubt.

Noodles: Be careful with your silent b's, Bill Martin.
My ear doesn't hear them.

Bill: But your ear knows to skip over them
and tells your eyes to do the same.

Noodles: My *nose* has nothing to do with it.
It's my ears!

Bill:	That's what I said.
Noodles:	My *eyes* said it too.
Bill:	So we're agreed.
Noodles:	Yes, I think.
Bill:	On what!
Noodles:	The eyes cannot read anything the ears have not heard.
Bill:	Robert Frost said that.
Noodles:	So did I. And now I'm going to test your ears, Bill Martin.
Bill:	I thought you didn't like tests.
Noodles:	For you they're okay, Bill Martin. Four me their knot sew good. Hear, reed this:

One, Two, Three – Gough!

To make some bread you must have dough,
Isn't that sough?

If the sky is clear all through,
Is the color of it blough?

When is the time to put your hand to the plough?
Nough!

The handle on the pump near the trough
Nearly fell ough.

Bullies sound rough and tough enough,
But you can often call their blough.

BY EVE MERRIAM

Bill: Touché! Nudlz, u'v mayed yor poynt.

Noodles: Aye thinque aisle gow nau, Bil Mar'n.

Bill: Doughn't luz yure eerz, Newduhlz.
U nede them evrie tiem yeau reed.
Thuh speling uv wirdz in hour langwidge
sometimes can be counted on
to tell us how to pronounce them,
but other times—Waugh!—
thuh speling iz a mishmash
uhntil thee ier goze tu werk.

Noodles: Gouldbigh! Gudbahee.

Bill: Noodles, your confusing me.

Noodles: Then trust your ears.
Goodbye, Bill.
Oodeley! Oodeley.

Bill: Eye'll never be the same.

The Conjure Wives

Once on a time,
when a Halloween night came
on the dark o' the moon,
a lot o' old conjure wives
was a-sittin' by the fire
an' a-cookin' a big supper
for theirselves.
The wind was a-howlin' 'round
like it does on Halloween nights,
an' the old conjure wives
they hitched theirselves
up to the fire
an' talked about the spells
they was a-goin' to weave
long come midnight.

The children will enjoy hearing you read
this story aloud the first time. From then on,
they'll be reading it on their own,
over and over and
over again.

a folktale for reading aloud, with pictures by Albert Pucci

"The Conjure Wives" is an example of home-rooted language, language that was framed at the fireside. Our literature is enriched by stories that are told in language of this kind, such as *Huckleberry Finn*, *Uncle Remus Stories*, the *Jack Tales*, *Smoky*. This is not language to be ashamed of or to be avoided in the classroom. It's language to be appreciated for its color, zest, rhythm, and impact. Will Rogers, years ago, made a professional career of exploiting his home-rooted language. The children will easily latch onto the music and suspense of "The Conjure Wives." Sit back and enjoy it.

By an' by

there come a-knockin' at the door.

"*Who's there?*"

called an old conjure wife.

"*Who-o? Who-o?*
One who is hungry
and cold,"

said a voice.

Then the old conjure wives
they all burst out laughin'
an' they called out:

"*We's a-cookin' for ourselves.*
Who'll cook for you?
Who? Who?"

The voice didn't say nothin',
but the knockin' just kept on.

For a discussion of ways to help children appreciate home-rooted language, see page 120 TE.

This tale lends itself to reading aloud, choral reading, and storytelling. Since it's very short and one that we never tire of hearing, you might like to invite children to form their own groups to work out a presentation that they dream up. This will lead naturally into creative dramatics. Won't it be interesting to see how the children create the effect of the dough swelling and swelling until it fills the room? And won't it be interesting to see how they create the presence of the "voice" without the audience ever seeing him?

"*Who's that a-knockin'?*"
called out another conjure wife.
"*Who? Who?*"

Then there come a whistlin',
wailin' sound:

"*Let me in, do-o-o-o!*
I'se cold thro-o-o-o
an' thro-o-o-o,
an' I'se hungry too-o-o!"

Then the old conjure wives
they all burst out laughin',
an' they commenced
to sing out:

"Git along, do!
  We's a-cookin' for ourselves.
  Who'll cook for you?
  Who? Who?"

An' the voice didn't say nothin',
but the knockin' just kept on.

Then the old conjure wives
began to get scared-like,
an' one of 'em says,
  "Let's give it somethin'
    an' get it away
    before it spoils our spells."

An' the voice didn't say nothin',
but the knockin' just kept on.
Then the conjure wives
they took the littlest piece of dough,

as big as a pea,
an' they put it in the fry pan.
An' the voice didn't say nothin',
but the knockin' just kept on.
An' when they put the dough
in the fry pan,
it begun to swell an' swell,
an' it swelled over the fry pan
an' it swelled over the top
o' the stove
an' it swelled out on the floor.
An' the voice didn't say nothin',
but the knockin' just kept on.
Then the old conjure wives
got scared
an' they ran for the door,
an' the door was *shut tight.*
An' the voice didn't say nothin',
but the knockin' just kept on.
An' then the dough
it swelled an' it swelled
all over the floor
an' it swelled up into the chairs.

An' the old conjure wives
they climbed up
on the backs of the chairs
an' they were scareder
and scareder.
An' they called out,
"Who's that a-knockin'
at the door? Who? Who?"

An' the voice didn't say nothin',
but the knockin' just kept on.
An' the dough kept a-swellin'
an' a-swellin',
an' the old conjure wives
begun to scrooge up
smaller an' smaller,
an' their eyes
got bigger an' bigger
with scaredness,

Have you noticed how regular
the dialectic spellings are
in this story?
Once *d* is omitted from the word *and,*
it is always omitted from the word *and.*
Once *g* is dropped on an *ing* ending,
it is always omitted.
It will be profitable to invite
the children to read the story,
searching out these
regular irregularities.
As they recognize the system,
it can lead to the generalization
that all language is system.

an' they kept a-callin',
"Who's that a-knockin'?
Who? Who?"

An' then the knockin' stopped,
and the voice called out,
"Fly out the window, do!
There's no more house for you!"

An' the old conjure wives
they spread their wings
an' they flew out the windows
an' off into the woods,
all a-callin',

"Who'll cook for you?
Who? Who?"

An' now if you go into the woods
in the dark o' the moon,
you'll see
the old conjure wife owls
an' hear 'em callin',
  "Who'll cook for you?
  Who-o! Who-o!"

Only on a Halloween night
you don't want to go
'round the old owls,
because *then*
they turns to old conjure wives
a-weavin' their spells.

111

My Old 'Coon Dog

My old 'coon dog,
my old 'coon dog,
I wish you'd bring him back.
He chased the old sow
over the fence
And the little pig
through
the crack, crack, crack.
And the little pig
through the crack.

My old 'coon dog,
my old 'coon dog,
He chased a 'coon up a tree.
And when I shot
that racoon down,
It was twice as big
as me, me, me.
It was twice as big
as me.

My old 'coon dog,
my old 'coon dog,
He went to chase a 'coon;
He started the chase
at the first of March
And ended the tenth
of June, June, June.
And ended the tenth
of June.

My old 'coon dog,
my old 'coon dog,
He died one afternoon;
I woke with a fright
that very same night
And heard him chasing
a 'coon, 'coon, 'coon.
And heard him chasing
a 'coon.

My old 'coon dog,
my old 'coon dog,
I wish you'd bring him back.
He chased the old sow
over the fence
And the little pig
through
the crack, crack, crack.
And the little pig
through the crack.

An American folk song

i heard a
couple of fleas
talking the other
day says one come
to lunch with
me i can lead you
to a pedigreed
dog says the
other one
i do not care
what a dogs
pedigree may be
safety first
is my motto what
i want to know
is whether he
has got a
muzzle on
millionaires and
bums taste
about alike to me

The lack of punctuation in his poem
is not a handicap in reading
it aloud. The sound of
the sentences create their
own punctuation. It is this
built-in ability to hear
and recreate
the sentence melodies
that allows children to speak
with the sound of sense.
Likewise they need
the sound of sense
(sentence melodies)
in developing
reading and writing
fluency.

archy the cockroach speaks,
from *certain maxims of archy*
by don marquis

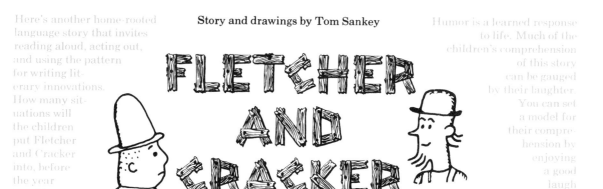

Story and drawings by Tom Sankey

When Fletcher went to town
to buy a new pump,
he found a "One Cent Sale."
He bought two pumps
for the price of one pump,
plus 1 cent.

"Shucks," says Fletcher,
"I only need *one* pump.
I got no use for the other.
Might as well see if Cracker has
something to swap for it."

So he went off to Cracker's house.

"Hello, Fletcher," says Cracker.
"Whatcha got there in the wagon?"

"This here's a brand new pump,"
says Fletcher.
"I thought you might
have something
you'd wanta swap for it."

"Well ..." says Cracker,
"that's hard to say.

I can't think of anything I have
that you might want, Fletcher."

"Oh, you must have something,"
says Fletcher.
"Look around."
This sentence can really stand *expanding*.
For suggestions, see page 80 TE.

"Well," says Cracker,
"I have a cow
that gives chocolate milk."

"Oh, you do not," says Fletcher.

"Yes, I do," says Cracker.
"Come on, I'll show you her."

Inside the barn,
Cracker showed Fletcher a small cow.

"Heck," says Fletcher,
"that's a *red* cow."

"I know it is," says Cracker.
"But she gives *chocolate* milk."
And he set in to milk the cow.
After a minute he handed Fletcher
a cup of chocolate milk.

Fletcher tasted it.
"By golly!" says Fletcher,
"she *does* give chocolate milk!"

"That's right," says Cracker.
"Wanta swap?"

"You bet!" says Fletcher.
"The pump is yours
and the chocolate-milk-giving-cow
is mine."

Fletcher tied the cow to the back
of his wagon and went home.

He put the cow in the barn,
fed her some hay,
and went in the house to bed.

The next morning
Fletcher went out to milk the cow,
but all she would give
was ordinary milk.

"That Cracker has thrown me
a crooked stick," says Fletcher.
"This is no chocolate-milk-giving-cow!
I'm going to fetch her
right back to him."

Fletcher tied the cow
to the back of his wagon
and drove over to Cracker's house.

"Hey you, Cracker," says Fletcher.
"This here red cow gives white milk."

"Not chocolate?" says Cracker.

"Not chocolate!" says Fletcher. "White!"

"What did ya feed her?" says Cracker.

"Why, I fed her hay, just like
I feed all my cows," says Fletcher.

"Oh, well, that's the problem,"
says Cracker.
"You have to feed her cocoa beans."

"Cocoa beans?" says Fletcher.
"Just where am I going to get
cocoa beans?"

"I don't know," says Cracker.
"I don't have any more."

"Come on now, Cracker," says Fletcher.
"You tricked me!
You tricked your best friend!"

"Well," says Cracker, "I have a sheep
that grows tailor-made suits.
Would you like the sheep instead?"

"Oh . . ." says Fletcher, "I might."

"Come along," says Cracker,
and he led the way to the barn.

Sure enough, there was the sheep
wearing a suit coat and matching pants
complete with buttons and pockets.

"How did such a thing happen?"
says Fletcher.

"It was an accident," says Cracker.

"The sheep accidentally ate
 a suit pattern
 and grew this suit of clothes
 all ready for wearing."

"Stop right there," says Fletcher.
"I'll just take that sheep.
 It's a good trade."

Fletcher hurried home
 with the sheep.
"Why, I can easily feed this sheep
 all sorts of patterns," says he,
"I can have it grow me an overcoat
 and a sweater and woolly underwear
 and all kinds of things."

He peeled the coat and the pants
 off the sheep, and tried them on.
The pants were too short
 and the coat too small.

"Oh, no!" says he to himself.
"That Cracker has done it again.
 He has dunked my doughnut,
 but I'm going right back
 and squeeze the coffee out."

He rode back to Cracker's house
 with the sheep and the suit
 to find Cracker sitting as before
 on his front porch in the rocker.

"Hello, there, Fletcher," says Cracker.
"How does the suit fit?"

"It don't fit at all," says Fletcher.
"I'd have to be four feet tall
 and three feet wide
 for this suit to fit me."

"Sounds about right," says Cracker.
"I bet it fit the sheep just perfect."

Fletcher was so mad, he couldn't talk
 for a long while and then he said,
"Gimme back my pump."

"Well," says Cracker. "I can't do that."

"Why not?" says Fletcher.

"Well, because," says Cracker,
"I sold it to Hiram Handy.
 Tell you what I'll do, though."

"What's that?" says Fletcher.

"I'll pay you for it," says Cracker.
"How much did you pay for it?"

"One cent," says Fletcher.
"I paid one cent for it,
 and it was the best buy I ever made."

"Well, that's fine," says Cracker.
"I'll just pay you
 double what you paid for it."

"You will?" says Fletcher.

"Yes sir!" says Cracker.
"And just think:
 That's twice what you paid for it.
 You sure made a good deal
 for yourself this time, Fletcher."

And all the way home,
 Fletcher told himself,
"I really am smart.
 Even Cracker says so."

I know a large dune rat

whose first name is Joe
And he skips beneath the boardwalk medium slow
Out to the edge where the daylight glisters
And he hasn't any brothers and he hasn't any sisters
And he hasn't any uncles and he hasn't any aunts
And he hasn't any Sunday-go-to-meeting pants.

Oh, he lives all alone in the big tall grassages
And through the brush piles he has secret passages.

He dines on moonbeams and washed-up scobbles
And he never has the toothache or the collywobbles.
He comes out at night and he dances by the sea
And he's a pretty nice dune rat, if you're asking me.

A POEM BY EUGENE F. KINKEAD
ART BY JANE ARMSTRONG WALWORTH

Some children might like to do their science
reports in rhyme, particularly if you give
them freedom to coin rhyming words as
needed. A leavening of tomfoolery is crucial
to any learning atmosphere. How long can
you stand a deadly serious diet of either food
or words?

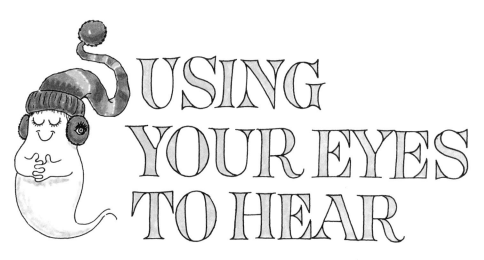

USING YOUR EYES TO HEAR

APPEAR
APPEAR
APPEAR
APPEAR
APPEAR

Bill: Noodles, are those earmuffs?

Noodles: Speak a little louder, Bill.
I can't hear you.

Bill: I said, WHY ARE YOU WEARING EARMUFFS?

Noodles: I think I can't hear you.

Bill: WHY THE EARMUFFS?

Noodles: Bill Martin, you don't talk very good sometimes.

Bill: TAKE OFF THOSE EARMUFFS, NOODLES!

Noodles: I'll take them off, Bill Martin,
but why are you shouting?

Bill: I'm sorry, Noodles.
I was trying to make you hear.

Noodles:	It won't work, Bill. Today I'm just listening with my eyes.
Bill:	That's a good reading skill, Noodles. I didn't know you knew so much about reading.
Noodles:	I know many, many things that you don't know I know, Bill Martin.
Bill:	That's true, Noodles. Each one of us carries a lot of knowledge in our heads that even we don't know we have.
Noodles:	I'm filled with knowledge. Didn't you know that?
Bill:	Yes, Noodles, you're a very knowledgeable ghost. Now tell me more about listening with your eyes.
Noodles:	Well, Bill Martin, if you had written down what you just said, I would have known you were shouting.
Bill:	You would have?
Noodles:	Sure, because the letters would have gotten bigger and blacker and louder all the time.
Bill:	Not everybody writes in big black letters to signal that he's shouting.
Noodles:	The funny papers always do. That's why they're smarter. School books aren't that smart, I don't think. They just go on and on and on and on in the same old type, forever. All I know is I'd rather read words on a cereal box that snap, crackle and pop!

Bill: Granted, Noodles.
It's exciting to see type explode on the page,
but a reader finds other kinds of clues
to help him hear the sounds of spoken language.

Noodles: And shouted language!

Bill: An exclamation point can tell that a sentence is shouted
even if the letters all stay the same size.

Noodles: Then you keep the exclamation points, Bill Martin,
and I'll keep the big letters.

Bill: A period signals to your eyes that a sentence is ending.
If you listen to yourself reading aloud, Noodles,
you'll hear your voice bring the flow of words
to a rest—to a stopping place.

Noodles: You don't use enough periods, Bill Martin.
You just talk and talk and talk and never stop.
That's why I'm putting my earmuffs back on.
I'd rather listen to myself.

Bill: Well, let your eyes listen to this, Noodles.

WHOSE IZZY IZZY?
IZZY YOURS OR IZZY MINE?
I'M GETTING DIZZY
WATCHIN' IZZY ALL THE TIME.
SAID HE'D MARRY ME THIS SPRING.
NOW HE'S BUYING YOU THE RING!
WHOSE IZZY IZZY?
IZZY YOURS OR IZZY MINE?

Noodles: (reads) Whose Izzy is he?
Is he yours
or is he mine?
I'm gettin'.....
Say, Bill Martin,
I like it better this way:

WHOSE ISHY ISHY?
ISHY HIS OR ISHY MINE?
I'M GETTIN' WISHY
WATCHIN' ISHY ALL THE TIME.
SAID SHE'D MARRY ME THIS SPRING,
NOW SHE'S WEARIN' IZZY'S RING.
WHOSE ISHY ISHY?
ISHY HIS OR ISHY MINE?

Goodbye, Bill Martin.
Ishy is calling me, I think.
Maybe she's changed her mind.
Oodeley, oodeley.

DISAPPEAR
DISAPPEAR
DISAPPEAR
DISAPPEAR
DISAPPEAR

Bill: Goodbye, Noodles.

Aloha

Hawaii, paradise islands.
Green-robed mountains
towering over the land,
rich fields of sugar cane
and pineapples
dotting the landscape,
a friendly sun brightening
the day after a rain,
stretching beaches of white sand
that welcome in the blue sea,
friendly people of many races
mixing their lives and languages
and dreams
in beautiful Hawaii.
Most family names in Hawaii
are Oriental names
like Chan, Okum, Yank
and Fujita,
because many immigrants
came years ago to Hawaii
from China, Japan and Korea
to work in the sugar cane
and pineapple fields.
Many workers also came
from the Philippine Islands,
Portugal and other places.
Consequently,
many different languages
and combinations of languages
are now spoken in Hawaii.

An editorial feature
with watercolor, *Rain Forest*, by John Pike

Pronunciation Key
to Hawaiian Sounds

Hawaiian Vowel	As in English
a	*ah*
e	*gay*
i	*see*
o	*oh*
u	*shoot*

The seven consonants, *h, k, l, m, n, p, w,* are pronounced just as they are in English with one exception. When *w* is the next to the last letter in a word, it is sounded like *v. Hawi* is pronounced hah' vee. When *e* is the last letter in a word, it is sometimes pronounced to rhyme with *see. Wahine* (woman) is pronounced wah hee' nee, but *kane* (man) is pronounced kah' nay.

The accent in a Hawaiian word is almost always on the next to last syllable.

The Hawaiian language
is written with only five vowels
and seven consonants.
The vowels and consonants
always signal the same sounds,
with the two exceptions
shown in the chart above.
Because the language
is so easy to pronounce,
you may want to learn
a few Hawaiian words
to combine with English.
This is what many Hawaiians do—
mix languages.

Wiki (wee' kee) means "hurry."
Can't you hear yourself
telling your mother in the morning
when she's cooking breakfast,
"*Wiki, wiki*"?
Mele (may' lay) is "song."

"Sing along, gang! Here's
a great *mele!*"
Huhu (hoo' hoo) is "angry."
"Don't stop me! I'm *huhu!*"
Hapa (hah' pah) means "half."
"It's *hapa* past eight!"
You already know, probably,
that *aloha* (ah loh' hah)
means "welcome."
"*Aloha, malihinie.*"
(a-loh-hah mah-lee-hee-nee.)
"Welcome, stranger."
Here are more Hawaiian words
to play with:
luau (loo' ow) feast,
opu (oh' poo) stomach
keiki (kay' kee) child
kaukau (kow' kow) food,
popoke (poh poh' kee) cat
pupuli (poo poo' lee) crazy.

Here are a few English names translated into Hawaiian:

Cynthia	Kinikia	(kee nee kee' ah)
Jane	Kini	(kee' nee)
Judith	Iukiki	(ee oo kee' kee)
Margaret	Makaleka	(mah kah lay' kah)
Mary	Malia	(mah lee' ah)
Susan	Suse	(soo' say)
Arthur	Aka	(ah' kah)
David	Kawika	(kah wee' kah)
Edward	Eluwene	(ay loo way' nay)
Frank	Palakiki	(pah lah kee' kee)
Kenneth	Keneke	(kay nay' kay)
Walter	Wala	(wah' lah)

Perhaps you have wondered
why Hawaiian words
are written with English letters.
There is a logical reason.
The Hawaiians had no
    written language
at the time
the first English-speaking
    missionaries
came to the Islands.
As the missionaries began
writing down some
of the Hawaiian words,
they naturally spelled them
with English letters.
If it had been
Japanese missionaries
who had written down
the Hawaiian language,
the language today
very likely would be written
in Japanese characters.
And now for one more word:
humuhumuhunukunukuapuaa.
It's almost as good as
supercalifragilisticexpialidocious.
It's pronounced
(we'll take it in syllables)
hoo-moo-hoo-moo-hoo-noo-koo-noo-koo-
ah-poo-ah-ah.
It's a big name for a little fish
found in the waters around Hawaii.

ROWAN-TREE, AND RED THREAD PUT THE WARLOCKS TO THEIR SPEED.

A TRADITIONAL ENGLISH VERSE   DESIGN BY RAY BARBER

We're right behind you, Charlie Brown

An editorial feature,
with cartoons by Charles Schulz

Americans love popcorn,

hot dogs, ice cream cones—

and Charlie Brown.

He and his friends

are more popular today

than they have ever been

in seventeen years

of their lives.

Isn't it interesting

that these comic-strip characters

never grow older

and never really change.

Charlie is still

losing ball games,

one after another.

At last count

he had just lost

999 ball games in a row

Copyright © 1963 by United Features Syndicate, Inc.

128

Copyright © 1961 by United Features Syndicate, Inc.

Lucy is just as grumpy
as she ever was.
She "hollers" so loud
that she can be heard
for blocks around,
but this is no louder
than she "hollered" yesterday
or ten years ago.
Her little brother, Linus,
still carries his baby blanket
around and sucks his thumb.
He probably will never
outgrow those habits.

Snoopy, the dog,
never does anything right,
but nobody wants
to change Snoopy.
They like him just as he is.
Actually, there's much good
that can be said about the way
a comic is put together.
For one thing,
you don't have any trouble
knowing what's happening.
The pictures tell the story.

Notice that throughout this article the writer
is trying to convince you of his opinion that
comics are okay. Did you need convincing?

When words are spoken,
a "balloon" shows
who is doing the talking.

When a person shouts,
the words get larger
and blacker,
helping the reader know
how they sound.

Moreover, a comic story
is short.
In five minutes, or less,

you've been in and out
of the story
unless you are reading
one of your favorite comic books.

And finally,
the comic characters never change.
They become old friends
whom we love,
even though we know their faults
and what they will be doing
tomorrow.

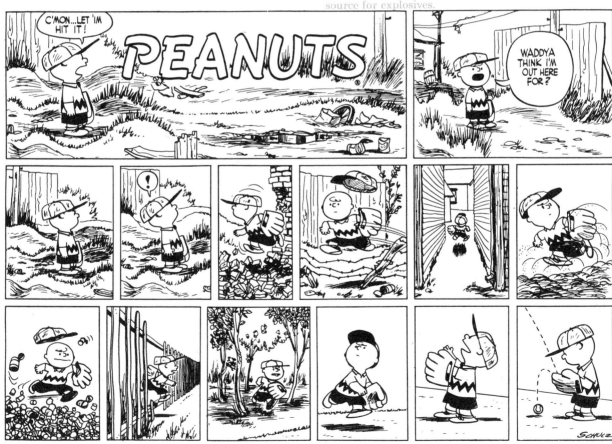

All: Giant Thunder striding home

wonders if his supper's done.

Boys: *'Hag wife, Hag wife, bring me my bones!'*

Girls: *'They are not done,'* the old hag moans.

Boys: *'Not done? not done?'* the giant roars

and heaves his old wife out of doors.

Cries he,

'I'll have them, cooked or not'

but overturned the cooking-pot.

All: He flings

the burning coals about;

see how the lightning

flashes out!

Upon the gale

the old hag rides,

the cloudy moon

for terror hides.

All the world with thunder

quakes;

forest shudders, mountain shakes;

from the cloud the rainstorm breaks;

every living creature wakes.

Stamp no more from hill to hill—

tomorrow you shall have your fill.

A POEM BY JAMES REEVES,
SCORED AS A CHORAL READING.
WHAT FUN!

Transforming
Sentences

LETTERING BY ERIC CARLE

When did the children discover that this is a description of a storm couched in the image of a giant? They might like to try writing some of their own descriptions in this imaginative way. And isn't it interesting how the title treatment becomes part of the mood of the poem?

USING LITERARY STRUCTURE IN READING

Bill: Noodles, what are you doing now?

Noodles: I'm building a story.

Bill: What's your story about?

Noodles: Three skunks.
The little bitty skunk,
the middle-size skunk
and the big skunk.
They really have a problem.

Think, good teachers, how literary structure has been belabored in schools, from elementary grades through college. Now along comes a ghost who discusses literary structure in the most natural, childlike way! You won't be surprised, will you, to know that this dialogue is a replica of a young child's spontaneous analysis after he had innovated on *The Three Billy-Goats Gruff*.

Bill: Well, that sounds like a story for sure.

Noodles: This story has a big problem, Bill Martin.
You see, the skunks have to get over the hill
to eat garbage.

Bill: Well, that's no problem.
Skunks know how to get over a hill.

Noodles: I know that
but you don't know what lives under the hill.
That's the problem.

Bill: Go on.

The linguistic and literary generalizations inherent in this and other dialogues throughout the book can be interwoven in any discussions you're having about reading. The better the children understand these premises, the better they'll approach each new reading experience.

Noodles: A great big troll lives under the hill
           and he won't let the skunks cross over.

Bill: Noodles, this sounds like a story I heard before.
           "The Three Billy-Goats Gruff."

Noodles: Yes, but ~~when you like a story~~, Bill Martin,
           ~~you can make another like it. It's so easy.~~ See page 19TE.
           You ought to try it sometime, Bill.

Bill: Well, let's hear more about the skunks.

Noodles: Well, the little skunk went trip-trapping up the hill.
           And the troll said, "No you don't, little skunk.
           I'm going to eat you up."
           The little skunk began to cry,
           "Oh, don't eat me, Mr. Troll.
           Wait for my brother.
           He's fatter."
           "Very well," said the troll.
           "I'll wait for your brother."
           So the little skunk crossed
           over the hill to eat garbage.

Bill: Then what happened?

Noodles: I don't have to tell you about the second skunk, Bill Martin.
           You already know, don't you?

Bill: If your story goes like other stories,
           I already know how the second episode goes.
           The second skunk meets the troll
           and convinces him to wait for his brother.

Noodles: "Very well," said the troll.
           "I'll wait for your brother.
           He's the fattest of all."
           And the second skunk crossed over the hill.
           to eat garbage.

Bill: And now comes the third skunk.

Noodles: Yes, here comes the third skunk trip-trapping up the hill.
Trip, trap! Trip, trap!
Trip, trap! Trip, trap!
And the old troll calls out,
"Who's that crossing over my hill?"
The big billy goat—oh, I mean the big skunk said,
"It is I, the big skunk!
I'm crossing over the hill to eat garbage."
"Not by the hair of my chinny-chin-chin!"
said the troll.
And he came up out of his hole.
"Now, I'm going to eat you up!"

Bill: Go on, Noodles.
This is a good story.

Noodles: Well, that skunk
didn't have a fatter brother
so he just yelled at the troll,
"Well, come along!
I've got two spears
and I'll poke your eyeballs
out at your ears!
I've got besides two curling stones
and I'll crush you to bits—
body and bones."

Bill: Then what?

Noodles: Oh, Bill, you know.
The big skunk stinked him good!
How else would you get rid of a troll
if you were a skunk?

Bill: That got rid of the problem, all right.

Noodles: Yes, the story's done
and the problem's all over.
Goodbye, Bill.
Oodeley, oodeley!

Bill: You know, boys and girls,
that ghost never ceases to amaze me.
Where did *he* learn that you can take the pattern of a story
to create another one?

Noodles: One more thing, Bill Martin.
If you wonder how I can read stories so easy,
even when I can't sound out all the words,
it's because I can figure out
how the author put his story together.
When you can tell what he's doing,
it makes the reading so easy
you don't even worry about the big words.

Bill: Noodles, you're just a con man.
Right now you're probably figuring out
how this next story is put together.

Noodles: Not me, Bill Martin.
I'm leaving.
I think Ishy is calling me.
Oodeley, oodeley!

DEVILISH MARY

A TRADITIONAL FOLKSONG, DESIGNED BY RAY BARBER

When I was a young man growin' up,
    thought I'd never marry;
saw so many pretty little girls,
    but none of them would have me.

RAH, RAH, RINKTUM, A HOODLEUM A RINKTUM!
RAH, RAH, RINKTUM A RAZY!
RAH, RAH, RINKTUM, A HOODLEUM A RINKTUM!
HER NAME WAS DEVILISH MARY!

One little girl I came across
    lived in London's Dairy,
her hair was red as golden thread,
    and her name was Devilish Mary.

RAH, RAH, RINKTUM, A HOODLEUM A RINKTUM!
RAH, RAH, RINKTUM A RAZY!
RAH, RAH, RINKTUM, A HOODLEUM A RINKTUM!
HER NAME WAS DEVILISH MARY!

138

Hadn't been courtin' but a week or two,
    we both got in a hurry;
both agreed right on the spot,
    and married the very next Thursday.

RAH, RAH, RINKTUM, A HOODLEUM A RINKTUM!
RAH, RAH, RINKTUM A RAZY!
RAH, RAH, RINKTUM, A HOODLEUM A RINKTUM!
HER NAME WAS DEVILISH MARY!

Hadn't been married but a week or two,
    she acted like the devil;
every time I'd open my mouth
    she'd crack my head with the shovel.

RAH, RAH, RINKTUM, A HOODLEUM A RINKTUM!
RAH, RAH, RINKTUM A RAZY!
RAH, RAH, RINKTUM, A HOODLEUM A RINKTUM!
HER NAME WAS DEVILISH MARY!

She wropped the broom all around my neck,
    striped my back with switches;
jumped on the floor and popped her fist
    and swore she'd wear the britches.

RAH, RAH, RINKTUM, A HOODLEUM A RINKTUM!
RAH, RAH, RINKTUM A RAZY!
RAH, RAH, RINKTUM, A HOODLEUM A RINKTUM!
HER NAME WAS DEVILISH MARY!

One night when I was late gettin' in,
   a-makin' an awful blunder,
she picked up a big old vinegar jug—
   I thought I' uz struck by thunder!

RAH, RAH, RINKTUM, A HOODLEUM A RINKTUM!
RAH, RAH, RINKTUM A RAZY!
RAH, RAH, RINKTUM, A HOODLEUM A RINKTUM!
HER NAME WAS DEVILISH MARY!

Hadn't been married but about two months,
   she decided we'd better be parted;
picked up her little bundle of duds,
   and down the road she started.

RAH, RAH, RINKTUM, A HOODLEUM A RINKTUM!
RAH, RAH, RINKTUM A RAZY!
RAH, RAH, RINKTUM, A HOODLEUM A RINKTUM!
HER NAME WAS DEVILISH MARY!

If ever I get married again
   it'll be for love nor riches,
it'll be a little gal sixteen foot high
   that can't get in my britches.

RAH, RAH, RINKTUM, A HOODLEUM A RINKTUM!
RAH, RAH, RINKTUM A RAZY!
RAH, RAH, RINKTUM, A HOODLEUM A RINKTUM!
HER NAME WAS DEVILISH MARY!

Here's a model sentence for expanding. Invite the children to add describing words in front of the word *river* and phrases or clauses after the word *river*. To help children frame clusters of words, suggest they begin the clusters

Can you figure out the missing words in this old jingle? How come?

with *near, by, under, that, which, when, where,* etc. Doesn't it delight you that children seldom, if ever, add anything that doesn't have the sound of sense? See page 80 TE.

I came to the river...

beautiful	that I had never seen before
roaring	near the old farmhouse
polluted	where the scouts were camping

I came to the river and I couldn't get across,

I jumped on a frog 'cause I thought he was a hoss,

The hoss wouldn't pull so I traded for a bull,

The bull wouldn't holler so I sold him for a dollar,

The dollar wouldn't pass so I threw it in the grass,

The grass wouldn't grow so I traded for a hoe,

The hoe wouldn't dig so I traded for a pig,

--- --- -------- squeal -- - ------ --- - wheel,

As the children fill in the missing words they are ex-

--- ----- -------- run -- - ------ --- - gun,

periencing the fact that the knowledge of a story or

--- --- -------- shoot -- - ------ --- - boot,

poem's literary structure can help a person decode print.

--- ---- -------- fit -- - thought I'd quit,

And I did.

American folklore

SNOOPY

A SONG BY CLARK GESNER
ILLUSTRATED BY CHARLES SCHULZ

Here are the words to a song in the musical comedy, "You're a Good Man,
Charlie Brown." The show was based on the comic strip "Peanuts" by
Charles M. Schulz. Imagine that you are Snoopy as you read this aloud. If
you have the recorded music of the show, you may want to sing along.

They like me. I think they're swell.
   Isn't it remarkable
How things work out so well?
   Pleasant day, pretty sky,
Life goes on, here I lie.
   Not bad, not bad at all.
Cozy home, board and bed,
   Sturdy roof beneath my head.
Not bad, not bad at all.

Faithful friends
   Always near me,
Bring me bones,
   Scratch my ear.
Little birds come to cheer me,
   Every day sitting here
On my stomach with their
   Sharp little claws
Which are usually cold
   And occasionally painful,
And sometimes there are
   So many that I can
Hardly stand it . . . .

I FEEL EV'RY NOW AND THEN
THAT I GOTTA BITE SOMEONE.

I know ev'ry now and then
   What I wanna be—
A fierce jungle animal
   Crouched on the limb of a tree.
I'd stay there very, very still
   Till I see a victim come
I'd wait knowing very well
   Ev'ry second counts.
And then like the fierce
   Jungle creature I am

I WOULD POUNCE!

I'D POUNCE!

I'd . . . you know, I never
   Quite realized it was
Such a long way down to
   The ground from here—
   Hm—
   Let me see, where was I?
Oh, that's right, the pretty sky,
   Not bad, not bad at all!

I WONDER IF IT WILL SNOW TONIGHT?

After we received permission to use the song, "Snoopy," we read *Peanuts* cartoons by the dozen until we found one strip that fit the theme of the song. It pleased us so to make a good match that we'd like to invite the children to go through their favorite comics to find an even better match. They may match all sorts of comics with songs and poems. It would be a great reading activity.

After you have read the song aloud, page 145, and the children have chimed in to the point of familiarity, their eyes will be prepared to pick up the syllabication/rhythm clues that are graphed on page 144.

KEMO   KIMO

	1	2	3	4
In	Car -	o -	li - na	the
	folks	all	go,	☐
	Sing	song	kitty,	can't you
	ki -	me -	oh?	☐
	There's	where the	folks	all
	plant	the	tow.	☐
	Sing	song	kitty,	can't you
	ki -	me -	oh?	☐
	Cover	the	ground	all
	over	with	smoke,	☐
	Sing	song	kitty,	can't you
	ki -	me -	oh?	☐
	Then	their	heads	a -
	round	they	poke.	☐
	Sing	song	kitty,	can't you
	ki -	me -	oh?	☐
	Ke -	mo	ki -	mo,
	there,	oh	where?	With my
	hi,	my	ho,	and
	in	comes	Sally,	singin'
	Some -	time	penny -	winkle
	ling -	tum	nip -	cat,
	Sing	song	kitty,	can't you
	ki -	me -	oh?	☐

144

In Carolina the folks all go,

Sing song kitty, can't you ki-me-oh?

There's where the folks all plant the tow.

Sing song kitty, can't you ki-me-oh?

Cover the ground all over with smoke,

Sing song kitty, can't you ki-me-oh?

Then their heads around they poke.

Sing song kitty, can't you ki-me-oh?

      Ke-mo ki-mo, there, oh where?

With my hi, my ho, and in comes Sally, singin'

Sometime penny-winkle ling-tum nip-cat,

Sing song kitty, can't you ki-me-oh?

There was a frog lived in a pool,

Sing song kitty, can't you ki-me-oh?

Sure he was the biggest fool.

Sing song kitty, can't you ki-me-oh?

He could dance and he could sing.

Sing song kitty, can't you ki-me-oh?

Make the woods around him ring.

Sing song kitty, can't you ki-me-oh?

      Ke-mo ki-mo, there, oh where?

With my hi, my ho, and in comes Sally, singin'

Sometime penny-winkle ling-tum nip-cat,

Sing song kitty, can't you ki-me-oh?

This lively song from the Kentucky mountains is sheer nonsense,
but its rhythm and use of strange words
have made it a favorite with people everywhere.
The first verse of the song has been set up
to help you fit the syllables of words to the 1-2-3-4 beat of the rhythm.
Isn't it interesting to see how the words are syllabicated to fit the rhythm?
The words should be chanted or sung
(to your own tune, if you don't know the original melody).

One of the great stories
of all time
by Rudyard Kipling,
adapted by Bill Martin , Jr.,
with drawings by Mel Hunter

RIKKI-
TIKKI-
TAVI

These two pages of type and pictures orient the reader to an adaptation of this famous story. Some of your better readers undoubtedly will enjoy reading the original story of Rikki-tikki-tavi, found in *The Jungle Book* by Rudyard Kipling.

Teddy found Rikki-tikki-tavi

in a ditch one summer morning after a heavy rain.

Rikki-tikki-tavi's name is pronounced to rhyme with Ricky and Davey.

The rising water  had washed the little

mongoose from its burrow, and Teddy had carried

A mongoose, when fighting, stands on his hind legs like a kangaroo.

it home inside his shirt. Teddy and

his father and his mother were English. They were

A mongoose has but one purpose in life — to fight and kill snakes.

living in India where Teddy's father

146

was doing business for the King. Teddy begged

to keep the little 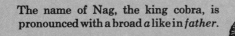 mongoose for a pet,

but Teddy's mother was fearful about having a

mongoose in the house. When Teddy's

father came home that evening, he reassured his

wife that a mon- goose would be good

protection against the danger of snakes in the

garden, and so 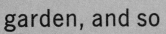 Teddy was given

permission to keep the homeless little mongoose.

Rikki-tikki meets Nag.

This is a storyteller's adaptation of a long story. A comparison of it with the original version about Rikki-tikki-tavi will show clearly how storytelling for a listening audience differs from storytelling for a reading audience.

Every morning
after his breakfast
of bits of banana and boiled egg,
Rikki-tikki-tavi
scuttled around the bushes
in the garden
just to see what was to be seen.
He was rather like a little cat
in his fur and tail,
but quite like a weasel
in his head and habits.
His eyes
and the end of his restless nose
were pink;
he could scratch himself
anywhere he pleased
with any leg, front or back;
he could fluff up his tail
till it looked like a bottle-brush;
and his war cry
as he scuttled
through the long grass
was:
Rikk-tikk-tikki-tikki-tchk!

This is to be read like an animal
sound, not like a human reading
words.

One morning
when Rikki-tikki-tavi
was in the garden,
he heard Darzee, the tailor-bird,
sitting on her nest
in the pine tree, crying.
A tailor-bird looks and sounds
something like a catbird.

Rikki-tikki stood up
on his hind legs and asked:
"What's the matter with you?"

"Oh, Rikki,
a terrible thing has happened.
One of my babies
fell out of the nest yesterday
and Nag ate him."

"Hm-m!" said Rikki-tikki,
"That is very sad —
but I am a stranger here.
Who is Nag?"

Just then the little mongoose
heard a cold, horrid sound
behind him
that made him jump
two feet into the air
and whirl around.

Inch by inch
out of the grass
rose up the head
and spread hood
of Nag, the black king cobra,
who was five feet long
from tongue to tail.

When he had lifted
one third of himself
clear of the ground,
he stayed balancing to and fro
exactly as a dandelion tuft
balances in the wind,
and he looked at Rikki-tikki
with wicked eyes
that never changed expression,
whatever the snake
might have been thinking.

"Who is Nag?" he said.
"I am Nag.
Look, and be afraid!"

It is true
that Rikki-tikki was afraid
for a moment;
but it was impossible
for him to stay frightened
for any length of time.

Though Rikki-tikki had never met
a live cobra before,
his mother had fed him
on dead ones,
and he knew
that a grown mongoose's
business in life
was to fight and eat snakes.
Nag knew that, too, and
at the bottom of his cold heart,
he, too, was afraid.

Suddenly
Darzee, the tailor-bird,
who was sitting on her nest
in the pine tree
watching the two below,
cried out:
"Behind you, Rikki!
Look behind you!"

Fortunately
Rikki-tikki knew better
than to waste time in looking.
He jumped up into the air
as high as he could go,
and just under him
whizzed the black blur
of another snake.

It was another cobra,
Nagaina,
Nag's wicked mate.
She had crept up behind Rikki
as he was talking
to make an end of him;
and he heard her savage hiss
as the stroke missed.
Rikki-tikki came down
almost across her back.
If he had been
a wise, full-grown mongoose,
he would have known
that then was the time
to scramble up the snake's back
and to break her neck
by biting sharply
just above her spread hood.
He bit, indeed,
in the middle of her back
where it did little damage.
Then he jumped clear
of the snake to avoid
the terrible lashing return-stroke
of the cobra,
which sometimes can be
just as deadly to a mongoose
as the cobra's bite.
Nagaina was left torn and angry.

Now it is said that
when a cobra misses its stroke,
it never says anything
or gives any sign
of what it means to do next.
Without a word
Nagaina slithered off
through the tall grass
to reconnoiter,
and Nag followed her.

Nag and Nagaina plan their attack.

That night
Teddy carried Rikki-tikki
off to bed with him.
Rikki-tikki was too well bred
to bite or scratch,
but as soon as Teddy was asleep,
he went off for his night walk
around the house.

Instantly Rikki-tikki knew
that something was strange
about this night.
The house was as still as still,
but he thought he could hear
the faintest scratch-scratch
in the world,
a noise as faint as that of a fly
walking on a windowpane.
He listened.
Then he recognized the sound
as that of snake scales
scratching on brickwork.
He knew immediately
that it was Nag or Nagaina
trying to enter the house.
But where?

He remembered a loose brick
at the back of the bathroom;
the brick could be pulled out
to drain the bath water
from the tub
to the creek near the house.
Plumbing facilities in India
are not always the same as ours.
Rikki-tikki crept
down the dark hall
and turned into the bathroom.

Pressing his lithe body
against the plastered wall,
he listened
and heard Nag and Nagaina
whispering together
outside in the moonlight.
Nag was saying,
"You go back to our nest
in the melon patch
at the back of the garden,
Nagaina.
Take care of our eggs.
They have been left alone too long.
I will creep into the bathroom
and wait
until the master comes in
for his bath in the morning.
Then I'll kill him
and his wife and his child.
When the family is dead,
the bungalow will be empty,
and Rikki-tikki will leave here.
And once again
the garden will belong to us.

Rikki-tikki heard
Nagaina slither off
toward the melon patch
at the back of the garden.

What kind of noise is a *slithering* noise?

151

Then he saw,
or thought he saw,
the black beady eyes
of the cobra
as Nag pushed his head
around the loose brick
and pulled
the cold five feet of his body
into the room after him.
Rikki-tikki heard the cobra
rise up and lap water
from the water jar.
Then he heard the cobra
wrap himself, coil by coil,
around the bulge
at the bottom of the water jar.

After an hour
Rikki-tikki began to move,
muscle by muscle,
towards the jar.

Nag was asleep,
and Rikki-Tikki looked
at his big back, wondering
which would be the best place
for a good hold.
"If I don't break his back
at the first jump," said Rikki,
"he can still fight;
and if he fights — O Rikki!"

He looked at the thickness
of the neck below the hood,
but that was too much for him;
and a bite near the tail
would only make Nag savage.
"It must be the head,"
he said at last.
"The head above the hood;
and, when I am once there,
I must not let go."

Then he jumped
and sank his teeth deep
into Nag's head
which was lying a little clear
of the water jar.

It took Nag only a moment
to uncoil.
Then he battered Rikki-tikki
to and fro,
as a rat is shaken by a dog,
to and fro on the floor,
up and down,
and around in great circles.
Rikki-tikki thought
he would surely be killed
in the encounter,
but he was certain of one thing:
when the family found him,
he would still be clinging
to the snake's head.

Here, in the middle of the ferocious fight, Kipling reminds us that Rikki-tikki is aware that he is protecting the family from danger. By giving the little animal human characteristics such as this, Kipling invites the reader to share vicariously the noble qualities of this valiant mongoose.

Then Rikki-tikki saw
a ball of fire shoot past him,
and he felt its hot breath...
When he regained consciousness,
Teddy was holding
the little mongoose
in his arms,
showering him
with praise and affection.
He was saying that Rikki-tikki
had saved the family.
Teddy's father
had been awakened
by the fight in the bathroom,
and he had fired two shots
into the cobra's hood.
Nag, the black king cobra,
was dead.

Without waiting for breakfast,
Rikki-tikki escaped
to the veranda
and nursed his tired
and bruised body
in the warm sunshine.
He stretched out
on the brickwork
and was almost asleep
when he heard Darzee singing,
"Nag is dead — is dead —
is dead!"

Nag is killed in a battle with the little mongoose.

The news of Nag's death
was all over the garden,
and the frogs and birds joined
in the chorus, "Nag is dead —
is dead — is dead!"

"Yes," said Darzee.
"The maid has thrown
Nag's lifeless body
out on the rubbish heap.
Nag will never eat my babies
again."

"Oh, you stupid
tuft of feathers,"
said Rikki angrily.
"Is this the time to sing?
Where is Nagaina?"

The content of the story communicates to the reader that the word *valiant* is laudatory. Whether the reader actually can unlock *valiant* and perceive its exact meaning is almost immaterial to the understanding of the story. Children, therefore, should be encouraged to skip over unknown words as long as they are getting the meaning of the story. It would be regrettable if a child bogged down on the word *valiant* and had not learned to proceed with the story until he had unlocked, pronounced, and figured out the meaning of every word. The *(continued below)*

"Nag is dead — is dead —
is dead!" Darzee went on,
singing at the top of her voice.
"The valiant Rikki-tikki
caught Nag by the head
and held fast.
The big man brought
the bang-stick,
and Nag fell in two pieces."

"Stop singing a minute, Darzee,"
said Rikki.
"Where is Nagaina?"

"What is it,
O Killer of the terrible Nag?"
asked Darzee.

"Where is Nagaina?"

"On the rubbish heap
by the stables,
mourning for Nag.
Great is Rikki-tikki
with the white teeth."

"Bother my white teeth!
Have you ever heard
where she keeps her eggs?"

"In the melon bed,
on the end nearest the wall,
where the sun strikes
nearly all day," said Darzee.
"She hid them there
three weeks ago."

Rikki-tikki turned
and flew down the garden path,
past the stable
and the tool shed,
on to the melon patch
near the wall.
There,
underneath the melon leaves,
he found Nagaina's nest
very cunningly concealed.
In it were twenty-six cobra eggs.

A cobra's nest
is nothing more than a hole
scooped out in the soft earth.
The cobra eggs
looked not unlike the eggs
that we keep in our refrigerator
at home,
except that the cobra eggs
were encased
in a soft, white, transparent skin
instead of in a hard shell.

subsequent context of the story will make the meaning of an unknown word clear. Children need to develop the art of skimming through different selections to give them the context needed for unlocking story meanings along with word meanings.

Rikki-tikki finds Nagaina's nest in the garden.

Inside of each egg
Rikki-tikki could see
a baby cobra curled up,
and he knew
that the eggs would hatch
within the day.

The little mongoose
chuckled to himself
as he clipped the end
of the first egg
and killed the little snake
within it.
He remembered
that his mother had told him
that a baby cobra
can kill a man or a mongoose.

Methodically,
Rikki-tikki fished egg after egg
from the nest
and destroyed them.
All the while
he was keeping a sharp watch
lest Nagaina should return.
At last
there was but one egg left.

As Rikki-tikki pulled it
from the nest,
Darzee, the tailor-bird,
flew to him
from her nest in the pine tree,
screaming,
"Rikki-tikki!
Come! Come!
Nagaina has gone
onto the veranda!
Oh, come quickly!
She means killing!"

Rikki-tikki grasped the last egg
in his mouth
and scuttled up the garden path
as hard
as he could put foot to ground.
He bounded up the veranda steps
two at a time.

What he saw
caused him to stop so short
that he skidded
halfway across the brickwork.
Teddy, his father and mother
were seated there
at early breakfast,
but Rikki-tikki saw
that they were not eating.
They sat stone-still,
and their faces were white.

Coiled at the foot
of Teddy's chair
within easy striking distance
of Teddy's bare leg
was Nagaina.
She was swaying to and fro,
singing a song of triumph.

**Rikki-tikki
fights
Nagaina
on the
veranda.**

"Son of the big man
that killed Nag!"
she hissed.
"Wait a little.
Keep very still,
all you three!
If you move
I strike,
and if you do not move
I strike.
Oh, foolish people
who killed my Nag!"

Teddy's eyes
were fixed on his father,
and all his father could do
was to whisper,
"Sit still, Teddy.
You mustn't move.
Teddy, you mustn't move."

Are the children aware
that a snake will not
strike a motionless
object?

Rikki-tikki
bounded out onto the veranda
behind Nagaina
and spit the last egg
from his mouth.
"Turn around, Nagaina.
Turn and fight!
Look at the last of your eggs.
I found your nest in the melon
patch and destroyed all
of the eggs but this one."

Why do you think, in a beautifully illustrated book such as this, that the story "Rikki-tikki-tavi" was not illustrated in detail?

Nagaina spun clear round,
forgetting everything
for the sake of her one egg.
At the same moment
Teddy's father
shot out a big hand,
caught Teddy by the shoulder,
and dragged him across the table,
spilling the dishes and the food
to the floor with a clatter.
"Tricked! Tricked! *Rikk-tck-tck!*"
chuckled Rikki-tikki.
"The boy is safe now,
and it was I — I — I
that caught Nag by the hood
last night in the bathroom."
The little mongoose began
to jump up and down,
all four feet together,
his head close to the floor.
"Nag threw me to and fro,
but he couldn't shake me off.
He was dead before the big man
blew him in two.
I did it!
Rikki-tikki-tck-tck!
Come, then, Nagaina.
Come and fight with me.
You shall not be a widow long."

Now the family drew back
against the porch railing,
watching the battle
of life and death
that was taking place
before them.
Nagaina was striking
again and again.
After each strike
she would recoil
as quickly as a watch-spring,
ready to strike again.
Rikki-tikki
was bounding all around Nagaina,
keeping just out of reach
of her stroke.
His little pink eyes
had turned red,
like hot coals.
He was standing up
on his hind feet
like a little kangaroo,
ready to spring
at the snake's neck
whenever he found the opening.
All the while
he was sounding his battle cry,
"*Rikki-tikki tck-tck!*"

Notice how the author has changed Rikki-tikki's battle cry, which previously was meant to be only an animal sound, into a human word without particularly distorting the animal sound.

Notice in this column the author's expert use of metaphor. Writers, particularly poets, have learned that the art of communication depends mainly upon the art of metaphor. In fact, Robert Frost once said that the use of metaphor *is* the poet's art.

You and the children might enjoy looking
through other pages for examples of
metaphor.

Again and again and again
she struck.
Each time her head came
with a whack
on the brickwork of the veranda,
she gathered herself
together to strike again.

Rikki-tikki danced in a circle
to get behind her,
and Nagaina spun round
to keep her head to his head.

Rikki had forgotten the egg.
He had moved so far from it,
that Nagaina came nearer
and nearer to it.
At last, she caught the egg
in her mouth,
turned to the veranda steps,
and flew like an arrow
down the path —
with Rikki-tikki right behind.

It is said
that when the cobra
runs for its life,
it goes like the whiplash
flicked across the horse's neck.
But Rikki-tikki was even faster.
He caught Nagaina by the tail
as she plunged into the rat hole
where she and Nag used to live.
Rikki-tikki tried to pull her back,
but Nagaina was the stronger
of the two,
and inch by inch,
she pulled the little mongoose
into the hole with her.

And Darzee, the tailor-bird,
who was sitting in the pine tree
watching the battle
taking place below,
set up a very mournful chant:
"It's all over
with Rikki-tikki-tavi!
Brave Rikki-tikki-tavi!
Even a wise, full-grown mongoose
would not follow a cobra
into its own hole."

Isn't it interesting that the word *with* in the
sentence above could be changed to *for*
without loss of meaning?

Rikki's triumph is complete.

Presently
the grass
that grew around the rat hole
quivered,
and Rikki-tikki-tavi,
covered with dirt,
dragged himself out of the hole
leg by leg.

He stopped
to shake the dust
from his whiskers;
then he looked up at Darzee,
the tailor-bird,
and said:
"It's all over.
Nagaina is dead."

And the red ants that lived
between the grass stems
heard him
and began trooping down
one after another
to see
if what Rikki-tikki-tavi had said
was true.

And as for Rikki-tikki-tavi,
he lay down in the sunshine
beside the rat hole
and went to sleep.
He slept all of that morning
and half of the afternoon,
because
for a little mongoose
he had done a hard day's work.

AFTERNOON ON A HILL

I will be the gladdest thing
   Under the sun!
I will touch a hundred flowers
   And not pick one.

I will look at cliffs and clouds
   With quiet eyes,
Watch the wind bow down the grass,
   And the grass rise.

And when lights begin to show
   Up from the town,
I will mark which must be mine,
   And then start down.

BY EDNA ST. VINCENT MILLAY

PUSSY-WILLOWS

Spring, Spring,
everything
you do is new and shiny.
Who, who
teaches you
to think of things as tiny
as all those velvet
willow cats
in furry coats
and furry hats
astride a twig
like acrobats,
soft, and sleek, and shiny?

BY AILEEN FISHER

Lines of poetry are written in lengths
and arrangements (chunks of
meaning) that cue the reader to rhyme,
rhythm and meaning. Look at the
different arrangements on these two
pages. How does the visual form of
these poems help you in the reading?

These poems and others throughout
the book invite many many repetitions.
Sometimes you will do the reading
to set the oral models in children's ears.
After they are familiar with the speech
melodies, they can take over,
sometimes reading individually,
sometimes in chorus, sometimes in
special groups with their own choral
reading arrangements.

Autumn

The morns are meeker than they were,
    The nuts are getting brown;
The berry's cheek is plumper,
    The rose is out of town.

The maple wears a gayer scarf,
    The field a scarlet gown.
Lest I should be old-fashioned,
    I'll put a trinket on.

BY EMILY DICKINSON

THE LAST WORD OF A BLUEBIRD

As I went out a Crow
In a low voice said 'Oh,
I was looking for you.
How do you do?
I just came to tell you
To tell Lesley (will you?)
That her little Bluebird
Wanted me to bring word
That the north wind last night
That made the stars bright
And made ice on the trough
Almost made him cough
His tail feathers off.
He just had to fly!
But he sent her Good-by,
And said to be good,
And wear her red hood,
And look for skunk tracks
In the snow with an ax—
And do everything!
And perhaps in the spring
He would come back and sing.'

BY ROBERT FROST

This double-page of poetry
can also be viewed as a
science experience.

PICTURE BY BETTY FRASER

161

Plugging into MEANINGS

Bill: Hey, Noodles, listen to this.
It's about your relatives.

Noodles: Now, what have they done?

Bill: Well, just listen and you'll find out.
"Nine Little Goblins."

They all climbed up
    on a high board-fence,
  Nine little goblins
    with green-glass eyes.
Nine little goblins that had no sense . . . . .

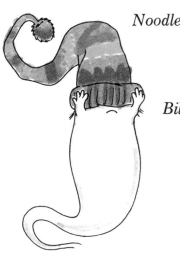

Noodles: Stop right there, Bill Martin.
This poem is not any good, I think.
Goblins have lots of sense.
They're not dumb.

Bill: . . . . Nine little goblins that had no sense.
And couldn't tell coppers
    from cold mince-pies;
And they all climbed up on the fence
    and sat—
And I asked them
    what they were staring at.

Noodles: This poem is not good, I think.
It's unfair to goblins.

Bill: And they sang: "You're asleep!
There is no board-fence,
And never a goblin
with green-glass eyes!

Noodles: There! Right there!
That poem's all wrong.
Goblins are real
and they have real eyes—not glass eyes.
I know I don't like this poem, Bill Martin.

Bill: 'Tis only a vision the mind invents
After a supper of cold mince-pies,
And you're doomed to dream this way,"
they said—
"And you sha'n't wake up till you're clean plum dead!"

Noodles: How can you like that poem, Bill Martin?
I think nobody likes that poem.

Bill: Well, this poem may not be your dish, Noodles.
You probably are so involved defending the goblins
that you didn't hear what the poet was saying.

Noodles: I heard him all right.
He said goblins are dumb.
Say, Bill Martin, who wrote this thing?

Bill: A man named James Whitcomb Riley.

Noodles:

Well, where does he live?

I'm going to go see him right now

and tell him a thing or two about goblins.

Bill:

Well, that's impossible, Noodles.

James Whitcomb Riley is dead.

He's been dead for a long long time.

Noodles:

That's no problem to me, Bill Martin.

I talk to dead people all the time.

Goodbye, Bill.

See you later.

Oodeley, oodeley!

DISAPPEAR
DISAPPEAR
DISAPPEAR
Disappear

Bill: Isn't it interesting, boys and girls,

what personal meanings Noodles brought to this poem.

This is the way it is with reading:

the author has his meanings,

the reader has his meanings,

and the two of them talk back and forth.

But I'm afraid in this case,

Noodles wasn't talking back and forth.

He blocked the author's meanings out

the moment he heard the author say,

"Nine little goblins that had no sense. . . . ."

From that time on

Noodles was talking to himself.

Good teachers, notice how easy it is for Bill to become pedantic when he's anxious to develop a particular awareness. Is it any wonder children *and ghosts* tune us out to preserve their sanity!

A good reader listens
both to what the author is saying
and to what he himself is thinking.
He can totally disagree with the author,
just so that he knows what the author says.
The reader can't always confront the author
as Noodles is doing right now,
but the reader develops a bag of know-how
for figuring out the author's meanings.

APPEAR
APPEAR
APPEAR
APPEAR
APPEAR
APPEAR

Noodles: Oh, Bill, you should have been there!
I like good old James Whitcomb Riley.
He's a very nice man I think.
And he wrote a very nice poem.

Bill: Well this is a real switch, Noodles.
What happened?

Noodles: He wasn't criticizing goblins at all, Bill Martin.
He was laughing at you people.
The goblins aren't even real, Bill Martin.
They're those fake goblins you people see
when you eat too much.
So, goodbye, Bill Martin.
I've got to go now
and read this poem to my relatives.
Oodeley, oodeley.

Bill: Well, boys and girls, now I really am stuck in meanings—
my meanings, the author's meanings, and Noodles'.
Maybe I *should* go get a piece of cold mince pie.

If you wonder why the central action of this picture falls in the gutter (center) of the double page, you share our concern. In granting reproduction rights, the Museum specified that the picture could not be cropped since the broad sweep of prairie background is essential to the artist's purpose. A good reason.

A Picture for Storytelling

After you have read this aloud to the children, invite them to read it aloud in unison, to make a choral reading of it, and to make a list of the facts that the poem reveals. Won't it be interesting to see if the children have any difficulties discovering that the title of the poem is the first line?

This poem invites children to observe living things in their natural habitat. This is science at its best.

A bat is born
    naked and blind and pale.
His mother makes a pocket of her tail
    and catches him.
He clings to her long fur
    by his thumbs and toes and teeth.
And then the mother dances through the night,
    doubling and looping,
    soaring, somersaulting —
    her baby hangs on underneath.

What is the difference in meaning between *underneath* and *beneath*?

Here is a great sentence to rearrange. See page 88 TE.

All night, in happiness, she hunts and flies.
Her sharp cries
    like shining needlepoints of sound
    go out into the night and,
    echoing back,
    tell her what they have touched.
She hears how far it is,
    how big it is,
    which way it's going:
    she lives by hearing.

Is it possible that a bat sees with its ears? Let us explore the meanings.

How many other words can you list that begin with a silent *g*?

The mother eats the moths and gnats she catches
    in full flight;

Is *gh* always silent as it is in *flight*?
    enough   daughter
    laughter   hiccough
This suggests making a list and coming to a generalization about the vagaries found in our language.

in full flight

How do you like this style of art as compared to other styles found in this book?

      the mother drinks the water of the pond
      she skims across.
Her baby hangs on tight.
Her baby drinks the milk she makes him
      in moonlight or starlight, in mid-air.
Their single shadow,
      printed on the moon
      or fluttering across the stars,
      whirls on all night;
      at daybreak
      the tired mother flaps home to her rafter.
The others all are there.
They hang themselves up by their toes,
      they wrap themselves in their brown wings.
Bunched upside down,
      they sleep in air.
Their sharp ears,
      their sharp teeth,
      their quick sharp faces
      are dull and slow and mild.
All the bright day, as the mother sleeps,
      she folds her wings
      about her sleeping child.

Notice the repetition of the word *sharp* and the sub-contrast of meanings achieved by the last six words in the sentence.

Has the picture of bats created by the poet changed any of your former notions about bats?

A POEM BY RANDALL JARRELL,
DRAWING BY MAURICE SENDAK

LITTLE CHARLIE CHIPMUNK
HE CHATTERED
AND HE CHATTERED
HE CHATTERED
AND HE CHATTERED
HE CHATTERED
AND HE CHATTERED
HE CHATTERED

OH,

The typography and typographical design suggests fun with language. Children will enjoy writing some of the poems or articles as display pieces as well as reading experiences. Incidentally, notice the emphasis of words in boldface type and words in color type.

WAS A TALKER, MERCY ME!
AFTER BREAKFAST
AFTER TEA!
TO HIS FATHER
TO HIS MOTHER!
TO HIS SISTER
TO HIS BROTHER!
TILL HIS FAMILY WAS ALMOST
DRIVEN WILD.
LITTLE CHARLIE CHIPMUNK
WAS A VERY TIRESOME
CHILD!

Do you agree with the poet that a talkative child is very tiresome to others? Do you think that the poet was really talking about a chipmunk, or was he laughing at some of our human antics?

A poem by Helen Cowles LeCron

Cardinal

Chickadee

How Birds Keep Warm in Winter

When you see a chickadee huddled on a snowy branch or a duck swimming in icy water, do you wonder how birds keep warm in winter?

A bird has several layers of winter feathers to keep him warm. Next to his skin is a blanket of filmy feathers called *down* and some fluffy body feathers. This blanket of feathers traps the bird's body heat in millions of tiny air pockets, keeping it warm. The bird's outer feathers are staggered like shingles on a roof to keep out the rain and snow. The strong outer feathers can withstand all kinds of wind and weather.

A bird regulates his body temperature by changing the position of his feathers. When he is perched or sleeping in the cold, he fluffs out the feathers to trap the warm air near his skin. When he is too warm and wants to cool off, he hugs his feathers close to his body to squeeze out the warm air.

An article
written and illustrated
by Bernard Martin

After you've finished with this article, it will be interesting to re-read *The Web of Winter*, page 56. The two selections beautifully cross pollenate.

Pigeon

Crop

Stomach

Gizzard

Intestines

Do you recall how Bill, in "The Web of Winter," kept Quick-Quick's *furnace* burning?

You may be surprised to discover that a bird has a "furnace" that makes heat to keep him warm.

The bird's stomach is his furnace. When a pigeon eats a seed, a wonderful process begins within its body. The seed is stored in the bird's crop until it is needed for heat and energy. Then the seed goes into the stomach where it is softened by gastric juices. Later the seed moves into the gizzard where it is ground by strong, gritty muscles into fine particles that can be digested easily. These fine particles, like fiercely burning wood or coal, flow through the small intestines. They are absorbed by the intestinal walls and released into the blood stream, to be used by the body as heat and power. Your body digests food for heat and energy in much the same way.

A bird that lives in the snow and cold must eat from dawn until dusk to "keep his furnace roaring." The fuel burns quickly, and if the "fire" goes out, the bird will freeze to death.

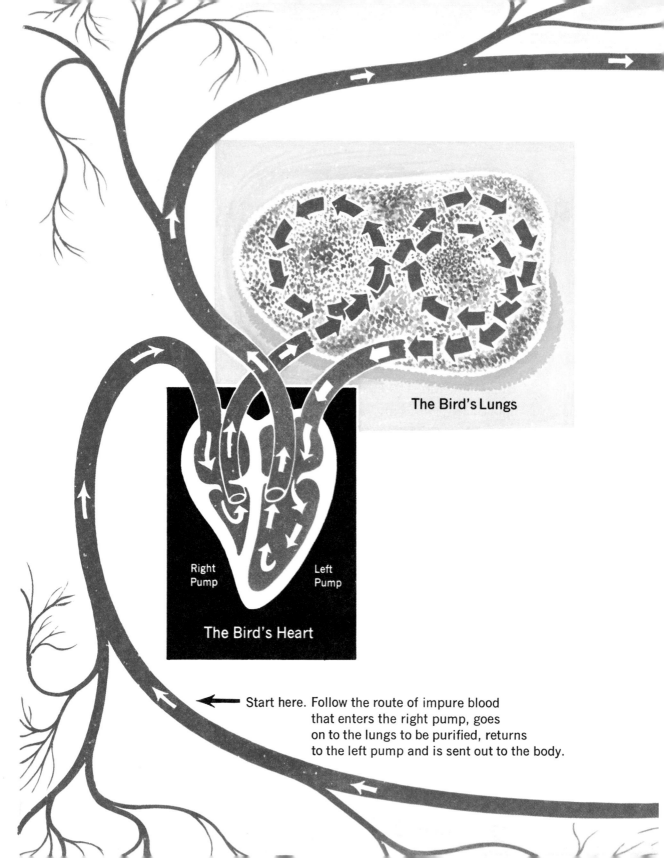

The Bird's Lungs

The Bird's Heart

Right Pump

Left Pump

Start here. Follow the route of impure blood that enters the right pump, goes on to the lungs to be purified, returns to the left pump and is sent out to the body.

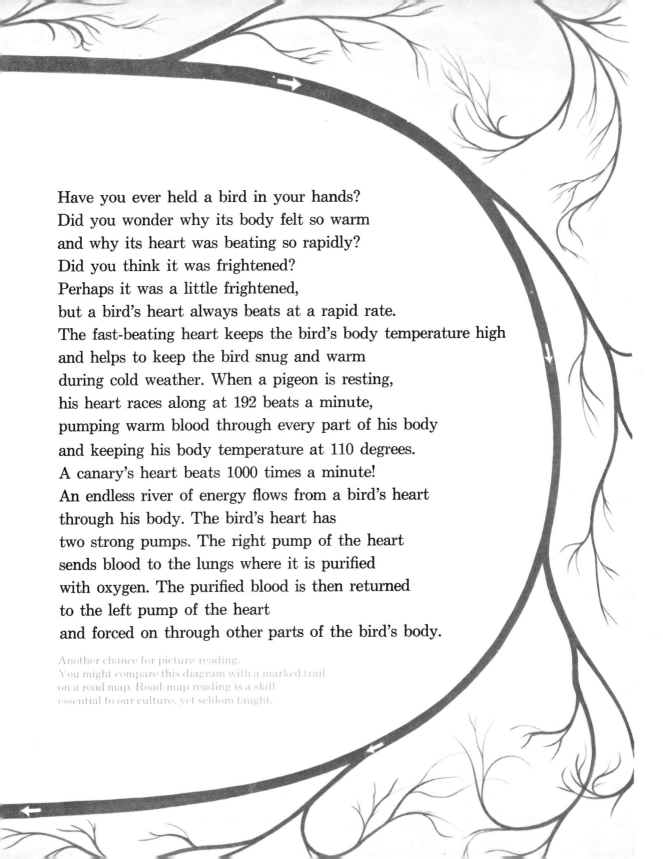

Have you ever held a bird in your hands?
Did you wonder why its body felt so warm
and why its heart was beating so rapidly?
Did you think it was frightened?
Perhaps it was a little frightened,
but a bird's heart always beats at a rapid rate.
The fast-beating heart keeps the bird's body temperature high
and helps to keep the bird snug and warm
during cold weather. When a pigeon is resting,
his heart races along at 192 beats a minute,
pumping warm blood through every part of his body
and keeping his body temperature at 110 degrees.
A canary's heart beats 1000 times a minute!
An endless river of energy flows from a bird's heart
through his body. The bird's heart has
two strong pumps. The right pump of the heart
sends blood to the lungs where it is purified
with oxygen. The purified blood is then returned
to the left pump of the heart
and forced on through other parts of the bird's body.

Another chance for picture reading.
You might compare this diagram with a marked trail
on a road map. Road-map reading is a skill
essential to our culture, yet seldom taught.

A bird also has another way to help keep himself warm in winter.

He oils his feathers, squeezing oil from a gland on his back. This waterproofs his feathers, providing him with a raincoat for protection from cold and rainy weather.

There is a way that you can help keep birds warm in winter. By seeing to it that the birds near your home have plenty to eat, you can help "keep their furnaces roaring" and their bodies warm in winter.

Isn't it pleasant to come upon two lovely poems about birds right on the heels of this fact-laden article? Both types of writing add to our appreciation of birds.

Titmouse

I Heard a Bird Sing

All: I heard a bird sing
    In the dark of December
A magical thing
    And sweet to remember.

Solo: "We are nearer to Spring
    Than we were in September,"
All: I heard a bird sing
    In the dark of December.   A POEM BY OLIVER HERFORD

The Robin

The robin comes in spring
And fills the air with merry song,
And makes the fields and meadows ring,
    Cheer-up!
    Cheer-up!
O robin, sing,
Lift your voice,
The air is warm,
The flowers are born,
Sing ... sing ... sing ... sing,
O lovely robin, *sing.*   A POEM BY HELEN I. MAY

This is a science story with rich language experiences that should be read aloud by you, the teacher, to the children. Subsequently, they will read the story silently and aloud and perhaps eventually use it as an oral reading for a classroom or auditorium program. Because of the unique language patterns in this story, you will want to read it aloud to yourself several times before you present it to the children, paying close attention to the flurries of excitement and resultant climaxes that occur throughout the story.

"Mool" is a particularly graphic story that lends itself to picture reading. Invite the children to study the pictures from page to page and discuss the meanings that the pictures convey. You will be surprised how much science information they will bring to and derive from their reading of the pictures. This type of reading activity is especially helpful for those children who are not strong readers of printed language. It helps build their self-respect to participate enthusiastically and significantly in a post-reading discussion based on picture reading. You may want to take their stories and comments down in dictation for them to read and later compare with the author's story.

Adapted by Bill Martin, Jr.,
from a German story *Mool,*
by Klaus Winter and
Helmut Bischoff.

**Something in the earth
is digging upward,
digging upward,
moving and lifting,
lifting and pushing,
pressing outward,
pressing upward and downward.**

To simplify this example, we have omitted this portion of the sentence.

Who is it that is digging, that seems to be stuck in the ground? It is Mool, the mole.

Who	is	it	that	is	digging?	It	is	Mool,	the	mole.
What	was	that	who	was	slithering	He	was	Jake,	a	snake
	are	this		will be	diving	She		Olive,	an	acrobat
		they		isn't	flying	That		Boo,		ghost

181

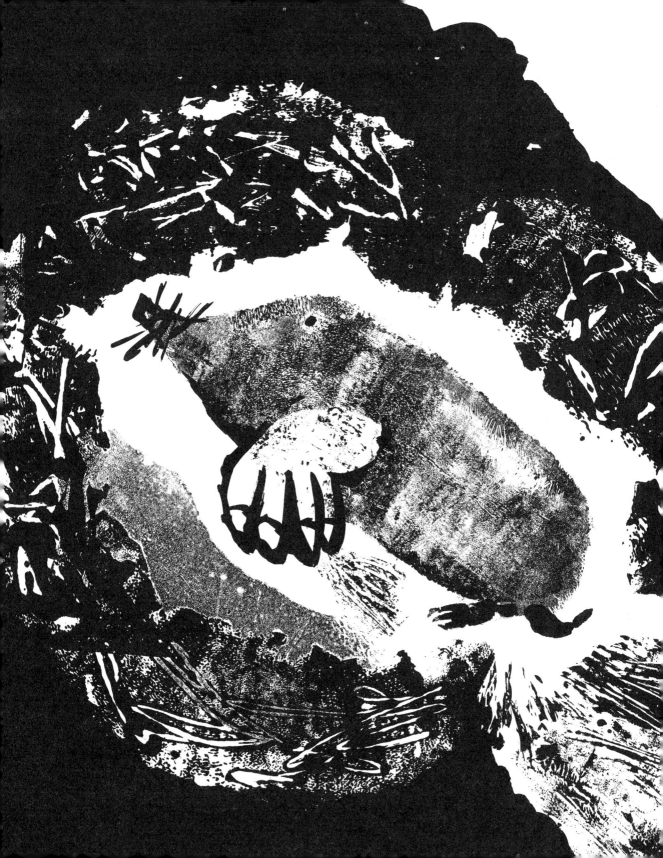

He is small and black,
with tiny eyes
that scarcely see
and two giant flippers
that are good for digging.
He has a snout and a long beard.
His body is covered
with velvety fur.
Mool, the mole,
crafty and shy,
constantly hungry.

This description of Mool may serve as a reference and pattern for children when they write a description of an animal. It provides them with a sequence of ideas with enough language patterns to trigger them into a full-blown use of their own writing skills. If a child should write an incomplete sentence such as the last language segment on this page, you might use it as an opportunity to discuss the appropriateness of fragments in certain types of writing. For a discussion of ways to help children link writing to reading, see page 114 TE in the back of this book.

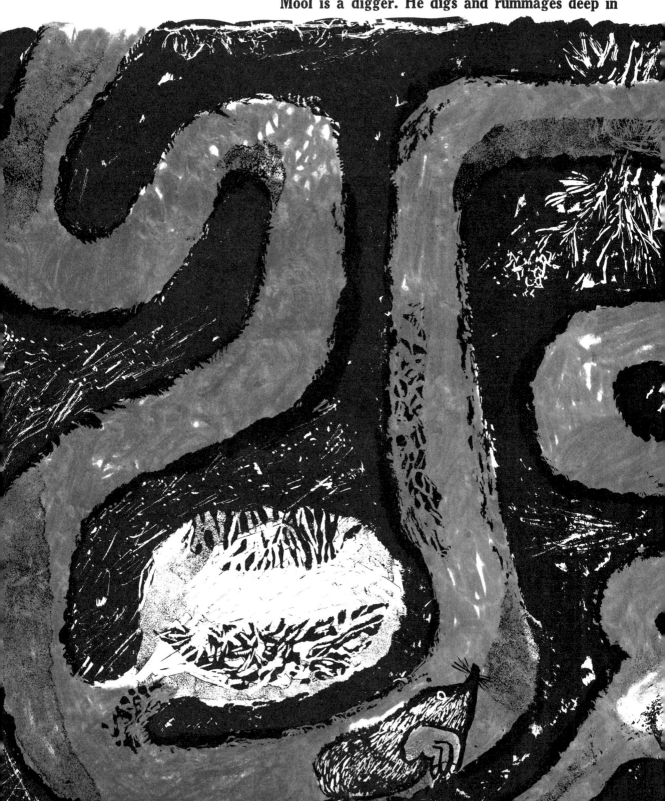

Mool is a digger. He digs and rummages deep in

the earth. He digs a tunnel to the sweet ivy roots.

He digs a hole to cool water.
He digs a pipeline
to the bed of young turnips.
Wherever he goes,
he digs a hole,
a tunnel, a pipeline.
Mool, the mole, is a digger.

But where does the earth go
when Mool is digging a hole?
Up, up, out of the hole.
He pushes the dirt
out of his tunnel.
Up with it! Out with it!
He leaves a mountain of dirt
at the mouth of his tunnel.
Mool is a pesky animal
if he digs in your yard.

Transforming Sentence. You don't have to confine yourself to this book in looking for model sentences to transform. You'll find them everywhere. Here, for example, is the beginning sentence from a familiar poem, "Someone," by Walter de la Mare.

Someone	*came*	*knocking*	*at*	*my*	*wee,*	*small*	*door.*
Something	began	creeping	up	the	dark	narrow	stair!
Somebody	was	walking	down	his	dim	unlighted	alley.
Milly	is	jumping	through	her	old	screen	door.
What	started	sliding	down	my	long	skinny	neck?
	likes						

This time you may wish to discuss some of the word groupings or punctuation marks.

1. *Isn't it interesting what a difference the question mark or exclamation point makes in the meaning of a given sentence?*

2. *Isn't it interesting that only the "ing" form of the action words can be substituted for the word "knocking."* If the children experiment, they will see that the present form of the verb or the *"ed"* form or any other form simply will not work.

3. *Aren't the describing words interesting? Isn't it fascinating that in our language they nearly always precede the described word? "Someone came knocking at my door small wee" just wouldn't sound right.*

4. *And how about the words that pattern like "his," "her," "my?" Isn't it interesting that they can represent an unlimited number of people?*

5. *And what about the words "at," "down," "through"?* Whenever a person encounters one of these words in his reading, he can make certain predictions about the kind of language that will follow.

It is these excursions into language that help children verbalize their own intuitive hunches about the workings of language and that help them claim new insights.

Now Mool is playing.

He is playing with a centipede
caught in his passageways.
He is playing with a worm
and a cricket and a snail.
They, too, are caught in the tunnel.

Smack!

Crackle!

Slurp

Mool has eaten them.
He has filled his stomach,
and now he is drowsy.
The mole is going to sleep.

From far at the end
of his passageways
come the sounds
of crawling and puffing,
puffing and scratching.
Mool hears it.
He's on his feet.
     After them!
        Out with them!
The fur tousles!
     They squeal!
        They squeak!
He chases the mouse sisters
out of his tunnel.

Here is a good model for transforming.

Mool wants to be alone.

Vocabulary Development: What better vocabulary-building and language-enriching experience can children have than to go back to this story and find all of the different words and phrases that are used to discuss and describe how Mool moves about?

Smack! Slap!
Mool is digging upward.
Suddenly, he is out of the ground.
Oh, how light it is!
The sun blinds him,
but it is warm on his fur.
He lies down to sleep
at the mouth of his tunnel.
High above him,
high in the clouds,
there is a black spot
that Mool does not see.

The spot has keen eyes
and sharp, pointed claws.
It dives from the sky
like a big shadow
. . . getting bigger
. . . bigger
. . . gigantic!
A fierce, hungry buzzard
is diving down at Mool!
Mool squeals!
He scuttles back into the ground.
The buzzard flies away
with only a stone in its claws.

Notice the recurring *k* sound in this column. The author has accented the *k* sound in keeping with the mole's chewing noises.

Mool digs deeper and wider.

He is hungry again.

His stomach can bear

something tasty!

And what has he found?

A fat turnip.

    Crunch, crunch!

A beautiful cabbage.

    Crunch, crunch!

A garden filled

with tasty, fresh vegetables.

    Crunch, crunch!

And here comes the farmer,

the angry farmer.

Here he comes with a frown,

waving his shovel.

How do you pronounce the word *vegetables*? All three are used.

    vej•te•belz
    vej•de•belz
    vej•e•te•belz

But Mool escapes.

He scuttles deep in his burrows.

No one can catch Mool

with a shovel.

"If I can't catch him,"

says the farmer,

"then I will drive him away.

I'll stick oily rags

in his burrows

to make a terrible smell.

And I'll put empty bottles

in his burrows

to whistle in the wind."

Mool stops.
"What do I smell?
What is that noise?
Oh, what a foul smell!
Oh, what a dreadful racket!
Away from here,
as fast as possible!
My delicate ears,
my sensitive nose
cannot bear this!"

Mool runs out of his burrow.
He swims across the lake,
his head above water.
On the other shore,
Mool starts burrowing
a new hole in the ground
with passageways all around
and a mountain of dirt
on the grass.

You and the children will find many sentence patterns in this poetic story that are comfortable examples of public language—the clear, direct, precise language that serves us best in everyday affairs. Whenever you find an interesting sentence in a story or poem, invite the children to try it out, reading it aloud many times and later trying to write it naturally into one of their own stories. This is the way language is claimed. See page 120 TE for further discussion of the levels of language.

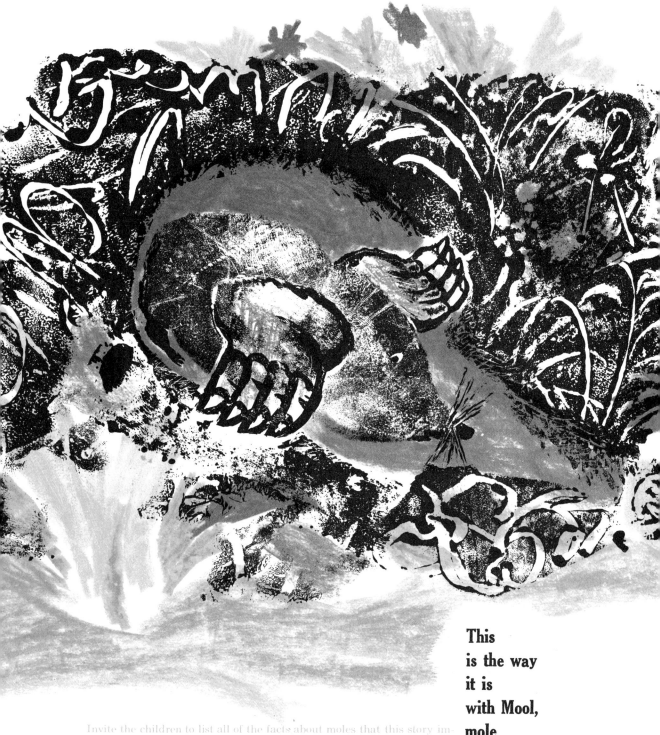

This
is the way
it is
with Mool,
mole
in the
ground.

What is the way with Mool?
What is your way?

This way of describing the mole's hole was pictured in "Mool," but it was not mentioned in the text. How long will it take the children to discover this fact? And won't it be interesting to notice whether any child responds to both the poet's and the artists's reference to *four* claws?

Rearranging Sentences: When children learn to recognize parts of sentences that can be moved within the sentence without changing sentence meanings, they become better readers and writers. The first three stanzas of this poem offer wonderful possibilities for this kind of rearranging. Ask the children to consider each stanza as a sentence. Throughout this book we have marked certain sentences that especially lend themselves to rearranging. You will find others on every page of the book. The children will learn much as they join in the search for sentences. See page 88 TE for further discussion of this linguistic manipulation.

The poet has used the *s* and *b* sounds for heightening his description of the mole. Do one reading asking the children just to listen to the sounds.

All but blind
  In his chambered hole
Gropes for worms
  The four-clawed Mole.

All but blind
  In the evening sky,
The hooded Bat
  Twirls softly by.

All but blind
  In the burning day
The Barn-Owl blunders
  On the way.

And blind as are
  These three to me,
So, blind to Someone
  I must be.

ALL BUT BLIND

A POEM BY WALTER DE LA MARE

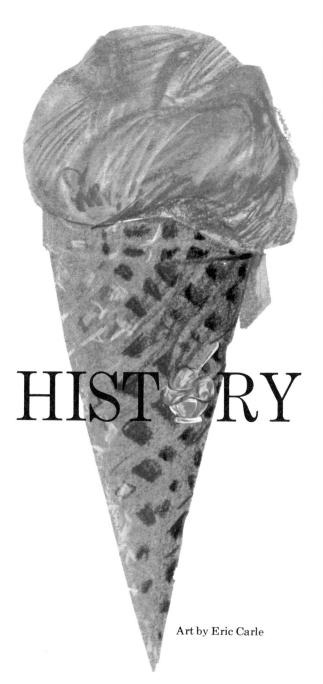

HIST RY

Art by Eric Carle

Bite by bite,
lick by lick,
Americans consume more
than four billion ice cream cones
each year.
The ice cream cone has become
a taken-for-granted part
of everyday life in America.
But it wasn't always so.
Until the turn of this century,
ice cream sold by street vendors
was served in glass dishes,
which required a great deal
of washing and care.
And customers were always
breaking the glasses
or walking away with them.
This unsatisfactory and expensive
means of serving ice cream
was changed in 1896
when the first
ice cream cone was invented.
The inventor
was an Italian immigrant,
named Italo Marchiony,
who sold ice cream
from a pushcart
in the streets of New York City.

Mr. Marchiony got tired
of washing his serving dishes
and buying new ones
to replace those
that had been broken,
so he decided to make
a new kind of container
for ice cream.
He baked a thin cooky
and rolled it up
into the shape of a cone.
Then he scooped ice cream
into the cone.

of the
ICE CREAM
CONE

His customers were delighted
with his new way
of serving ice cream,
and Mr. Marchiony was glad
to be free of dishes
and dishwashing.
These edible ice cream containers
became popular in New York.

They were called "toot" cones,
probably because
they resembled little horns.
Mr. Marchiony made a fortune
in New York
with his toot cones,
but somehow
the idea of the toot cone
never "caught on"
in the rest of the country.
It wasn't until
the St. Louis World's Fair in 1904
that the ice cream cone
was introduced to the world.
It so happened
that an ice cream vendor
at the Fair
was enjoying a brisk business
selling dishes of ice cream
for 5 cents and 10 cents.
One day he ran out of dishes
for ice cream
and didn't know what to do.
A Syrian waffle-maker
named Ernest Hamwi
had a waffle stand nearby.
When Mr. Hamwi
saw the problem
facing the ice cream vendor,
he suggested a simple solution.

Proper names in a story sometimes can be confusing to the reader unless he has actually heard
those names pronounced. This is especially true
when names come from another language as both
of these do. It is a good habit for a reader coming upon a name to stop, then and there, and decide how
he is going to pronounce it thereafter, right or wrong. The fact that he has decided on one pronunciation
makes the word more meaningful and more descriptive each time he reads it. To slip over a name willy-
nilly is like seeing a picture of a faceless man. It never comes alive as a person.

He took one of his waffles,
which was very thin,
and rolled it up into a cone.
It cooled quickly
and became hard and dry.

Then the ice cream vendor
filled the cone with ice cream,
and his customers
"ate it up" so to speak.
The ice cream cone
was on its way to becoming
an all-American treat.

Expanding Sentences: Here is a useful sentence to write on the board for expanding. How many words can the children list for describing the vendor? the cone? the ice cream? the customers?

The ice cream cone customers
at the St. Louis World's Fair
loved the cone so much
that they took the idea
back to their home towns
all across the country,
and before long
ice cream vendors
were selling the waffle-cones
at fair grounds,
carnivals, beaches,
amusement parks,
and, of course,
in all the neighborhood
ice cream parlors.

Isn't this a descriptive term?

Soon the national demand
for the cones
became so great
that the old method
of rolling cones by hand
proved too slow.
In order to supply
the growing demand,
machines were built in 1905
that could make
1,500 cones a day.
Cone-making machines
have been greatly improved
since then.
Now there are machines that,
with the press of a button,
automatically produce in a day
150,000 cones by themselves.

There are two kinds
of cone-making machines.
One is called
a baking-and-rolling machine,
which first bakes the waffles
and then automatically
rolls them into cones.
The other is called
a split-mold machine.
It pours waffle batter
into a cone-shaped mold
and then bakes the batter.
After the cone cools and hardens,
the mold automatically
comes apart,
and the cone is removed.

Strawberry?
Vanilla?
Double-decker?
Triple-decker?   Have you ever sat in the third
                 deck of a ball stadium?
What's your favorite kind
of ice cream cone?
Make mine a triple-decker —
a scoop of chocolate,
then a scoop of pineapple sherbet,
and crown that with
a scoop of peppermint stick.
Wow!

PART II

RESPONDING TO READING

Noodles: Oodeley, oodeley!
Here I come, Bill Martin,
full of response-ability.

Bill: Hello, Noodles.
I see you've already noticed
we're starting the second half of the book—
Responding to Reading.

Noodles: Oh, I've been reading this part
for a long long time.
I didn't tell you all this, did I?
I sneaked ahead.

Bill: That's all right, Noodles.
I hope the boys and girls and teachers and everybody
know that you can skip around in this book
from front to back to middle to in-between
any time you like.

Noodles: That's what I like...
skipping around and around and around,
reading here, reading there,
reading reading everywhere.
Sometimes I see things and I just can't wait.
I have to look at it right that very minute.

Bill: Now we're going to think of ways
to respond to what we read, Noodles.
Reading has to be for something
besides just recognizing words.

Noodles: Like having a real whole lot of fun.
Don't you like to have fun, Bill Martin?
I like to laugh when I read sometimes.
And I'm going to tell you something else,
but don't you tell anybody.
Do you promise?

Bill: I promise.

Noodles: Then I'll whisper it in your ear.

Bill: Just say it out loud, Noodles.
Nobody is here to hear you.

Noodles: That's not the way you do with a secret.
You don't tell the whole wide world.
I'm going to whisper in your nice little ear.

Bill: Alright, whisper it then.

Noodles: Which ear do you want me to tell it in, Bill,
the one right here
or the one on the other side of your little head?

Bill: Take your choice, Noodles.

Noodles: I think I like this one.
It's cleaner.
Pss...pss...pss...pss...pss...pss...pss...
pss...pss...pss...pss...pss...pss...pss!

Bill:	I never knew you ever cried, Noodles.
Noodles:	Sometimes I do when the story is sad, but I don't let anybody see me.
Bill:	Well, I cry too when the story is sad, Noodles. Many people do. "The Steadfast Tin Soldier" is the story of a brave man but it makes me cry every time I read it. There's nothing wrong with shedding tears. That's one way to respond to reading.
Noodles:	I'll betcha an astronaut wouldn't cry, I'll betcha. He's too brave.
Bill:	That isn't true, Noodles. You're not a sissy just because you cry. Crying is part of being a human being. Sometimes we cry because we're sad, sometimes because we're glad.
Noodles:	Cry when you're glad? I never did it that way.
Bill:	Why, Noodles, I've seen football players cry with joy because they won a game. I've seen people cry with joy because they're glad to be back together again. I've seen people laugh until they cried.
Noodles:	I know one time I almost cried, Bill Martin. That was when you were reading about those goblins. I was just so very very mad, I was sad.

Bill: Anger is another way of responding to reading.
And there are many other ways
which we will be discussing
in this part of the book:
storytelling,
reading aloud,
choral reading,
creative dramatics,
wondering about words,
choosing what you like and don't like,
and finding out more than the story told you.

Noodles: Girls and boys and ba-bees,
teachers and principals and parents,
protect your ears!
Bill Martin is making another speech.
I don't know what you boys and girls are going to do,
but I'm really getting out of here right now.
Goodbye, everybody!
Oodeley, oodeley!

Bill: Well, that's another way
to respond to reading, boys and girls.
You can always walk out on the author
by closing the book.

My Favorite Things

Raindrops on roses and whiskers on kittens,
  Bright copper kettles and warm woolen mittens,
Brown paper packages tied up with strings,
  These are a few of my favorite things.

Cream-colored ponies
  and crisp apple strudels,
Doorbells and sleighbells
  and schnitzel with noodles,
Wild geese that fly with
  the moon on their wings,
These are a few
  of my favorite things.

A song by Richard Rodgers and Oscar Hammerstein II,
picture by Bill Goldsmith

*Girls in white dresses
   with blue satin sashes,
Snowflakes that stay
   on my nose and eyelashes,
Silver-white winters
   that melt into springs,
These are a few
   of my favorite things.*

*When the dog bites,
When the bee stings,
When I'm feeling sad,
  I simply remember
     my favorite things
        And then
           I don't feel so bad.*

Antelope

Elk

Animals that helped

Beaver

Mule Deer

The first trailblazers
of the American West
were wild animals.
For thousands of years
before the coming
of trappers and settlers,
wild animals roamed the land
west of the Mississippi River.
Enormous herds of buffalo
and elk and deer and antelope
surged across the prairies
and through the mountain passes
in their never-ending search
for new grazing grounds.
By instinct,
by trial
and error,
they found
and followed the easiest
and most natural pathways
across the continent.
And it was these very trails
that made it possible
for the American pioneers
to settle the lands
west of the Mississippi.
The pioneers would not have known
the best ways to cross
the mountains and rivers
and grudging slopes
if they had not followed
the animal trails.

Buffalo

win the West

An essay by Bernard Martin,
pictures by Chet Reneson

This picture of an old-time trapper was painted by a
distinguished contemporary artist, John Clymer. In
what ways is this a picture of trapping? How does
212   the picture tell what Mr. Clymer wanted it to tell?

Other wild animals
that were instrumental
in the settlement of the West
were those that tempted trappers
into the unsettled territory
with their valuable furs.
One such animal was the beaver.
Prior to 1800,
fifty million beaver
were believed to have inhabited
the region west
of the Mississippi.
The beaver's coat
of rich, lustrous, brown fur
was worth ten dollars or more
to fur traders
in St. Louis and New York.
The presence
of millions of beaver
in the streams and rivers
of the frontier
represented a great opportunity
for riches
to many buckskin-clad trappers.
It lured[1] them   [1]enticed, beckoned
into every nook and cranny
of the vast wilderness.
    The trappers raced
up the Missouri River
to set beaver traps
on the Platte,
the Snake, the Clearwater
and the Yellowstone rivers.

Here is another picture by John Clymer about trappers in the olden days. The picture communicates much about a trapper's life that the story doesn't. How does this picture tell you what it wants to say?

Others ventured
into the Southwest
along the Colorado River
and its tributaries.
   As the trappers
continually searched
for new and better
trapping territory,
they used the trails
made by the buffalo
and other animals,
and they made maps of the land
to guide others
through the wilderness.
   When settlers began
to flow westward,
many trappers were paid
to guide them
across the hard
and often hostile[2] land.   [2]unfriendly
Basing their routes on the trails
that had been used by animals
for thousands of years,
the trappers laid out
the Santa Fe, the Oregon
and the Mormon trails,
plus dozens of minor[3] routes   [3]less important
leading across the continent
to the Pacific Ocean.

As the frontier
moved slowly westward
year by year,
animals of all kinds
were killed for food, clothes,
shelter and sport.
By 1890,
the great herds of buffalo
and untold millions
of brown-furred beaver
had almost become extinct.[4]   [4]no longer living
And with the disappearance
of the animals,
the trapper, too, soon vanished
and receded into history.
However, he left a legacy[5]   [5]gift from the past
of trails over which
a stream of settlers
poured across the prairies
and mountains to the Pacific.
Stagecoaches followed
the wagon trains,
and the railroad
followed the stagecoaches,
and all of them followed
the animal trails
of the old West.
Even trains and cars traveling
across the country today
are following those routes
which, not so very long ago,
thundered under the hoofs
of mighty buffalo herds.

White Snow Bright Snow

A POEM BY ALVIN TRESSELT

Softly, gently in the secret night,
Down from the North came the quiet white.
Drifting, sifting, silent flight,
Softly, gently, in the secret night.

White snow, bright snow, smooth and deep.
Light snow, night snow, quiet as sleep.
Down, down, without a sound;
Down, down, to the frozen ground.

Covering roads and hiding fences,
Sifting in cracks and filling up trenches.
Millions of snowflakes, tiny and light,
Softly, gently, in the secret night.

The use of white space on this double-page spread
magnifies the importance of the selections, and creates a
picture of its own. If you are concerned that there are too
few words for the space involved, you can take comfort in
the majesty of language which imprints itself indelibly on
the mind and probably achieves in brevity what a
thousand more words would have destroyed.

Spring Rain

The storm came up so very quick
    It couldn't have been quicker.
I should have brought my hat along,
    I should have brought my slicker.

My hair is wet, my feet are wet,
    I couldn't be much wetter.
I fell into a river once
    But this is even better.

A POEM BY MARCHETTE CHUTE,
PHOTOGRAPH BY DENNIS STOCK

Rain Sizes

Rain comes in various sizes.
Some rain is as small as a mist.
It tickles your face with surprises,
And tingles as if you'd been kissed.

Some rain is the size of a sprinkle
And doesn't put out all the sun.
You can see the drops sparkle and twinkle,
And a rainbow comes out when it's done.

Some rain is as big as a nickel
And comes with a crash and a hiss.
It comes down too heavy to tickle.
It's more like a splash than a kiss.

When it rains the right size
        and you're wrapped in
Your rainclothes, it's fun out of doors.
But run home before you get trapped in
The big rain that rattles and roars.

A POEM BY JOHN CIARDI

Contrast in your mind's eye
how a poet and a mathematician
use language to describe rain sizes.
Which language do you prefer?

Storytelling is the basic technique used in making this essay come alive. It's a technique you may want to explore for your own teaching. It never fails.

READING ALOUD AND STORYTELLING

If you are not already using your experiences "in the olden days," for storytelling in the classroom, make a point to do so at the next convenient time. The children's response to your bit of Americana will be proof enough of its value.

APPEAR
APPEAR
APPEAR
APPEAR
APPEAR

Noodles: Oh, hello, Bill Martin,
but don't say nothin' to me
'cause I'm busy reading.

Bill: Reading what?

Noodles: Soup.

Bill: Reading what?

Noodles: Beautiful soup!
Do you want some?

Bill: No, but I'd like to hear about it.

Noodles: I was hoping you'd ask me to do that, Bill.
Put on your napkin
and get out of my way, Bill,
'cause here comes the soup!

Bill: Is it chicken-noodle?

Noodles: NOOOOOODLES!
How can you say that?
You're not making soup out of me!

Bill: Oh, come on, Noodles.
No one wants a ghost in his soup.

Noodles: I don't think you have ever tried
a ghost in your soup, Bill Martin.
A ghost might be a very very tasty treat.
Come to think of it,
I eat ghost soup all the time at my house.

Bill: Well, get on with the reading, Noodles.
I'm waiting for that beautiful soup.

Beautiful Soup
by
Lewis Carroll

Beautiful Soup, so rich and green,
Waiting in a hot tureen!
Who for such dainties would not stoop?
Soup of the evening, beautiful Soup!

Soup of the evening, beautiful Soup!
Beau-ootiful Soo-oop!
Beau-ootiful Soo-oop!
Soo-oop of the e-e-evening,
Beautiful, beautiful Soup!

Beautiful Soup! Who cares for fish,
Game, or any other dish?
Who would not give all else for two
Pennyworth only of beautiful Soup?
Pennyworth only of beautiful Soup?
Beau-ootiful Soo-oop!
Beau-ootiful Soo-oop!
Soo-oop of the e-e-evening,
Beautiful, beauti-FUL SOUP!

Bill: Bravo! Bravo!
You read that well, Noodles!

Noodles: Yes, I did read that very very well, Bill Martin.
That is one of my most favorite stories
because I really do like soup.

Bill: Well, here's a soup story, Noodles,
I can tell you.
I remember it from my childhood,
when my grandmother used to tell stories
while she was ironing shirts
or getting a meal on the table.
She was a great storyteller,
telling the stories in a simple natural way,
just as if she were talking
about the coming and going of the weather.

Sometimes
I sway
like a tree
and
whisper.

Once upon a time there was an old woodcutter and his wife
who lived at the edge of a road going through the woods.
They were very poor with little in their pantry,
but they took all of their vegetables and a little piece of ham
and made a kettle of soup, just enough for three.
Then they invited the Lord to supper,
and he sent word that he would come that night.

Sometimes
I tell
stories to
the kids.

Along about suppertime,
an old beggar came to the door
and asked
for something to eat.
The old woman thought,
"I'll let him have
my part of the soup.
He needs it worse than I do."
So she fed the beggar and he thanked her and left.

Sometimes
I
CHANT!

Before long a little ragged boy came knocking on the door.
He looked so cold and starved that the old folks took him in.

And the old man thought, "I'll let him have
  my part of the soup.
  I'm not much hungry."
   So he fed the boy and let him sit and get warm.
The old lady asked the boy to stay the night
but he said he couldn't and thanked them and left.

By and by the old man and the old woman
  saw the Lord coming.
  They met him at the gate and said,
  "We've waited so long!
  We were afraid you had forgotten to come."
 "No," said the Lord, "I didn't forget.
 I've been here twice already."

And from that day onwards,
the old man and his wife
always found the kettle full of soup
no matter how much or how often they ate.

Noodles: Oh, I do like that story very very much.
     It makes me feel so good.

   Bill: I like it, too, Noodles.

Noodles: Bill Martin, did I hear you
     invite me to your house for soup tonight?

   Bill: Well . . . yes, Noodles.
     It'll be beef-noodle.

Noodles: Oh, I did just remember,
     I can't come tonight I think.
     Goodbye, Bill.
     Oodeley, oodeley.

223

A folktale adapted by Bill Martin, Jr.

Woodcuts by Susan Blair

The Gunny Wolf

Compare these woodcuts with the
linoleum cuts on page 268.

Here is a story told in home-rooted language
that has the grandeur of literary language.

A man and his little daughter lived alone in a forest—
oh, how he loved her—
and there were wolves in the forest.
So the man built a fence round the house
and told his little daughter,
"You must on no account go outside the gate
while I am away."

This story is so rooted in oral tradition that the ears tend to unlock the words.

One morning when he had gone away,
the little girl was hunting for flowers
and thought it would do no harm
just to peep through the gate.
So she did.
She saw a little flower so near
that she stepped outside to pick it.
Then she saw another a little farther off
and went for that.
Then she saw another and went for that,

and so she kept getting
farther and farther
away from home.

As she picked the flowers,
she sang a little song,
 "*Tray-blah,*
  tray-blah,
  cum-qua,
  ki-mo."

(This is sung
in a childish voice.)

Suddenly she heard a noise
and looked up
and saw a great gunny wolf,
and he said,

(This is said
in a low, gruff voice.)
"Sing that sweeten,
gooden song again."

(Childish voice)
She sang,
"Tray-blah,
tray-blah,
cum-qua,
ki-mo."

Wolf, he gone.

(This is said softly and quickly
to represent the child's footsteps.)
Pit-a-pat, pit-a-pat,
pit-a-pat, pit-a-pat.
She goes back.

(This is said rapidly
in a coarse, deep voice.)
Presently she hears
pit-a-pat, pit-a-pat,
pit-a-pat, pit-a-pat
coming behind her,
and there was the wolf,
an' 'e says,

(Gruff voice)
"You move?"

(Childish voice)
"Oh no, my dear.
What 'casion I move?"

How could these sentences be expanded to
give the information in the parentheses?

Wolf: "Sing that sweeten
gooden song again."

She sang,
Child: *"Tray-blah,*
tray-blah,
cum-qua,
ki-mo."

Wolf, he gone.

(Delicately)   *Pit-a-pat, pit-a-pat,*
pit-a-pat, pit-a-pat.
She goes back some more.

(Coarsely)   Presently she hears
pit-a-pat, pit-a-pat,
pit-a-pat, pit-a-pat
coming behind her,
and there was the wolf,
an' 'e says,

Wolf: "You move!"

Child: "Oh no, my dear.
What 'casion I move?"

Wolf: "Sing that sweeten,
gooden song again."

       She sang,
Child: *"Tray,*
      blah-tray,
      blah-cum
      qua-ki-mo."

       Wolf, he gone.

(Delicately)   *Pit-a-pat, pit-a-pat.*
She goes back some more.

       Presently she hears
(Coarsely)   *pit-a-pat, pit-a-pat*
coming behind her,
and there was the wolf,
an' 'e says,

Wolf: "YOU MOVE!"

Child:	"Oh no, my dear. What 'casion I move?"
Wolf:	"Sing that sweeten, gooden song again."
Child:	She sang, *"Tray-blah-tray,* *blah-cum-qua,* *ki-mo."*
	Wolf, he gone.
(Delicately)	*Pit-a-pat, pit-a-pat, pit-a-pat,* *pit-a-pat, pit-a-pat, pit-a-pat.* She goes back some more,
(Coarsely)	and this time when she hears *pit-a-pat, pit-a-pat, pit-a-pat,* *pit-a-pat, pit-a-pat, pit-a-pat* coming behind her, she slips inside the gate
(Read the word *shuts* like the sound of a gate slamming.)	and SHUTS it, and wolf, he can't get her.

This story lends itself to choral reading. It makes a
dramatic yet simple auditorium program in which all
children in your class can participate. A group of girls
may read the child's part, a group of boys the wolf's
part, and all other children the narration. This is valid
reading instruction.

What storytelling and storywriting these pictures suggest!
Won't it be interesting if some children
connect the action of the three pictures with a plot?

Three Pictures Tell a Prairie Story

Here are three paintings
by the well-known painter
Harvey Dunn,
who loved the prairies
and prairie people.
He was a prairie boy himself.
You can read his pictures
like you read a book,
for the pictures are alive
with prairie experiences.
In looking at these pictures,
it is useful to ask,

"How do the lines and colors
and shapes tell me
what Harvey Dunn wanted me
to know about the prairie?"
How does the grass
in the first picture
tell you that the land
is rich for farming?
How does the girl's hair
in the last picture
tell that the wind is blowing?

PHONE CALL

by Adam Arthur
drawings by Peter Lippman

I'm so glad you called.
I keep hearing funny noises.
They're coming from the garden
and I don't know what they are.
It's a strange sort of rustling sound
but there's no wind at all
so it can't be that.

Children have always enjoyed
weird stories, and here is one
written by a 13-year-old. As
children indicate they have
inculcated a feeling of suspense
from the story, you have proof of
their comprehension. The story

**Yes, I know it's late
but I can't get to sleep
with that eerie sound out there.
Hang on a moment.
I'm going to make sure
all the doors are locked.**

lends itself to choral reading with
sound effects and spooky
intonations. You may get tired of it,
but chances are the children won't.
Have you noticed that the
illustrations are done by the same
artist who did *The Electric Paint*
pictures? You may wish to compare
his style

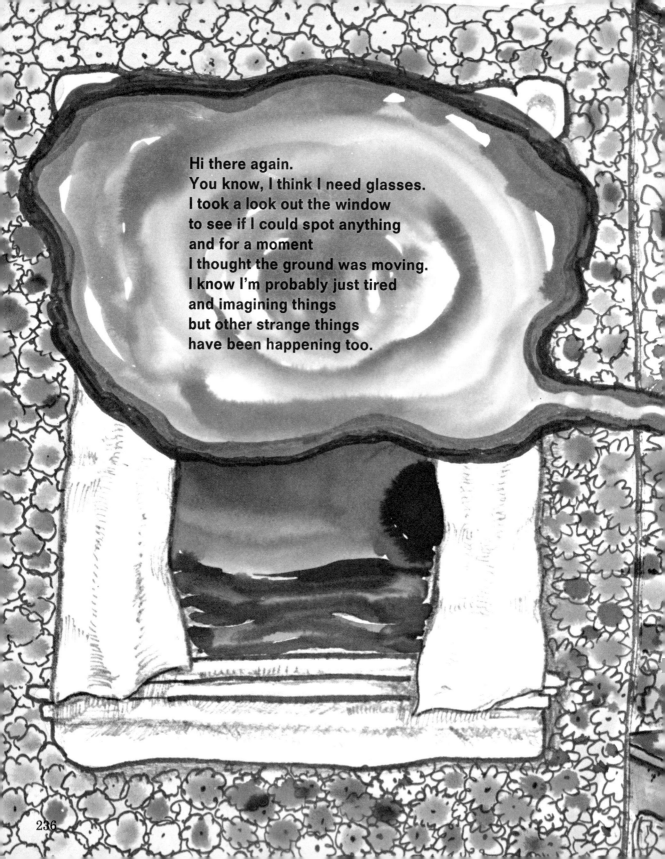

Hi there again.
You know, I think I need glasses.
I took a look out the window
to see if I could spot anything
and for a moment
I thought the ground was moving.
I know I'm probably just tired
and imagining things
but other strange things
have been happening too.

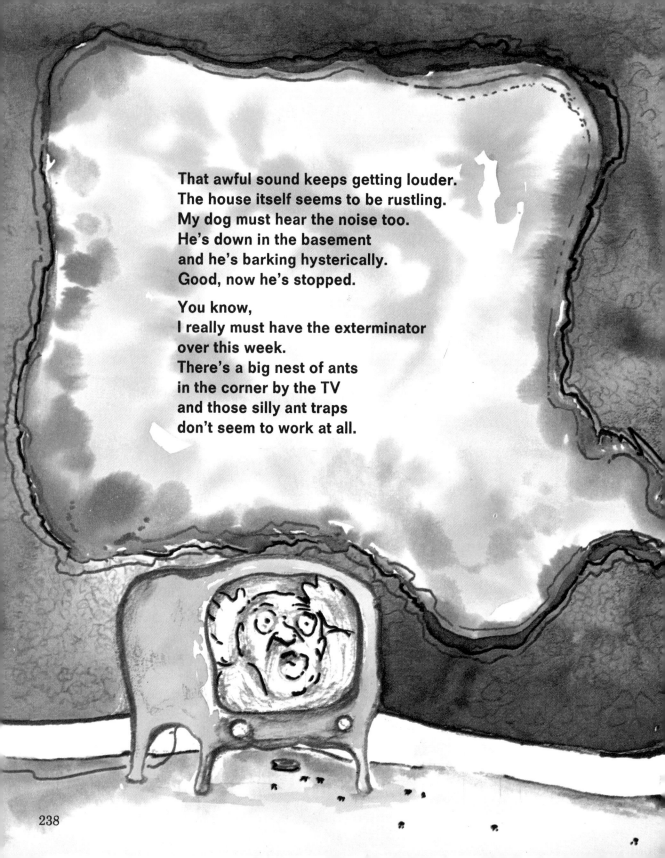

That awful sound keeps getting louder.
The house itself seems to be rustling.
My dog must hear the noise too.
He's down in the basement
and he's barking hysterically.
Good, now he's stopped.

You know,
I really must have the exterminator
over this week.
There's a big nest of ants
in the corner by the TV
and those silly ant traps
don't seem to work at all.

Oh dear!
Now there's a lot of those pesty ants
on the dinner table and in the dog's food dish.
I've never had this much of a problem before.
Ouch! . . .
One of those little devils
just bit my toe.
Oh no! The window is cracking.

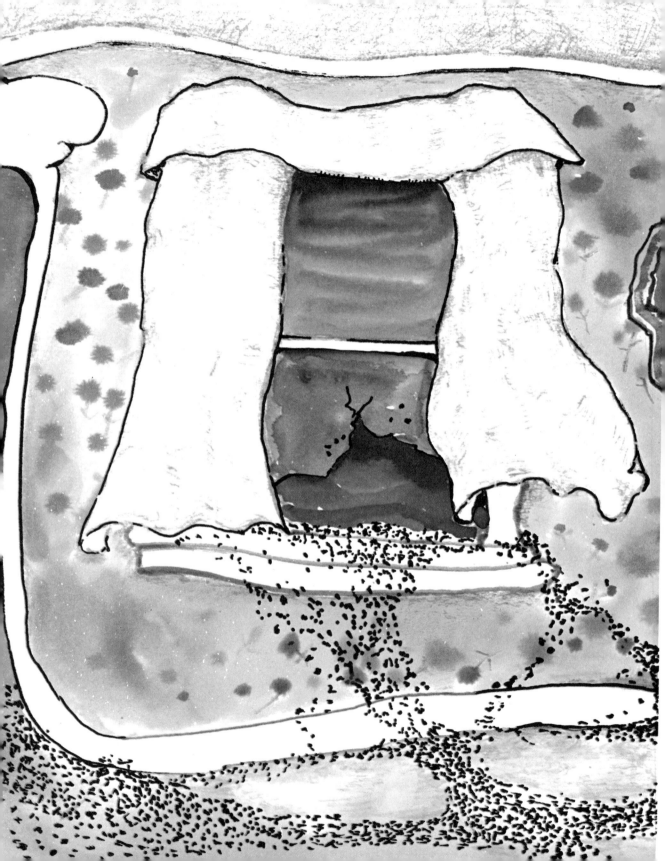

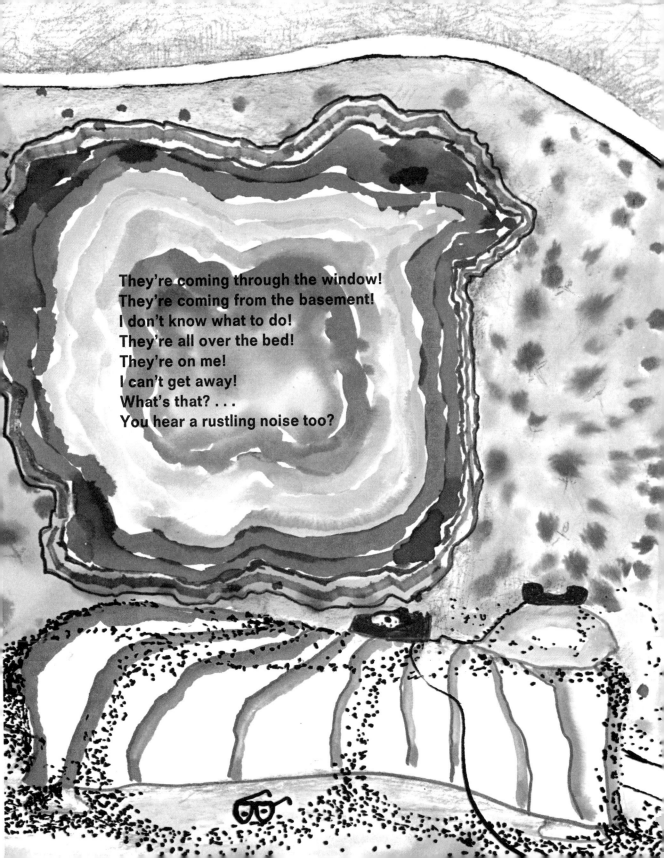

They're coming through the window!
They're coming from the basement!
I don't know what to do!
They're all over the bed!
They're on me!
I can't get away!
What's that? . . .
You hear a rustling noise too?

CHORAL READING

APPEAR
APPEAR
APPEAR
APPEAR
APPEAR

Noodles: Hey, Bill Martin!
They're here, they're there, here they are!
Just like I said they would be.

Bill: Who's here, Noodles?

Noodles: All the boys and girls, can't you see them?
I invited them to help us,
just like I said I would.

Bill: Oh, hello, boys and girls.
Welcome to our party.

Noodles: And say, kids,
you better smile or you won't get any dessert.
I betcha never did know that, did you?
The bigger you smile, the more pie you get.

Bill: This isn't that kind of a party, Noodles.
We're going to do some choral reading.

Noodles: Nothin' to eat?
Oh me, I think I have to leave now.

Bill: Wait a minute, Noodles.
We'll have a choral reading party this time,
but the next time
you boys and girls get together
to read your favorite poems and stories,
why not make a party out of it,
with treats for everybody?

Noodles: Well, if there's treats,
don't forget to invite me, O.K.?
Let's start reading.
Sound your do, do, do ...
I'm in pretty good voice today.
Did you hear my sweet sounds?

Bill: Well, here's the story, "Tatty Mae and Catty Mae"
which I have scored for choral reading.
Let's all choose parts and have a go at it.
There are solo parts and chorus parts.
Everyone will have something to do.

Noodles: Well, I can tell you something right now, Bill Martin,
I'm going to do a solo part
and be in the chorus.
And since this story is about cats,
I'll probably put in a few meows.

Bill: That's a good idea, Noodles.
Boys and girls, you may want to add
sound effects of your own,
such as the sound of sea gulls, and boat whistles,
and cat calls.
Here we go:

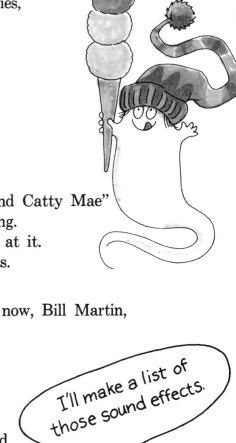

> Ice cream sure would pep up this party!

> I'll make a list of those sound effects.

ALL: Two old cats lived on a houseboat.
BOYS: One was named Tatty Mae.
GIRLS: The other was named Catty Mae.

SOLO 1: Tatty Mae was a good fisherman.
SOLO 2: Catty Mae was a good fisherman.
ALL: So they both were good fishermen.

SOLO 3: Tatty Mae left her fish pole in the middle of the room.
SOLO 4: Catty Mae left her fish pole in the middle of the room.
ALL: So they both left their fish poles in the middle of the room.

SOLO 5: Tatty Mae left her fish net hanging on the doorknob.
SOLO 6: Catty Mae left her fish net hanging on the doorknob.
ALL: So they both left their fish nets hanging on the doorknob.

SOLO 7: Tatty Mae left her fish hooks in the bathtub.
SOLO 8: Catty Mae left her fish hooks in the bathtub.
ALL: So they both left their fish hooks in the bathtub.

SOLO 9: Tatty Mae left her fish worms on the dresser.
SOLO 10: Catty Mae left her fish worms on the dresser.
ALL: So they both left their fish worms on the dresser.

SOLO 11: Tatty Mae left her fishing coat on the chair.
SOLO 12: Catty Mae left her fishing coat on the chair.
ALL: So they both left their fishing coats on the chair.

SOLO 13: Tatty Mae put her fishing boots on the bedpost.
SOLO 14: Catty Mae put her fishing boots on the bedpost.
ALL: So they both put their fishing boots on the bedpost.

SOLO 15: Tatty Mae left her fishing cap on the pump handle.
SOLO 16: Catty Mae left her fishing cap on the pump handle.
ALL: So they both left their fishing caps on the pump handle.

ALL:	One day Tatty Mae said to Catty Mae,
TATTY MAE:	I declare, you're a litterbug!
ALL:	One day Catty Mae said to Tatty Mae,
CATTY MAE:	I declare, you're a litterbug!
ALL:	So they both said to each other,
TM & CM:	I declare, you're a litterbug!

Tatty Mae and Catty Mae is available both in book form and cassette recording. Listening to Bill Martin and guitarist Al Caiola will enhance the children's appreciation of their own performances.

ALL:	Tatty Mae said,
TATTY MAE:	I think we're both litterbugs!
ALL:	Catty Mae said,
CATTY MAE:	I know we're both litterbugs!
ALL:	So they both said,
TM & CM:	We're both litterbugs!

BOYS:	So Tatty Mae cleaned up and picked up and put away her litter.
GIRLS:	So Catty Mae cleaned up and picked up and put away her litter.
ALL:	So they both cleaned up and picked up and put away their litter.

Maybe you'd like to tape record your choral readings.

ALL:	The next day Tatty Mae said,
TATTY MAE:	Where is my fish pole?
ALL:	The next day Catty Mae said,
CATTY MAE:	Where is my fish net?
ALL:	The next day they both said,
TM & CM:	Where are my fish worms?

ALL:	Tatty Mae said,
TATTY MAE:	Now, I'm all mixed up.
ALL:	Catty Mae said,
CATTY MAE:	Yes, the clean-up was a mix-up.
ALL:	So they both said,
TM & CM:	We'll never do it again.

ALL:	And they didn't.

THE HORSEMAN

I heard a horseman
  Ride over the hill;
The moon shone clear,
The night was still;
His helm was silver,
  And pale was he;
And the horse he rode
  Was of ivory.

WALTER DE LA MARE

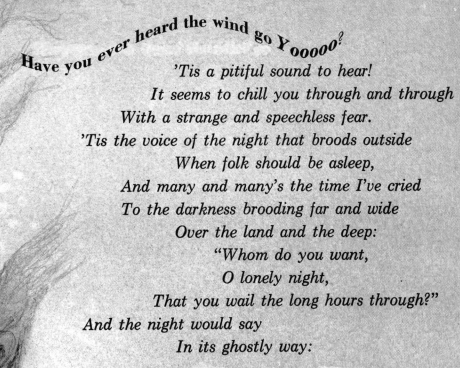

Have you ever heard the wind go Yoooooo?
'Tis a pitiful sound to hear!
It seems to chill you through and through
With a strange and speechless fear.
'Tis the voice of the night that broods outside
When folk should be asleep,
And many and many's the time I've cried
To the darkness brooding far and wide
Over the land and the deep:
"Whom do you want,
O lonely night,
That you wail the long hours through?"
And the night would say
In its ghostly way:

Yoooooooooooooo
Yoooooooooooooo
Yoooooooooooooo

THE NIGHT WIND
**A POEM BY EUGENE FIELD,
PICTURE BY GEORGE BUCKETT**

Before reading the poems, invite the children to analyze the design of the page. What does the mood of the drawing and the arrangement of the type tell about the poems and the reading of the poems? (Practically every page in this book invites this kind of discussion.) You, the teacher, should do the first reading of each of these poems so children will experience them as poetry and not as reading exercises. Then invite the children to read aloud with you. This leads naturally to various groups of children using the poems as choral readings, wherein poetry enriches their lives, while it perfects their reading skills.

Foal

Come trotting up
Beside your mother,
Little skinny.

Lay your neck across
Her back, and whinny,
Little foal.

You think you're a horse
Because you can trot—
But you're not.

Your eyes are so wild,
And each leg is as tall
As a pole;

And you're only a skittish
Child, after all,
Little foal.

A POEM BY MARY BRITTON MILLER, WATERCOLOR BY STANLEY M. LONG

One of the best ways to understand a poem is to analyze its structure. By looking at its rhyme scheme and rhythm, as well as at its verse patterns and configuration (the visual shape of the poem as determined by the length of the lines, the space between verses, the number of verses, and the shape of the right- and left-handed margins), children tend to develop a better understanding and deeper appreciation than if they attempted to tell what the poem means. In this program we never tamper with a poem's meanings. That's a matter of individual choice, which never can be prescribed.

Teevee

In the house
of Mr. and Mrs. Spouse
he and she
would watch teevee
and never a word
between them spoken
until the day
the set was broken.

Then "How do you do?"
said he to she,
"I don't believe
that we've met yet.
Spouse is my name.
What's yours?" he asked.

"Why, mine's the same!"
said she to he,
"Do you suppose that we could be—?"

But the set came suddenly right about,
and so they never did find out.

A POEM BY EVE MERRIAM

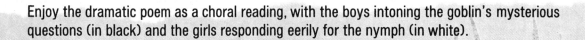

Enjoy the dramatic poem as a choral reading, with the boys intoning the goblin's mysterious questions (in black) and the girls responding eerily for the nymph (in white).

Overheard on a Saltmarsh

NYMPH, NYMPH, WHAT ARE YOUR BEADS?

Green glass, goblin. Why do you stare at them?

GIVE THEM ME.

No

GIVE THEM ME...

GIVE THEM ME.

No

THEN I WILL HOWL ALL NIGHT IN THE
REEDS, LIE IN THE MUD AND
        HOWL FOR THEM

        Goblin, why do you love them so?

THEY ARE BETTER THAN STARS OR WATER,
BETTER THAN VOICES OF WINDS THAT SING,
BETTER THAN ANY MAN'S FAIR
DAUGHTER, YOUR GREEN
GLASS BEADS ON A
SILVER STRING.

Hush, I stole them out of the moon.

        GIVE ME YOUR BEADS, I WANT THEM.

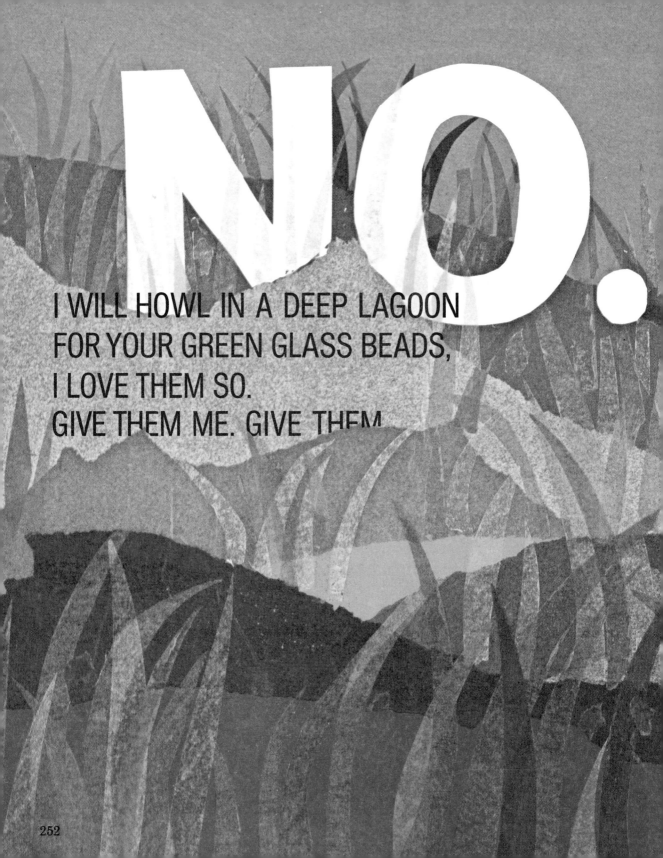

NO.

I WILL HOWL IN A DEEP LAGOON
FOR YOUR GREEN GLASS BEADS,
I LOVE THEM SO.
GIVE THEM ME. GIVE THEM

NO.

A dramatic dialogue by Harold Monro,
illustrated by Eric Carle

253

Did You Feed My Cow?

A POEM BY MARGARET BURROUGHS

CALL: Did you feed my cow?
RESPONSE: *Yes, ma'am!*
Will you tell me how?
Yes, ma'am!
Oh, what did you give her?
Corn and hay.
Oh, what did you give her?
Corn and hay.

Did you milk her good?
Yes, ma'am!
Did you do like you should?
Yes, ma'am!
Oh, how did you milk her?
Swish! Swish! Swish!
Oh, how did you milk her?
Swish! Swish! Swish!

Did my cow get sick?
Yes, ma'am!
Was she covered with tick?
Yes, ma'am!
Oh, how was she sick?
All bloated up.
Oh, how was she sick?
All bloated up.

Did my cow die?
Yes, ma'am!
Did my cow die?
Yes, ma'am!
Oh, how did she die?
Ugh! Ugh! Ugh!
Oh, how did she die?
Ugh! Ugh! Ugh!

Did the buzzards come?
Yes, ma'am!
For to pick her bones?
Yes, ma'am!
Oh, how did they come?
Flop! Flop! Flop!
Oh, how did they come?
Flop! Flop! Flop!

Beans, Beans, Beans

Baked beans,
Butter beans,
Big fat lima beans,
Long thin string beans—
Those are just a few.
Green beans,
Black beans,
Big fat kidney beans,
Red hot chili beans,
Jumping beans too.
Pea beans,
Pinto beans,
Don't forget shelly beans.
Last of all, best of all,
I like jelly beans!

A POEM BY LUCIA AND
JAMES L. HYMES, JR.

'Twas Midnight

AMERICAN FOLKLORE

'Twas midnight on the ocean,
 Not a streetcar was in sight;
 The sun was shining brightly,
 For it rained all day that night.
'Twas a summer day in winter
 And snow was raining fast,
 As a barefoot boy with shoes on
 Stood sitting in the grass.

Dr. Hack

Hello,
I'm a magician.
Now watch closely!
I shall cut Miss Partly into two parts.
In this case, the hand
   is not quicker than the eye,
because I'm using a saw.

Cut! Cut! Cut!

I'm cutting Miss Partly in two.

HE MUST DO IT WITH MIRRORS.

Note the author's fun with language.

Children, here's a story that asks to be read aloud. Who would like to begin? Here is one time it makes sense to choose your better readers.

A monologue by Henry W. Ford,
pictures by Bob Shein

256

THE TWO PARTS OF PARTLY ARE NOT EXACTLY HALVES.

What does the art suggest to you about the mood of this story and also about the kind of language one might encounter?

And here she is,
        Miss Bonnie Partly,
in two parts, but not in halves.
Thank you for your generous
                    applause!

The children will have no problem in this zany story finding intriguing words to add to their notebook lists.

Not all arithmetic lessons look alike. Here is one that will tickle your funny bone at the same time that it provokes you into dealing with fractions and proportions.

too-hard-for-me
too-sweet-to-eat
too-long-to-remember

And now,

problem
candy
title

I shall attempt that once-in-a-lifetime,
butcher-boy rope trick
which I learned from a tattooed sailor in Siam.

traveling
talented
knowledgeable

Do the usual
pronunciation
rules or the
ear's fondness
for rhyming
words help most
with unlocking
the name
Kaknowkus?

Hocus-pocus,
Jimmy Kaknowkus,
watch closely
for
what you can't see!

Just listen
to the *k* sounds
in this sentence!

258

$\frac{1}{2}$

$\frac{1}{4}$

$\frac{1}{8}$

$\frac{1}{16}$

$\frac{1}{32}$

$\frac{1}{64}$

$\frac{1}{64}$

Halve the whole,
then halve one of the halves,
then halve one quarter,
halve that half,
then halve the last half,
and what do you have?

You can readily identify
your mathematicians as the
children react to this story.

THE SMALLER
THE PART,
THE BIGGER
THE NUMBER.

Isn't this a rare excursion in the vagaries of our language?

half, halves—nouns
halve—a verb
have—a verb

Halve and *have* are pronounced alike, but, oh, the
difference! Another interesting facet of our language is the
relationship between letters like *f* and *v*, *p* and *b*, *t* and *d*.
They are formed exactly alike on the tongue; but in each
case the first is voiceless, the second is voiced.

Now,
busykabuzzy,
rosykablat!
Out of my hat
come names for the fractions!

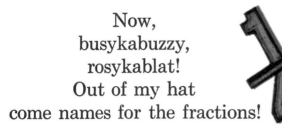

Isn't it interesting
that our language storehouse
gives us an anticipated
pronunciation for words
like *busykabuzzy*?

COME ON,
ONE-EIGHTH!
GET INTO
POSITION!

Is the *s* in *position*
a *z* or an *s* sound?

260

How many words can you list which, like *busy*, have an *s* pronounced as a *z?*

    busy
    rosy
    nose
    etc.

And now
for my gr-r-r-reatest wizardry,
an infinity
of
fractions!

BOOM!
BOOM!
GET A
BROOM!

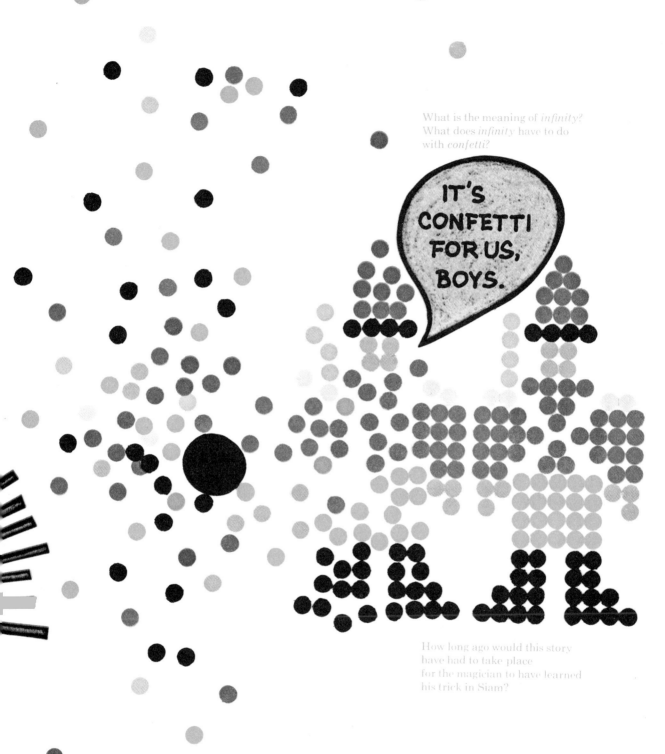

What is the meaning of *infinity*?
What does *infinity* have to do
with *confetti*?

How long ago would this story
have had to take place
for the magician to have learned
his trick in Siam?

263

CREATIVE DRAMATICS

Are the children enjoying Noodles' home-rooted language? They might as well. He'll never change.

APPEAR
APPEAR
APPEAR
APPEAR
APPEAR

Noodles: Hello, Bill Martin.
I'm all ready.
I brought all the stuff...
the costumes
and two homemade spotlights
and the big old black kettle for the soup.

Bill: Noodles, what are you talking about?

Noodles: We're going to give a show, Bill.
Did you forget all about that?

Bill: What show, Noodles?
Do I know it?

Noodles: Heck, yes!
It's the story you told
us about the old man and the old woman
who had the Lord come for supper.
Don't you remember?
It's on page 222.
I always did like that story
so we're going to make a play out of it.

A GHOST STORY FOR THOSE WHO DARE

Bill: That's a good choice, Noodles.
It divides easily into scenes.
The first thing you do in making a play
is to figure out the scenes
and what happens in each scene.

Noodles: The first scene could be the old man and woman
making the soup, couldn't it?
And they'll be talking about the Lord coming to supper.
And maybe they'll be singing my song,
"Soup of the evening, beautiful soup!"

Bill: That's the nice part of making a play, Noodles.
You can have the characters say a lot of things
to round out the story.

Noodles: I'm a very good rounder-outer, Bill.

Bill: Just to get things started,
here are some questions
that might help you work out the first scene:
1) What does the little house look like?
2) What and where are the pieces of furniture?
3) Is it a warm day or a cold day?
4) What can the old man and old woman do and say
    that show how very poor they are?
5) Why do they decide to invite the Lord to supper?
6) How do they send him the invitation?

Noodles: Those things really do make us think, Bill,
and I really am a very good thinker.
When we come to those other scenes,
I'll really have some very good questions.

Bill: So will the boys and girls, Noodles.

Noodles: And the best part
is that we don't have to learn any lines, Bill.
We don't even have to write anything down.
We know how the story goes into scenes
so we can just say whatever comes into our little heads.

Bill:
That's right, Noodles.
Knowing what is supposed to happen in a scene
let's you think on your feet.
And if you come upon a good way
to say something, you'll probably say it that way
again and again until it becomes part of the show.

Noodles: Watch me walk like an old man, Bill Martin.
I think I could do that part.

Bill: Wow! Noodles, you're good as the old man.
Now let's see some of the boys and girls try it.

Noodles: All right, kids, all you have to do
is walk and talk old,
and you really use an old creaky voice
for the old man and the old lady.

Bill: The boys and girls can choose the actors they like best.

Noodles: And parts can be passed around
so everybody gets a chance
to be the old man if they want to, O.K.?

Bill: Everybody can be in the show
because we'll add a lot of extra parts.

Noodles: Sure, we'll think of a lot of things.
There can be a lot of travelers
passing by the old man's door...

Bill: And there can be an announcer to introduce the play...

Noodles: Bill, do you think there could be a kitty in this play?

Bill: Yes, I think that old man would have a cat...
and maybe a dog.

Noodles: If I was the kitty cat,
I know I would want to smell the soup
and probably sneak a little bitty bite.

266

Bill: And there could be a stage crew
to handle the lights and the furniture.

Noodles: And some kids can make all that scenery.

Bill: Oh, as the boys and girls practice the play,
they'll find more and more ways to let everybody take part.

Noodles: Here's another great idea.
You probably didn't know
I had so many good ideas, did you, Bill?
The boys and girls can make lists of things
for the old man and the old lady to do
and for the stranger and the two visitors
and the cat and the dog.

Bill: Thinking it through ahead of time
makes it easy for actors to become the characters.

Noodles: I surely do hope they invite me to the show, Bill.
Do you suppose they will?

Bill: Of course, they will, Noodles.
You gave them the idea in the first place.

Noodles: Good old Noodles!
Always right there to think of the good stuff to do.
Well, I'll be seeing you.

Bill: Where are you going, Noodles?

Noodles: To my house to wash my face
and sew up the hole in my hat.
I really want to look good when I come to the show.
Oodeley, oodeley.

DISAPPEAR
DISAPPEAR
DISAPPEAR
DISAPPEAR
DISAPPEAR

267

ONCE upon a time there was a king who was the wisest in all of the world. So wise was he that no one had ever befooled him, which is a rare thing, I can tell you.

Now, this king had a daughter who was as pretty as a ripe apple, so that there was no end to the number of the lads who came asking to marry her. Every day there were two or three of them dawdling around the house, so that at last the old king grew tired of having them always about.

This classic story is beautifully told in a series of episodes
that lend themselves to acting out.
It is a worthwhile project
if you wish to make a full-scale production of the story,
bearing in mind that it takes a great deal of time and effort.
The rewards to the children, however, will be great.

HOW BOOTS

BEFOOLED

THE KING

The author has used
a "stream of consciousness" technique
in lieu of direct quotations.
The italicized sentences throughout the
story indicate this writing technique.

**An Irish folktale
retold by Howard P. Pyle,
linoleum cuts by Eric Carle**

So he sent word far and near
that whoever should befool him
might have the princess
and half of the kingdom to boot,
for he thought that it would be
a wise man indeed
who could trick him.

But the king also said
that whoever should try
to befool him and should fail
should have a good whipping.
This was to keep
all foolish fellows away.
But the princess was so pretty
that there was no lack of lads
who came to have a try
for her and half of the kingdom,
but every one of these went away
with a sore back and no luck.

Do you think
that the father of Peter, Paul, and Boots
was prejudiced in favor of his two older sons?
Do you think it humanly possible
that a parent could be more fond of one of his
children than of another?
Could a child be more fond of one parent?

Now, there was a man
who was well off in the world,
and who had three sons;
the first was named Peter,
and the second was named Paul.
Peter and Paul thought themselves
as wise as anybody
in all of the world,
and their father thought
as they did.
As for the youngest son,
he was named Boots.
Nobody thought anything of him
except that he was silly,
for he did nothing but sit
poking warm ashes all of the day.

One morning Peter spoke up
and said that he was going
to the town
to have a try
at befooling the king,
for it would be a fine thing
to have a princess
in the family.

His father did not say *no*,
for if anybody was wise enough
to befool the king,
Peter was the lad.

So, after Peter had eaten
a good breakfast,
off he set for the town,
right foot foremost.
After a while
he came to the king's house
and—*rap! tap! tap!*—
he knocked at the door.
Well, what did he want?
Oh! he would only like
to have a try
at befooling the king.
Very good;
he should have his try.
He was not the first one
who had been there that morning,
early as it was.
So Peter was shown in
to the king.

271

"Oh, look!" said he,
"yonder are three black geese
out in the courtyard!"

But no,
the king was not to be fooled
so easily as all that.
"One goose is enough
to look at at a time," said he;
"take him away
and give him a whipping!"
And so they did,
and Peter went home
bleating like a sheep.

One day Paul spoke up.
"I should like to go
and have a try
for the princess, too," said he.

Well,
his father did not say *no*,
for, after all,
Paul was the more clever of the two.
So off Paul went
as merrily as a duck
in the rain.

By and by he came to the castle,
and then he, too,
was brought before the king
just as Peter had been.

"Oh, look!" said he,
"yonder is a crow
sitting in the tree
with three white stripes
on his back!"

But the king was not so silly
as to be fooled in that way.
"Here is a Jack," said he,
"who will soon have more stripes
on his back
than he will like;
take him away
and give him his whipping!"
Then it was done
as the king had said,
and Paul went away home
bawling like a calf.

One day up spoke Boots.
"I should like to go
and have a try
for the pretty princess, too,"
said he.

At this

they all stared and sniggered.
*What! He go
where his clever brothers
had failed,
and had nothing to show
for the trying
but a good beating?
What had come over the lout!
Here was a pretty business,
to be sure!*
That was what they all said.

But all of this
rolled away from Boots
like water from a duck's back.

No matter,
he would like to go
and have a try
like the others.
So he begged and begged
until his father was glad
to let him go
to be rid of his teasing,
if nothing else.
Then Boots asked
if he might have
the old tattered hat
that hung back of the chimney.

Oh, yes,
he might have that
if he wanted it,
for nobody with good wits
was likely to wear such a thing.
So Boots took the hat,
and after he had brushed the ashes
from his shoes,
set off for the town,
whistling as he went.

The first body whom he met
was an old woman
with a great load
of earthenware pots and crocks
on her shoulders.

"Good-day, mother," said Boots.

"Good-day, son," said she.

"What will you take
  for all of your pots and crocks?"
said Boots.

"Three shillings," said she.

"I will give you five shillings
  if you will come and stand
  in front of the king's house,
  and do thus and so
  when I say this and that,"
said Boots.

Oh, yes!
She would do that
willingly enough.

So Boots and the old woman
went on together,
and presently came
to the king's house.
When they had come there,
Boots sat down
in front of the door
and began bawling as loud as he could—
"No, I will not!
I will not do it, I say!
No, I will not do it!"

So he kept on,
bawling louder and louder
until he made such a noise
that, at last,
the king himself came out
to see what all the hubbub was about.
But when Boots saw him,
he only bawled out louder than ever.

"No, I will not!
I will not do it, I say!"

"Stop! Stop!" cried the king,
"What is all this about?"

"Why," said Boots,
"everybody wants to buy my cap,
but I will not sell it!

I will not do it, I say!"

"But why should anybody
want to buy
such a cap as that?" said the king

"Because," said Boots,
"it is a fooling cap
and the only one
in all of the world."

"A fooling cap!" said the king,
for he did not like to hear
of such a cap as that
coming into the town.
"Hum-m-m-m!
I should like to see you
fool somebody with it.
Could you fool
that old body yonder
with the pots and the crocks?"

"Oh, yes!
That is easily enough done,"
said Boots, and without more ado
he took off his tattered cap
and blew into it.
Then he put it on his head again
and bawled out,
"Break pots! Break pots!"

No sooner had he spoken these words
than the old woman jumped up
and began breaking and smashing
her pots and crocks
as though she had gone crazy.
(That was what Boots
had paid her five shillings
for doing,
but of it the king knew nothing.)

"Hui!" said he to himself,
"I must buy that hat
from the fellow
or he will fool the princess
away from me for sure and certain."

What an intriguing sentence to transform!

Then he began talking to Boots
as sweetly as though
he had honey in his mouth.
*Perhaps Boots would sell
the hat to him?*

*Oh, no!
Boots could not think of
such a thing
as selling his fooling cap.*

*Come, come;
the king wanted that hat,
and sooner than miss buying it,
he would give
a whole bag of gold money for it.*

At this Boots looked up
and looked down,
scratching his head.
*Well, he supposed he would have
to sell the hat some time,
and the king
might as well have it
as anybody else.
But for all that
he did not like parting with it.*

So the king gave Boots
the bag of gold,
and Boots gave the king
the old tattered hat,
and then he went his way.

After Boots had gone,
the king blew into the hat
and blew into the hat,
but though he blew enough
breath into it
to sail a big ship,
he did not befool
so much as a single titmouse.
Then, at last, he began to see
that the fooling cap was good
on nobody else's head
but Boots';
and he was none too pleased at that,
you may be sure.

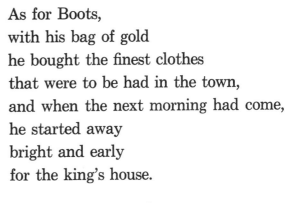

As for Boots,
with his bag of gold
he bought the finest clothes
that were to be had in the town,
and when the next morning had come,
he started away
bright and early
for the king's house.

"I have come," said he,
"to marry the princess,
if you please."

At this
the king hemmed and hawed
and scratched his head.
Yes, Boots had befooled him
sure enough,
but, after all,
he could not give up the princess
for such a thing as that.
Still,
he would give Boots
another chance.
Now there was the high-councillor,
who was the wisest man
in all of the world.
Did Boots think
that he could fool him also?

Oh, yes!
Boots thought
that it might be done.

Very well;
if he could befool the high-councillor
so as to bring him
to the castle
the next morning
against his will,
Boots should have the princess
and the half of the kingdom;
if he did not do so,
he should have his beating.

Then Boots went away
and the king thought
that he was rid of him now
for good and all.

As for the high-councillor,
he was not pleased
with the matter at all,
for he did not like the thought
of being fooled
by a clever rogue,
and taken here and there
against his will.

So when he had come home,
he armed all of his servants
with blunderbusses,
and then waited
to give Boots a *welcome*
when he should come.

But Boots was not going to fall
into any such trap as that!
No indeed! Not he!

The next morning he went quietly
and bought a fine large meal-sack.
Then he put a wig
over his beautiful hair,
so that no one might know him.

After that
he went to the place
where the high-councillor lived,
and when he had come there,
he crawled inside the sack
and lay just beside
the door of the house.
By and by
came one of the maid servants
to the door,
and there lay
the great meal-sack
with somebody in it.

"Ach!" cried she,
"who is there?"

But Boots only said, "Sh-h-h-h!"

Then the serving maid
went back into the house
and told the high-councillor

that one lay outside
in a great meal-sack
and that all that he said was,
"Sh-h-h-h-h."
So the councillor went himself
to see what it was all about.

"What do you want here?" said he.

"Sh-h-h-h-h!" said Boots,
"I am not to be talked to now.
This is a wisdom-sack,
and I am learning wisdom
as fast as a drake
can eat peas."

"And what wisdom have you learned?"
said the councillor.

Oh! Boots had learned wisdom
about everything in the world.
He had learned

*that the clever scamp
who had fooled the king yesterday
was coming
with seventeen tall men
to take the high-councillor,
willy-nilly,
to the castle that morning.*

When the high-councillor
heard this,
he fell to trembling
till his teeth rattled
in his head.

These illustrations
have been done with linoleum cuts.
A linoleum cut differs
from a woodcut
only in the texture of the two materials.
The artist's technique in using
both linoleum and wood
blocks is virtually the same.

281

Would anyone today
be as naive as the councillor
and pay fifteen dollars or so
to crawl into a "wisdom-sack" to "wise up?"
What is the most foolish thing
you know of a person doing today?

"And have you learned
how I can get the better
of this clever scamp?"
said he.

Oh, yes!
Boots had learned that
easily enough.

So, good!
Then if the wise man in the sack
would tell the high-councillor
how to escape the clever rogue,
the high-councillor
would give the wise man
twenty shillings.

But no,
that was not to be done;
wisdom was not bought so cheaply
as the high-councillor
seemed to think.

Well,
the councillor would give him
a hundred shillings, then.
That was good!
A hundred shillings
was a hundred shillings.
If the councillor

would give him that much,
he might get into the sack
himself,
and then he could learn
all the wisdom that he wanted,
and more besides.

So Boots crawled out of the sack,
and the councillor
paid his hundred shillings
and crawled in.
As soon as he was in
all snug and safe,
Boots drew
the mouth of the sack together
and tied it tightly.
Then he flung sack,
councillor and all,
over his shoulder
and started away to the king's house,
and anybody who met them
could see with half an eye
that the councillor was going
against his will.

When Boots came
to the king's castle,
he laid the councillor down
in the goose-house,
and then he went to the king.

When the king saw Boots again,
he bit his lips
with vexation.

"Well," said he,
"have you fooled the councillor?"

"Oh, yes!" said Boots,
"I have done that."

And where was the councillor now?

*Oh, Boots had just left him
down in the goose-house.
He was tied up
safe and sound
in a sack,
waiting*

*till the king
should send for him.*

So the councillor was sent for,
and when he came,
the king saw at once
that he had been brought
against his will.

"And now
may I marry the princess?"
said Boots.

But the king was not willing
for him to marry the princess yet;
no! no!

Was the king dishonest
in refusing Boots permission
to marry the princess
after he had performed
the king's two requests?

Boots must not go so fast.
There was more to be done yet.
If he would come
tomorrow morning,
he might have the princess
and welcome,
but he would have to pick her out
from among fourscore other maids
just like her;
did he think
that he could do that?

Oh, yes!
Boots thought
that might be easy enough to do.

So, good!
Then come tomorrow;
but he must understand
that if he failed,
he should have a good whipping
and be sent packing
from the town.

So off went Boots,
and the king thought
that he was rid of him now,
for he had never seen the princess,
and how could he pick her out
from eighty others?

But Boots was not going
to give up so easily
as all that!

No, not he!
He made a little box,
and then he hunted up and down
until he had caught a live mouse
to put into it.

When the next morning came,
he started away
to the king's house,
taking his mouse along with him
in the box.
There was the king,
standing in the doorway,
looking out into the street.
When he saw Boots
coming towards him,
he made a wry face.

"What!" said he,
"are you back again?"

Oh, yes!
Boots was back again.
And now
if the princess was ready,
he would like
to go and find her,
for lost time
was not to be gathered again
like fallen apples.

The children may enjoy rehashing the story
identifying those points of action
where they were so in tune with the author's plot structure
that they could predict certain happenings
or certain language.

So off they marched
to a great room,
and there stood
eighty-and-one maidens,
all as much alike
as peas in the same dish.
Boots looked here and there,
but even if he had known
the princess,
he could not have told her
from the others.
But he was ready
for all that.
Before anyone knew
what he was about,
he opened the box,
and out ran the little mouse
among them all.
Then what a screaming
and a hubbub
there was.
Many looked as though
they would have liked to swoon,
but only one of them did so.

As soon as the others
saw what had happened,

they forgot all about the mouse
and ran to her
and fell to fanning her
and slapping her hands
and chafing her temples.

"This is the princess,"
said Boots.

And so it was.

After that
the king could think
of nothing more
to set Boots to do,
so he let him
marry the princess
as he had promised
and have half of the kingdom
to boot.

That is all
of this story.
Only this:
It is not always Transforming Sentences
the silliest one
that sits kicking his feet
in the ashes at home.

You may wish to
explain to the
children that the
use of pictures in
a sentence to sub-
stitute for words
is called *rebus*.
They probably
will enjoy trying
this technique in
writing some of
their own stories
and poems.

COMPARISONS

As wet as a 🐟 — as dry as a bone;

As live as a bird — as dead as a stone;

As plump as a partridge — as poor as a rat;

As strong as a 🐴 — as weak as a 🐱 ;

As hard as a flint — as soft as a mole;

As white as a lily — as black as a coal;

As plain as a staff — as rough as a 🐻 ;

As tight as a 👜 — as free as the air;

As heavy as lead — as light as a 🪶 ;

As steady as time — as uncertain as weather;

As hot as an oven — as cold as a 🐸 ;

As gay as a lark — as sick as a 🐕 ;

As savage as tigers — as mild as a dove;

As stiff as a poker — as limp as a 🧤 ;

As blind as a bat — as deaf as a post;

As cool as a 🥒 — as warm as toast;

As blunt as a 🔨 — as sharp as an awl;

As flat as a flounder — as round as a ⚪ ;

As brittle as glass — as tough as gristle;

As neat as a pin — as clean as a 🧵 ;

As red as a 🌹 — as square as a box;

As bold as a thief — as sly as a 🦊 .

Anonymous   pictures by Betty Fraser

Come Dance with Me

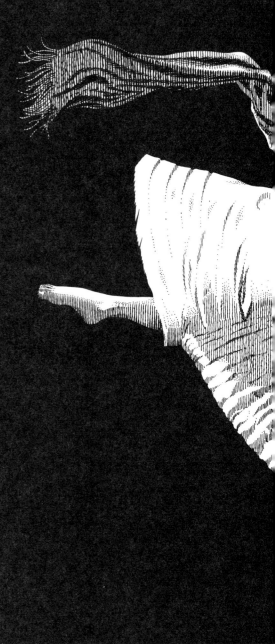

Once upon a time in a country
where the people were fond
of music and dancing,
there lived a prince
who was the best dancer of all.
He moved to the music
like a soaring bird
and, seemingly, never tired.
Then one day the Prince was injured
in the jungle
and, thereafter,
walked with a stiffness
in his right knee.
The Prince grieved
that this should happen to him,
for his dancing days were over.
His father, the King,
shared his son's grief
and sent to every corner
of the land,
seeking someone to help.
Many came but none succeeded,
and, at last, the Prince lost hope
that he would ever dance again.

A story by Bill Martin Jr.,
paintings by Vic Herman

Then, one day, a young girl
came from the far mountains
to give her help to the Prince.

"Are you a physician?"
 he asked gloomily,
 knowing that she was not.
"How can you help me?"

"I am not a physician," she said,
"but I, too, like to dance.
 Come, dance with me."

"But my knee is stiff," he said.
"My dancing days are over."

"Have you not noticed?"
 replied the girl.
"I, too, have a stiff knee."
 The Prince, at first,
 was taken back.

Then he rose stiffly
and led her to the village square
to join in the dancing.
The townspeople were overjoyed
to see the Prince dancing again.

They wanted to cheer.
Instead, so that the Prince
and his partner
would not feel shy,
they, too, joined in the dance,
all dancing with stiff right knees.

Noodles: Did you know what I've been doing now, Bill?
I have a new friend and you know what his name is?
His name is Dick.
And we were out hunting for ooley bugs.
Did you know what an ooley bug is?

Bill: I never heard of an ooley bug, Noodles.
What's an ooley bug?

Noodles: Well, I never did really see one but I'm looking,
and you have to wear your hat
when you look for them—that's why I have my hat on—
because you wait until it gets dark
and you go out the front door
and you go into the bushes—

then you keep bending
low to the ground and saying,
"Ooley bug! Ooley bug!"
and if there's one there,
it'll come right up to you.
You never did know this?

Bill: I never knew that, no.

Noodles: I know just about every thing in the world,
and if you just stay with me, Bill Martin,
you'll probably —

Bill: — catch an ooley bug, right?

Noodles: Yes, but if you don't catch one,
I'll put one in my pocket and bring him to you.

Bill: That's an interesting word, Noodles,
ooley bug!

Noodles: I just made it up, Bill.
When I get tired of the old words,
I just make up new ones.
I write them on the wings of paper airplanes
and sail them out into the world for everybody.

Bill: What are some of your home-made words, Noodles?

Noodles: Fingertonguelingersome is one.

Bill: What?

Noodles: Fingertonguelingersome.
And you're supposed to say it very very fast.

Bill: What does it mean?

Noodles: Bill Martin, do you know what?

Bill: What?

ANTIDISESTABLISHMENTARIANISM

Noodles: You sound like a school teacher.
They think you have to know what every word means.
Sometimes you just say a word because it's pretty
or because you like the way it rolls around on your tongue.
Fingertonguelingersome is a loop-de-looper.
It just flies around your mouth
and sometimes it comes out differently
than it's supposed to.

Bill: I'll remember that one, Noodles.

Noodles: And do you see these cards, Bill?
They're my word cards.
I write my special words on cards
and carry them around with my flashlight.
So I can look at them day and night.

Bill: That's an interesting pack of words, Noodles.

Noodles: And that isn't all I do. I write my special special
favorite words on colored paper and paste them
on a great big potato chip can,
and use that same can for my waste basket.
Nobody's going to throw
my good words away.

Bill: Where do you find your words, Noodles?

Noodles: Every place.
Sometimes when I hear a word I like,
I just say, "That's my word."
And I take it.
Did you know something, Bill?

Bill: What?

Noodles: Sometimes I hang some words
on a string that goes
from one side of my room to the other.
Right now the words on my string say,
"Chickamungus is amazable."

superfluous

lunar module

powwow

eventide

miracle

Superstar

halo

kingpin

Stupidhead

flashback

rough 'n ready

Bill: Say, that's a good word — *amazable.*

Noodles: I made it up, Bill.
And do you know something else?
I've got my best words
right here on my arm.

Bill: Noodles, you're kidding.

Noodles: Do you want to see?
But first you gotta promise
you won't wash them off.

Bill: I promise.

Noodles: Then take a little look, Bill Martin.

Bill: Wouldn't you know it!
"Oodles of Noodles!"

Noodles: That's the true one.
Do you know where I found these words?

Bill: Where, Noodles?

Noodles: I made them up out of my own little head.
When I was in the Hall of Mirrors once,
I saw myself 53 times all at once.
And I just said,
"There's oodles of that dear sweet little Noodles."
And now I've got to go.

Bill: Where, Noodles?

Noodles: Word hunting.
Goodbye, Bill.
Oodeley, oodeley!

THE HAPPIEST DAY OF MY LIFE

PRETTY COLORS...SUNNY SKIES...DEEPEST DEEPS

...OH, IT'S THE HAPPIEST HAPPIEST HAP·HAP·HAP·HAPPIEST HAPPIEST HAPPIEST IS THE HAPPIEST DAY OF MY LIFE...OH, THIS IS THE HAPPIEST HAPPIEST DAY OF MY LIFE HAPPIEST DAY OF MY LIFE

OH, THIS

song by Rita Abrams, design by Jane Mutshnick, lettering by Ray Barber

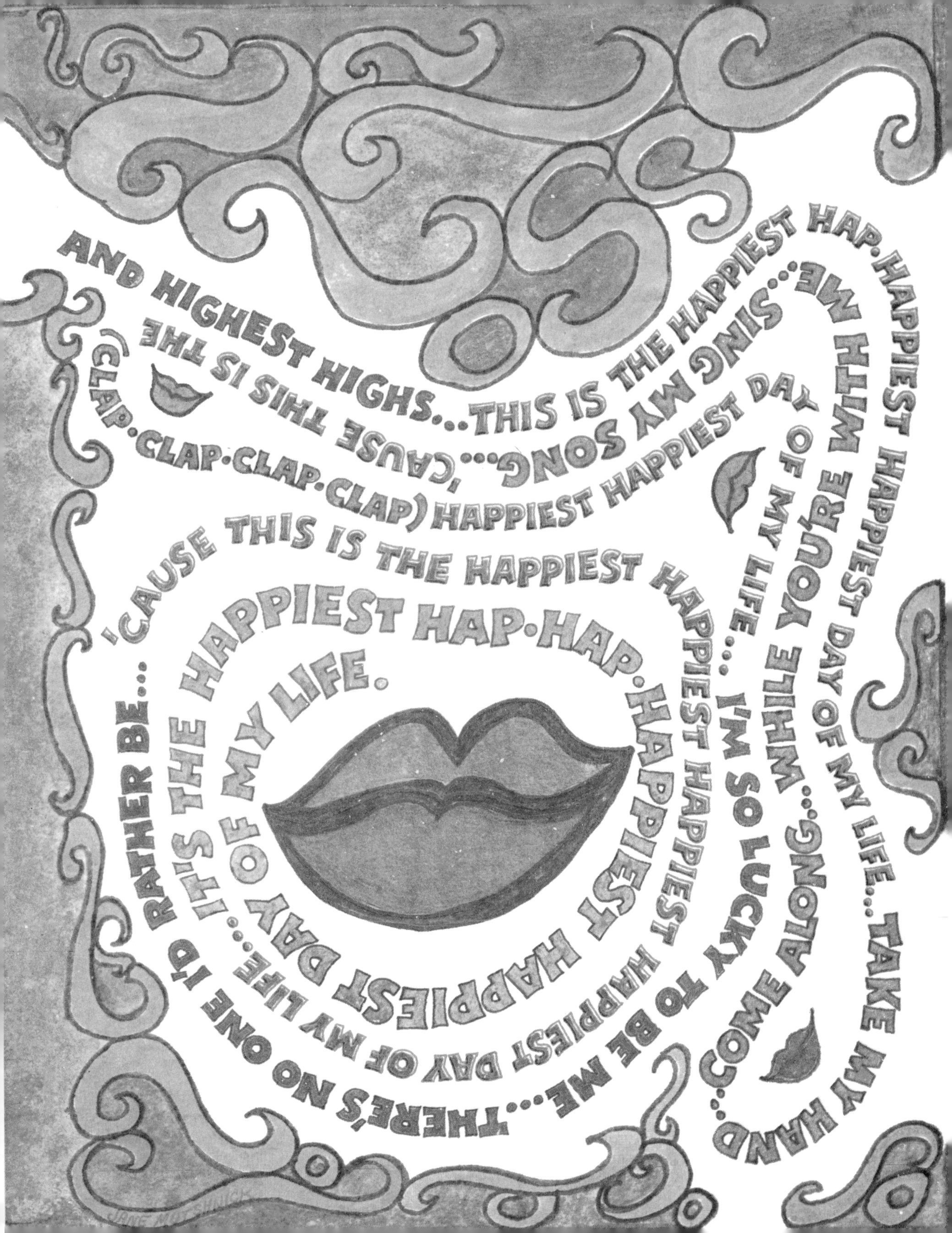

Here's a story the children can read silently. Remind them that it's all right to skip over unknown words if the absence of the word doesn't destroy the meaning. After their reading of the story, you might ask the children to identify words in the story which at first were unknown and then became known as they read on.

302

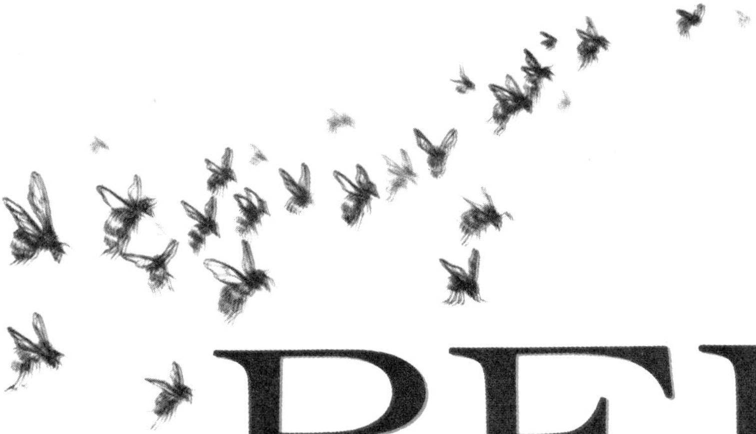

BEES

A true story by Gene Fulks, pictures by Zena Bernstein

It seems like
Did you know that

before the sun rises.
while dew is still on the grass.

Expanding Sentences: Are the children aware that sentences can be expanded by adding chunks of meaning?

*^It is early in the morning.^*
The bees are waking up.
Flights of worker bees are swarming
out of the beehive...
up, up,
over the tree,
over the meadows,
over the fields of clover,
across the river,
straight to the orange grove,
far, far away.
They fly so far away from the beehive,
so far away from home,
oh, how will they find their long way back?

Here is another science story that leads naturally to an accumulation of facts about living things. Despite the literary language, many of the sentences have the matter-of-fact ring of public language.

Buzz ... buzz ... buzz.
Thousands of worker bees
swarm down into the orange trees, Reducing Sentences
swarm down into the sweetness
of the sweet white orange blossoms.
Burrowing deep into the blossoms,
they gather the sweet nectar
and buzz from blossom to blossom.
Their honey sacs, now filled with nectar,
their pollen baskets bulging with golden pollen,
the worker bees fly homeward,
carrying their heavy loads.

Ask the children to rewrite the facts on these two pages
using the kind of language they would ordinarily use in a science report.
Do they prefer one kind of writing over the other?

With eyes as keen as the eyes of a bird,
they see the bend in the river,
they see the fence through the clover,
they see the tree in the meadow,
and they see the narrow little lane
that leads them back to the beehive.
The worker bees never get lost.
The worker bees always come home.

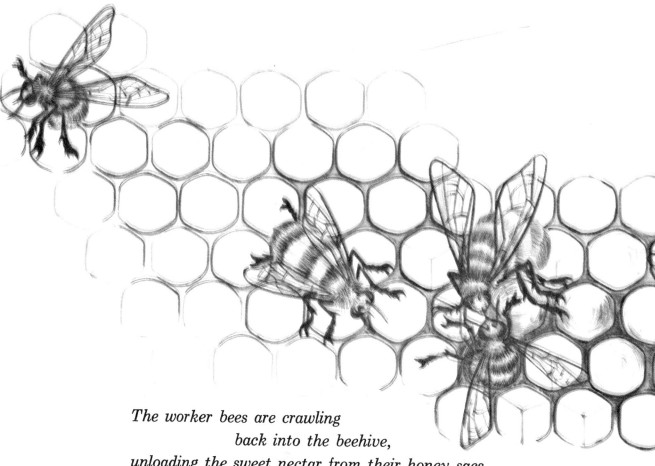

The worker bees are crawling
       back into the beehive,
unloading the sweet nectar from their honey sacs
and the golden pollen from their pollen baskets.
Most of the worker bees are ready to go
    to the orange grove again,
but some will not return.
Weary with work,
their wings tattered and torn,
some drop to the floor of the hive and die.
But the work goes on.
Other worker bees take their places
and swarm out of the beehive
    to fly toward the orange grove.
The endless search for nectar and golden pollen
    goes on and on and on.

Won't it be interesting
if some children remember
This is the man all "tattered and torn"
from "The House That Jack Built"?

But back inside the beehive,
thousands of other worker bees
are swarming over the honeycomb,
turning the nectar from the orange
    blossoms into honey,
chewing the golden pollen to feed the baby bees,
making wax from some of the nectar
    to build the honeycomb,
buzz...buzz...buzzing.
So many bees you couldn't count them all,
all of them busy from morning till dark—
all except the drone bees.

How do you like this style of art
as compared to that in "Mool" or "A Bat Is Born"
or any other selection in the book?

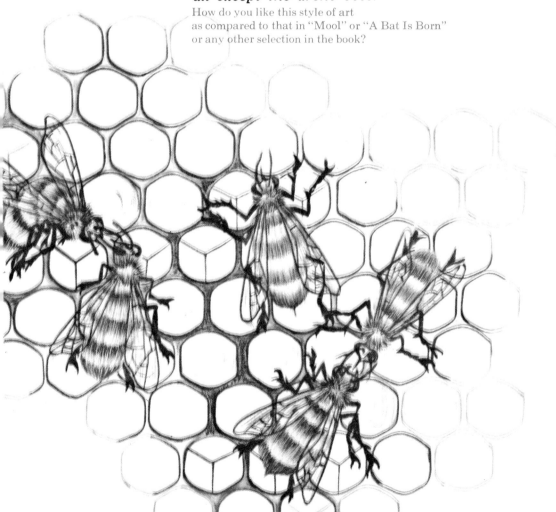

The drone bees are men bees.

They keep the queen bee company.

They dawdle around the beehive,

begging the busy nurse bees for droplets of honey,

> *pestering,*
>
> *begging*
>
> *and buzzing*
>
> *all day long.*

One of the drone bees

will one day mate with the queen bee

and become the father of new baby bees.

The queen bee is the largest bee.

She is the queen of the beehive.

From morning till night,   Rearranging Sentences

after she has mated,

she crawls over the honeycomb

laying eggs to hatch baby bees.

The queen bee is a busy bee.

She sometimes lays 4,000 eggs in a day,

4,000 eggs...4,000 baby bees.

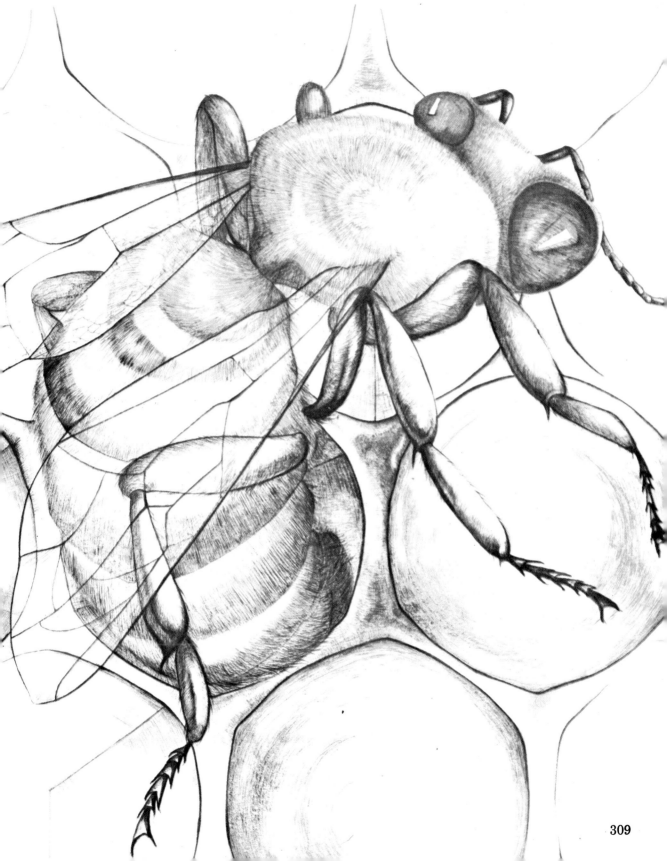

A beekeeper is coming down the narrow lane.
He wears heavy gloves and a netting over his hat.
He is coming to rob the beehive of its
    rich golden honey.
Step...step...step.
The beekeeper is walking away
with a bucketful
    of rich golden honey.
And still there comes another intruder.
Scratch...scratch...scratch.
A mother skunk and her four kittens
    come to the beehive.
They come at night
when the bees cannot fly and sting them.
Oh how wise, Mother Skunk!
Scratch...scratch...scratch.
The bees stir but they do not fly.
They do not fly at night
because they cannot see
    their way in the dark.
The bees, sensing the danger,
    crawl out of the beehive
    to see who is there.
Snap...snap...snap.
The skunks eat bees until they are full.

Does it seem to you
that the idea of the bees not flying at night
is being repeated?
Do you see a way to reduce any of the sentences
without destroying the meaning
but avoiding the repetitions?

Rearranging Sentences: "Bees eat skunks...."
There are some parts of a sentence
that defy rearrangement without changing meanings.

But soon it will be morning.
And soon there will be more nectar
     and more honey
     and more eggs
     and more bees.
The endless making of honey
goes on and on and on.

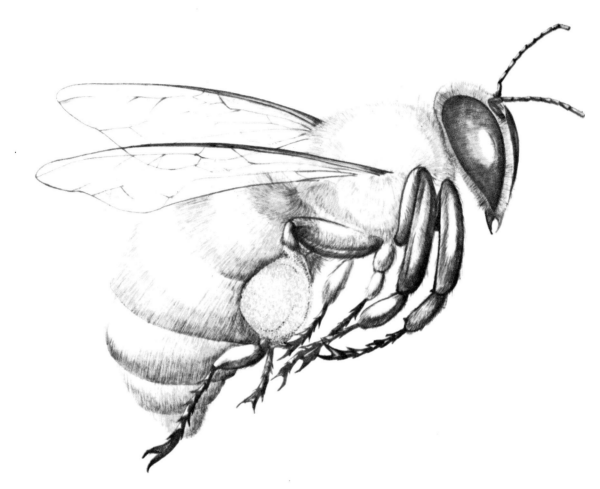

Ask the children to go through the story
and select phrases or sentences
that best describe the picture on this page.
The children's reuse of language found in a story
is one way they have of claiming that language as their own.

The Sea Wolf

*Here is a poem that will fill
the mind with haunting pictures of fishermen riding out
the fury of storms at sea. As
you read it aloud together, let
your voices show the rising and
the passing of the storm.*

The fishermen say, when your catch is done
    And you're sculling in with the tide,
You must take great care that the Sea Wolf's share
    Is tossed to him overside.

They say that the Sea Wolf rides by day,
    Unseen on the crested waves,
    And the sea mists rise from his cold green eyes
    When he comes from his salt sea caves.

The fishermen say, when it storms at night
    And the great seas bellow and roar,
    That the Sea Wolf rides on the plunging tides,
    And you hear his howl at the door.

And you must throw open your door at once,
    And fling your catch to the waves,
    Till he drags his share to his cold sea lair,
    Straight down to his salt sea caves.

Then the storm will pass, and the still stars shine,
    In peace — so the fishermen say —
But the Sea Wolf waits by the cold Sea Gates
    For the dawn of another day.

A POEM BY VIOLET MC DOUGAL,
    PICTURE BY TERRI PAYOR

GOING BEYOND READING

"I CALL IT 'RESEARCH'".

Bill: Noodles! Noodles!
          I thought he was here.
          I'm sure I heard him. . . .
          Noodles!
          Oh Noodles, where are you?

If you have heard Noodles
on a cassette recording,
you know how impossible it is
for print to recreate
the sound of the human voice.
The skilled reader brings
the memory of human intonations
to the print
and thereby gives it the sound of sense
and human aliveness.

Noodles: Here I am, Bill.
              Couldn't you see me?

Bill: No. I looked everywhere
          but you weren't to be seen.

Noodles: I didn't want you to find me because
              I was researchin', didn't you know that?

Bill: Researching what?
          I didn't know you even knew what research is.

Noodles: You never do seem to know what I know.
I know a very lot of things if you would only ask me.

Bill: All right, Noodles, tell me about researching.

Noodles: Well, for one thing, Bill,
it's something you do yourself.

Bill: Like what?

Noodles: If you get to wondering about something,
and I do this many times,
you just ask yourself your own questions
and then you find out your own answers.

Bill: Give me an example, okay?

Noodles: Well, the other day I read an article in the paper
about wanting to have school all year long,
and so I just asked myself,
"Who in the world wants school all year long?"

Bill: That's a good research question.
How did you go about it?

Noodles: To start with I went right to the kids and asked them,
because they're the ones who are going to be involved.
I asked ten kids.
I have 8 no's, 1 yes and 1 undecided.
And I'll tell you something else, Bill Martin,
that you probably wouldn't know unless I tell you.
All 8 said it big, loud, and *NO.*

Bill: Did they explain why
they didn't want school all year long?

Noodles: That was my second question
that I asked them, "Why?"
Here's what they said,
I wrote it down:

The first one said,
    "What are you trying to do, kill me?"
The second one said,
    "What! Give up my vacation?"

317

The third one said, "I'm undecided. It all depends on
    what you're going to do in school those extra months."
The fourth one said, "Oh, my aching head!
    I couldn't stand that much learning!"
The fifth one said, "Why not? School's okay.
    It's better than doing nothing."
The sixth one said, "My mother wouldn't like that. She'd
    have to mow the grass herself if I went to school."
The seventh one said. "Never. What would teachers
    be like if they were stuck with us all year long!"
The eighth one said, "I'd lose my baby-sitting money
    if I went to school and I need my money."
The ninth one said, "What a gyp!
    Just when I'm old enough to go to camp,
    they start talking about school all summer."
The tenth one said, "You must be kidding!"

So there you have my research, Bill Martin.
Eight no's, 1 yes, and 1 undecided.

Bill: That's a good kind of action research, Noodles,
    getting people's opinions and counting them up.
    How did girls feel about this question
    as opposed to the boys?

Noodles: I don't know.
    I didn't ask any girls, but that's a good idea.

Bill: Boys and girls, why don't you do some research
    in your own classroom,
    and ask these same questions of each other
    and tally them as boys' opinions and girls' opinions.
    And see if boys and girls think alike on this question.

Noodles: And another thing, they might find out what the teachers
    in the school think.

Bill: And how about your mothers and your fathers?

Noodles: And if you want the opinion of a ghost,
    just let me know, kids.
    I'll get you a great big fat *NO* vote.

Bill: And there are other kinds of research you might like to do.
For example, if you read a poem that you really like,
you may want to try to find other poems by the same author.
Or poems about the same subject.
And there's action research, such as finding out who broad
jumps the farthest;
opinion research, such as finding out what people believe;
library research, such as reading to find more information;
experiment research, such as finding out whether a plant
grows better indoors or outdoors.

Noodles: And ooley bug research where on some dark and stormy night
you go hide in the bushes calling for ooley bugs
to come out of their little holes and be counted.

Bill: Or if you read about a place and get curious about it,
you may want to look at a map and find out where it is,
or you might want to call a travel agent
for a brochure about that place.

Noodles: Or if you're a ghost and want to go visit the place
you just say

Goodbye, Bill Martin.
This is too much research for me.
Oodeley, oodeley!

Bill: Noodles! Come back! Come back!
I have a lot more to tell you about research. . . .
Well, boys and girls, I can tell you. . . .
Boys and girls!
Now how could they do that?
They've disappeared too.

You may like to have a child volunteer to read a block of the type aloud, with the other children following the reading in their own books. Then stop and discuss the meanings. The article will have more meaning if you take some time to have Ecuador located on the map and discuss something about its climate in relation to its global position. Don't cue the children in advance to the wide range of temperatures found in this tropically located country.

MARKET DAY IN ECUADOR

An article and photographs by Peter Buckley

Monday is a very important day in Ambato. Monday is market day! Thousands of people come to this market, from the city itself and from far away, by foot, by bus, and on horseback. There are no supermarkets in Ambato, and there are very few stores. The marketplace is the one place to go if you want to buy or sell.

321

Ambato is almost two miles high in the Andes Mountains. It is always cool there, even though it is very near the equator. On either side of Ambato, the mountains drop down quickly to the hot tropic lowlands.

Were the children surprised, after their initial conjectures about the climate in Ecuador, to find the wide range of temperatures?

Far below Ambato, in the tropics, certain Indian tribes grow sugar. On Sunday they wrap some of their sugar in palm leaves and set out for the marketplace in Ambato to be ready for sale day, Monday.

Other Indian tribes come to the marketplace with rope to sell. The rope is made from grass which grows wild, in fields near their villages in the lowlands. The Indians labor long and hard to make the rope.

This picture suggests how rope is made.
The strands of grass are obviously
braided and twined into long lengths.
Is the woman to the left
holding yarn or colored grass?
What might be some uses of colored grass?

Indians of a tribe that raises cattle are trying to sell their cows.

Not far from them is the part of the market where horses are sold.

The children might like to investigate the extent to which a central square is part of our own city and village construction. How different is the market place in Ambato from the market place of some of our own modern shopping centers?

Transforming
Sentences

Sugar, rope, cows, horses: you can buy almost anything you want on Monday in Ambato. The market spreads out from the central square until it almost fills the city streets. There is a special place for every item, and everyone knows exactly where to go if he wants to sell a needle or if he wants to buy a bag of corn.

Many Indian languages are spoken in the market because each tribe has its own language. Everyone, however, speaks a little Spanish, and so it is easy for a man from one tribe to speak to a man from another tribe, even though their own languages may be different.

The market is a very important place. It is important not just because it is like a giant department store and

a giant supermarket put together so that people can buy and sell what they need, but it is important because people talk to each other.

They tell each other the news from the villages, their farms, their towns. Many men and many women with their babies firmly strapped to their backs come to the market to learn the news.

Rearranging
Sentences

This expression could be written *not only because?* What would happen if the word *just* were left out altogether?

Isn't it interesting to speculate how the word *giant* has come to be a familiar descriptive word in our time?

There are no newspapers in the villages or on the farms far from the city; and even if there were, they would be useless because many people cannot read. Instead of reading the news, the people gather together in the market on Monday.

When they are through with their business, the people of one tribe meet with the people of another tribe.

The news is very important. One man who raises sheep hears that floods in a distant valley have drowned many large flocks of sheep.

Knowing this, the sheep-farmer realizes that during the next year there will be a shortage of sheep in the market, and so he will be able to raise his prices when he brings his own sheep for sale.

An Indian boy, who has four sheep and a pig, each tied to the end of a rope, gets into trouble when the five animals decide to go in different directions.

Men from the Otavalo Tribe who live on the shores of a lake more than a hundred miles north of Ambato meet every Monday at the market.

327

A father learns that his son is no longer busy transporting bananas but, instead, is growing his own bananas.

People hear about their friends who have gotten married, a new baby and distant relatives who have died.

They hear about a new tractor, a better way to plow a field, a new hospital where they can take a sick child for free medical care and a good movie playing in Ambato.

A man who needs a job will ask for one in the market.

A man who wants to buy a house will ask if anyone knows of a good one for sale.

A man with a broken motor will ask where he can get it fixed.

A woman who is ill will ask for a doctor.

There is no end to the news you can hear on a Monday in Ambato.

A day at the market is busy from beginning to end. After hours of talk, friends who have not met for weeks eat together.

Then everyone has to think of going home. Some must catch a bus for the tropical lowlands. Others ride their horses to farms high in the cold mountains. The people who live in Ambato walk slowly home. In another week it will be market day once again in Ambato.

328

Late in the afternoon a farmer puts his son on the new donkey he has bought at the market, and together they start for home.

How would you feel if you were this boy? Do you think these people
are headed for the hot, tropical lowlands or the high, cold mountains?

Would you like to

on a star,

Carry moonbeams home in a jar,
And be better off than you are,
Or would you rather be a mule?

A mule is an animal with long funny ears,
He kicks up at anything he hears,
His back is brawny
And his brain is weak,
He's just plain stupid
With a stubborn streak,
And by the way if you hate to go to school,
You may grow up to be a mule.
Or would you like to swing on a star,
Carry moonbeams home in a jar,
And be better off than you are,
Or would you rather be a pig?

A pig is an animal with dirt on his face,
His shoes are a terrible disgrace,
He's got no manners
When he eats his food,
He's fat and lazy
And extremely rude,
But if you don't care a feather or a fig,
You may grow up to be a pig.
Or would you like to swing on a star,
Carry moonbeams home in a jar,
And be better off than you are,
Or would you rather be a fish?

A fish won't do anything but swim in a brook,
He can't write his name or read a book,
To fool the people
Is his only thought,
And though he's slippery,
He still gets caught,
But then if that sort of life is what you wish,
You may grow up to be a fish.

And all the monkeys aren't in the zoo,
Ev'ry day you meet quite a few,
So you see it's all up to you.
You can be better than you are,

You could be SWINGING on a ★

You are standing on Pluto.

You may be surprised at the amount of talk
and the depth of outer-space vocabulary
children will bring to these pictures.
This is a time for you to sit back and listen,
and let the children pursue these four pages
in their own way.
Any child who understands where the story places him
in relation to the sun and outer space
tells you without your having to ask a single question
that he has comprehended the inherent concepts.

The ninth planet is cold and dark.
The other planets in the sun's family
   look like tiny points of light
   because they are so far away.
Even the sun looks small.

If you looked out beyond Pluto into deep space,
    you would see other stars like our sun.
Some of those stars also have a family of planets
    like the family to which Earth belongs.
Do you think that people like us
    might be living on another planet,
    circling another sun,

Far, far out in deep space

Excerpts from *The Sun and Its Planets*
by Gerald S. Hawkins, illustrations by Fred Moore

Boa Constrictor

by Shel Silverstein

picture by Ray Barber

OH I'M BEING EATEN BY A BOA CONSTRICTOR, A BOA CONSTRICTOR, A BOA CONSTRICTOR, A BOA CONSTRICTOR, I'M BEING EATEN BY A BOA CONSTRICTOR, AND I DON'T LIKE IT... ONE BIT! A BOA CONSTRICTOR, ONE BOA CONSTRICTOR, WELL WHAT DO YOU KNOW...

Poor maligned boa! It doesn't eat people but the myth persists. Who'll look it up and explode the misconception?

Don't overlook the small type.
There's a gem of information there.

IT'S UP TO MY NECK, OH DREAD...

OH HECK

IT'S UP TO MY

MIDDLE, IT'S... MMFFF...

IT'S UP TO MY THIGH,

OH GEE...

OH FIDDLE...IT'S UP TO MY

IT'S UP TO MY KNEE, OH MY...

...IT'S NIBBLING MY TOE,

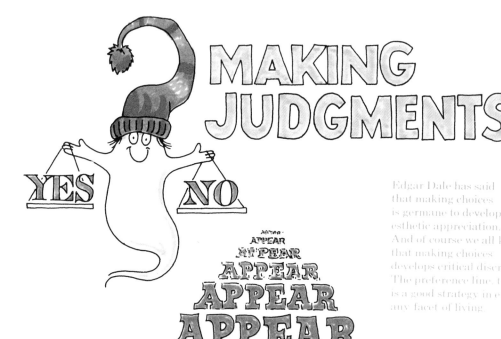

MAKING JUDGMENTS

YES NO

APPEAR
APPEAR
APPEAR
APPEAR
APPEAR

Edgar Dale has said
that making choices
is germane to developing
esthetic appreciation.
And of course we all know
that making choices
develops critical discrimination.
The preference line, therefore,
is a good strategy in evaluating
any facet of living.

Noodles: Say, Bill, like I told you,
my very favorite story is "Cracker and Fletcher."

Bill: Why, Noodles, just last week you told me
that your favorite story was "Freddy Freon."

Noodles: That's one of my problems.
I'm always changing my favorite.

Bill: Join the crowd, Noodles.
That's the problem everyone has.
Our favorite story generally
is the one we just finished reading.

Noodles: Sometimes that's true but sometimes
my favorite is something that I read a long time ago.

Bill: That's the way we come to make judgments
about our likes and dislikes, Noodles.
Sometimes a favorite story may lose its first place
the very next day,
while another favorite story
may stay on the list for years and years.

Noodles:	What list, Bill?
Bill:	Your hit parade of favorite stories.
Noodles:	And favorite poems and pictures.
Bill:	That's right, Noodles.
Noodles:	And favorite books and teachers and specially our favorite days.
Bill:	Noodles, let's make a preference line of your favorite stories.
Noodles:	A what line?
Bill:	A preference line. That's a way of deciding what stories you like best.
Noodles:	Oh, I already decided that, Bill. "The Three Billy Goats Gruff" is my favorite story of stories.
Bill:	Then let's put that story at the high end of your preference line.

The Three Billy-Goats Gruff

LOW   MIDDLE   HIGH

Noodles:	Can I put my awful story at the low end? It's that story called "The Twins Visit the Farm." It wasn't much of a story. It was just a lot of dry facts that somebody thought we should learn. And that dumb Susie! I was really disgusted with her. Facts, facts, facts.

Bill: All right, we'll put "The Twins Visit the Farm"
at the low end of your preference line.

Noodles: And I know another dumb one that goes at the low end,
"Mat Has A Fat Bat."
That's a fake story.
Just a bunch of words!

Bill: Noodles, you're sounding like my puppet.
Could it be that I'm putting words in your mouth?

Noodles: I don't need your words, Bill.
I've got plenty of my own.

Bill: Good for you, Noodles.
Now let's put "Fat Mat Cat" on the line.
Where do you want it?
Near the middle or near the bottom or at the bottom?

Noodles: Do you have a basement for such stuff?
It was the worst I've ever read,
so extend that low line, Bill.
Let's make room for one that is lower than the low.

Bill: Okay, Noodles, we'll put it here.

Noodles: Those two low ones are crowding each other
out of the picture.

Bill: And your favorites will crowd each other,
too, for the top slot, Noodles.
Choices are not easily made.

Noodles: Well, I'd rather move to the top.
It was sure crumby at the bottom.

Bill: But, Noodles, knowing what you don't like,
helps you know what you do like.
Every preference line has to have a bottom.

Noodles: Even for desserts.
I put all those delicious desserts at the top.

Bill: Oh no you don't Noodles.
Some people call stewed prunes dessert.

Noodles: They do?
And I don't even like the way they smell!

Bill: Boys and girls, now that you've seen
how a preference line works,
why don't you make a preference line of your own —
one for stories, another for poems,
another for songs, and so forth?
Every story that you read will fit
somewhere on the line.
A story may change places
from day to day or week to week,
but it can always be represented
after you've read it.

Noodles: That would really take a long line, Bill Martin,
longer that I have time to fill in,
so I've got an idea.
I'm only going to put ten stories on my line,
ten stories I've read this last month.

Bill: Well, you can do it anyway you please, Noodles,
and now before you beat me to it,
oodeley, oodeley!

Noodles: Do you believe that?
Ol' Bill Martin just did my disappearing act.
Just wait till tomorrow,
I'm really going to trick him.
I'm going to get him good.

Alligator on the Escalator

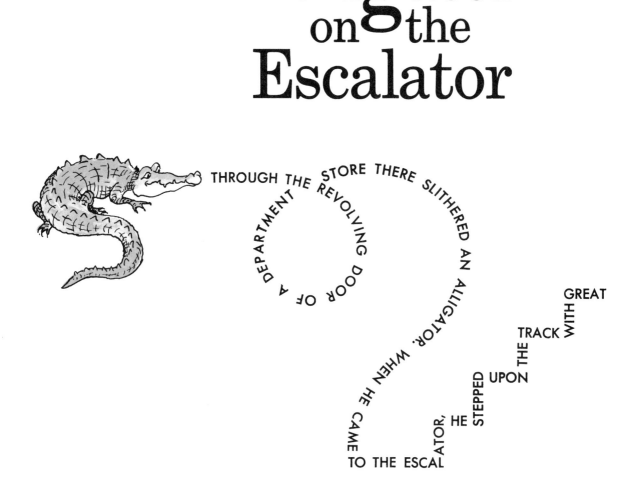

THROUGH THE STORE THERE SLITHERED AN ALLIGATOR. WHEN HE CAME TO THE ESCALATOR, HE STEPPED UPON THE TRACK WITH GREAT

DEXTERITY; HIS TAIL DRAPED OVER THE RAILING, AND HE CLICKED HIS TEETH IN GLEE; "YO, I'M OFF ON THE ESCALATOR,

EXCITED AS I CAN BE!

IT'S A *MOVING* EXPERIENCE,

AS YOU CAN PLAINLY SEE.

ON THE MOVING STAIR I GO ANYWHERE,

I RISE TO THE TOP,

PAST OUTERWEAR, INNERWEAR,

DINNERWARE, THINNERWARE—

THEN DOWN TO THE BASEMENT WITH BARGAINS GALORE, THEN BACK

ON THE TRACK TO THE TOP ONCE MORE!

OH, I MAY RIDE THE ESCALATOR

UNTIL CLOSING TIME OR LATER,

SO TELL THE TELEPHONE OPERATOR

TO CALL MRS. ALBERT Q. ALLIGATOR

AND TELL HER TO TAKE A HOT MUD BATH

AND NOT TO WAIT UP FOR ME!"

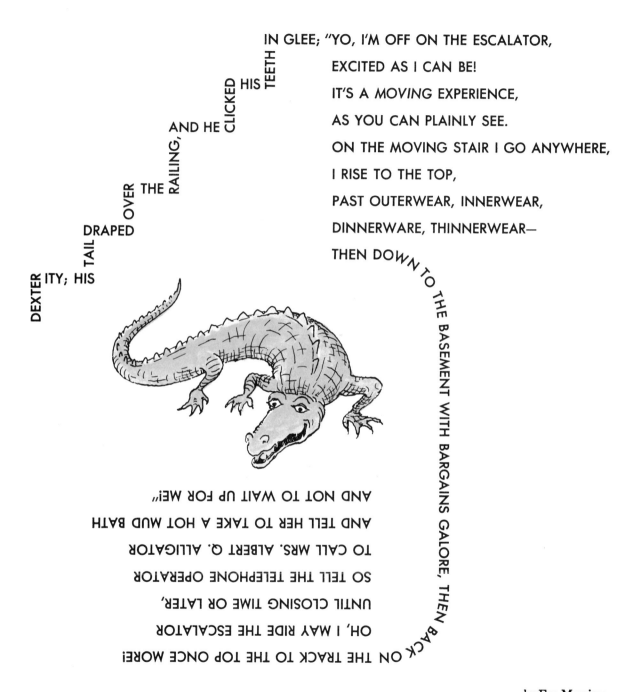

by **Eve Merriam,**
pictures by Kelly Oechsli

Trees Alone Do Not Make a Forest

A forest is more than a spread of trees. It is a "town," a community with a vast population of animal and plant life.

The members of the forest community could not survive without each other. They depend on each other for food. The plants wage a constant battle among themselves for the sunlight, soil, water and minerals necessary for life and growth. The animals, too, try to eat without being eaten.

The death of every plant and every animal feeds new forest life. Everything in the forest is part of the endless pattern of *growth and decay*, of *life and death* in the forest.

Forest Life in the Treetops

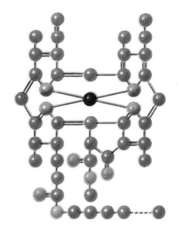

Leaves give life to the forest. Green leaves on trees, vines, shrubs and bushes make plant food. And in doing so, they provide food for all animals in the world.

This represents part of the atoms in a chlorophyll molecule. Chlorophyll is the green substance in leaves that enables them to combine water from the soil with carbon and oxygen from the air to produce the plant food called glucose.

Birds, too, live in the branches of trees. They feed on insects and prevent great armies of insects from destroying the trees. However, not all birds live on insects. Owls, hawks and eagles feed upon toads and squirrels and other small animals of the forest.

Squirrels not only live in trees but also feed upon their seeds. This is small loss to the trees, and being carried away by squirrels and other animals is an important way for seeds to get scattered throughout the forest.

Forest Life on the Forest Floor

The forest food cycle begins with leaves and ends with such animals as foxes, bears and wolves. These animals eat other animals of the forest. Their only enemies are dogs and man, disease and starvation.

Some insects help the life of the forest by carrying pollen from flower to flower. However, many insects are harmful, feeding upon the leaves of forest plants. If it were not for birds and toads, insects would soon destroy the forest.

Toads and frogs feed upon the millions of insects that live on the forest floor. But, in turn, toads and frogs often become food for other animals. The backs of many toads are covered with poison glands that cause pain or death to animals that try to eat them.

Plants such as mushrooms and toadstools do not produce their own food because they do not have leaves. These scavenger plants, known as fungi, feed on dead plants and thereby help rid the forest of rubbish.

Forest Life Underground

The food cycle of the forest begins and ends in the soil of the forest floor. The roots of plants take water from the soil to be used in making plant food. The roots also anchor the trees and help keep soil from being washed away.

Earthworms help the forest by plowing the soil in search for food. They dig passages that allow air and water to pass freely through the earth. Earthworms are just one of hundreds of kinds of animals that live on the forest floor.

Forest Life Inside Things

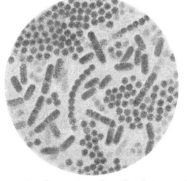

Many insects in their larval (worm) stage feed upon the wood of living trees, often destroying them. Other insects eat dead wood, thereby causing the wood to crumble and decay. This enriches the soil and helps clear away the rubbish in the forest.

Bacteria live in dead things like trees and leaves and animals and cause the dead matter to decay. The decay enriches the soil which helps things grow. And so, life in the forest is renewed by decay, year after year after year.

Pictures by J. Kunz, courtesy of

VIEWING THE PRINTED PAGE AS ART

After reading this
essay, you and the
children can profitably
leaf through the book
viewing the printed
page as art.
Learning to read
the *esthetic* dimensions
of print is essential
to learning to read.

Noodles: Say, Bill,
you're giving me
a headache.
You've got me hanging here upside down.

Bill: Sometimes a page in a book
needs a special touch to make it come alive, Noodles.

Noodles: Why did you do it to me?
Just let the old words do it.
They don't care if they're upside down.

Bill: We've done that, too, Noodles.
Sometimes the words in this book have run crossways,
sometimes downwards,
sometimes upwards,
sometimes round and round.

Noodles: And sometimes there aren't any words at all.

Bill: The important thing is that the page.
gives the reader a deep sense of aliveness.

Noodles:	That's what I like, Bill Martin.
Bill:	Sometimes the words alone possess the aliveness, sometimes it's the combination of words and pictures, and sometimes it's just pictures.
Noodles:	And sometimes it's Noodles. Don't forget me, Bill.
Bill:	That's right, Noodles. You've given many of these pages a keen sense of aliveness.
Noodles:	Well, I think I'll go now.
Bill:	Not yet, Noodles. I'm not finished.
Noodles:	I'll help you finish Bill. Don't look now but I'm going to turn you into a blot.
Bill:	Not again, Noodles, please.
Noodles:	We need some aliveness on this page. I think you'll look better as a blot.
Bill:	Please, Noodles, I'm not finished.
Noodles:	Here comes the big surprise: Hokus pokus diddeley dokus presto chango — Bill Martin is a blot!

As you go through this book, boys and girls,

Well, what do you know!
Nothing stops him.
Talk, talk, talk, talk, talk.
I think I'm going home
to get my earmuffs.

ask yourself what makes a page come alive for you.

Goodbye, everybody.
Oodeley, oodeley!

Sometimes it's the words, sometimes the white space, someti.....

a picture for storytelling

BY SYMEON SHIMIN

"AN-OUT-OF-THE-PARK" DEFINITION

by Bobby Mc Guire

lettered by Ray Barber

What a refreshing change from dictionary definitions!
Does it suggest what children might do with other games and sports?

A BASEBALL BAT IS....

the enemy to a slick infielder's
magnetic glove.... a sweeping sound
of torture to a pitcher's heart....
a maker of runs, rallies, and
champions.

A BASEBALL BAT IS....

a badge of courage against a blazing
fastball.... or a sneaky curve....
it is hanging in there on the
3-2 pitch.

A BASEBALL BAT CAN....

drill a ball.... line it, bunt it,

drive it .... drag it, p⚾p it,
smack it, smash it .... Texas
Leaguer it, foul it, miss it, homer it.

A BASEBA⚾LL BAT CAN....
bring 50,000 fans to their feet....
make them cheer in stereo.

A BASEBA⚾LL BAT IS....
the mem⚾ry of Babe Ruth....
Stan Musial.... The Sally League....
the 1927 Yankees.... all blended int⚾
the golden slow motion of yesterday.

BUT A BASEBA⚾LL BAT,
m⚾st of all, is.... the union of
boys on a neighborhood sandlot
swinging into manhood.

Here is a gallery of ten bird pictures, painted by the talented artist Basil Ede of Surrey, England. Many people think that Mr. Ede is the best painter of birds since Audubon made his prize collection of lifelike bird paintings in the early 1800's. Certainly Mr. Ede's pictures are lifelike, but he says that his aim is not to show his skill as a painter.

Birds in a Gallery

He wants people to see the character of each bird. That is why he paints them. It is impossible to look at these pictures without seeing the character of each bird, but it also is impossible to look at these paintings without knowing that you are having a rare experience. Just to see the beautiful coloring and shapes and movement makes you suddenly realize that you are alive, that the birds and artists and books and music contribute to the excitement of living.

Yellow-shafted Flicker has a strong bill for boring into tree bark for insects. His sharp claws hold him fast to the tree as he listens for insects under the bark. When something stirs, he attacks it.

Robin
is noted
for his red breast
and his cheery song
which begins at dawn.
Many people
consider the robin
the first sign
of spring.

Tree Swallow
might be nesting
in your birdhouse
in the backyard.
These birds
have strong wings.
They sometimes fly
10,000 miles
in a single year's
migration.

Compare this information
about feather preening with the
information given about birds' feathers
in "How Birds Keep Warm in Winter,"
pages 172-179.
What protective devices of this kind
does the human body have?
How about other animals
such as the hare, the bear, and the deer?

Belted Kingfisher
has been so busy fishing
it seems
that he hasn't had time
to preen his feathers.
Birds use their beaks
to dress their feathers
with oil which they take
from their bodies.

Black-capped Chickadee
is a gay
and active bird.
He darts about
in and out of trees
and open spaces,
calling his name,
*"Chickadee!
dee-dee-dee."*

357

Pileated Woodpecker ➤
is a "woodworking machine." He has a powerful neck, a heavy skull, and a chisel-like bill for working his way into hollow trees. Notice how he balances himself with his tail and claws as he chops at the tree.

Hairy Woodpecker
looks almost like the downy woodpecker, except it is larger. Both of these woodpeckers are "bark-stickers" looking for insects.

⬆
Baltimore Oriole is one of the prettiest of birds. His clear, loud whistle in May and June announces that he is in the neighborhood once again to build a hanging nest in a high tree.

Pileated Woodpecker

Eastern Evening Grosbeaks travel in flocks varying from three to a hundred. The plumes of the mother bird are less colorful than those of the males, which is true of many kinds of birds.

Grosbeaks

Great Horned Owl ➡ has eyes that collect light and ears that collect sounds, making him the best nighttime hunter of all birds. His feathers are so soft that they muffle the sound as he swoops down on his prey. Notice how his claws are shaped for grasping.

360

Princess Sylvia laying on the carving tray asked, "Haven't you ever heard of eating noodles?"

"Nope! I want to eat you!" said Mother Dragon running to call her family to dinner.

don't eat
the by Jay Ells
princess

SHE'S PROBABLY TOO TOUGH

Joe and Millicent Dragon had been helping Mother Dragon dress the dinner. They liked the dinner quite a bit. "Want to come to our playroom?" they asked their dinner.

Prepare for an adventure in fantasy. Prepare also for the keen delight the children will feel when they recognize that here is an author who uses the same intriguing kind of sequence that they so often like to create in their own writing. How fortunate that no one told this author he couldn't use great flights of fancy almost lacking continuity, and wonderful incongruities! The success of this story is its fidelity to the ways of childhood. In your first reading of it to the children and subsequently their reading of it for their own delight, the linguistic continuity should be maintained. If on occasions you wish to go through simply to discuss and react to the pictures, let that be an experience in itself. To try to integrate story continuity with open discussion tends to dilute the value of both.

"Yes, I do," Sylvia said leaping off the carving tray and running upstairs and into the playroom with Joe and Millicent. They locked the door.

As you look at a double page spread, do you have the feeling that the pictures and the words and the space all create the message? This was the intention of the author artist. The value of this story cannot be measured by the number of words on a page. Its message is in the utter delight it offers a child, helping him stay the chaos of the day. Throughout the SOUNDS OF LANGUAGE program we have introduced many experiences of this kind. We invite you to respond with joy knowing that "what the heart feels today, the head will know tomorrow."

Crash! Bang! "Open this door," yelled Mother Dragon.

"Bring that dinner out immediately," said Father Dragon.

"Whataya mean hogging the whole dinner for yourselves?" screamed brother and sister dragons.

Sylvia began to cry. "Don't cry, Sylvia," said Joe. "We'll save you." He opened the window. "Come on, Millicent."

They all flew out the window. Behind them they heard the crash
of the breaking door and the yell, "O.K. Now you're going to get it."

And the whole dragon family flew out the window after them.

Joe and Millicent flew with Sylvia until they were tired. They stopped to rest on a mountain top. Joe surrounded them with a ring of fire.

When the Dragon family flew up to the fire, they couldn't get through. Father Dragon said, "We'll wait. They'll come out when they get hungry."

But Sylvia went around to the other side of the big rock on the mountain top and found a sleeping knight and his horse. "My brother, Charles!" she exclaimed.

The knight woke up. "Sylvia! I've been looking everywhere for you. Where have you been?"

"This is Joe and Millie Dragon who rescued me from being eaten. The hungry Dragon family is waiting right outside the ring of fire." "You can all squeeze into my armor with me and hide. My horse Faithful Dobbin can jump so quickly through this fire that we won't be burned. If the Dragon family comes after us I'll stick them with my sword."

They popped into the armor

and Dobbin jumped through the flames.

Just outside the fire the bulging knight was stopped by Father Dragon.

Charles said, "I was sleeping on the mountain top and two dragons and a horrible little girl tried to eat me. I barely escaped with my horse."

Father Dragon chuckled. Charles rode quickly down the mountain and through many villages until he reached the castle where his mother and father lived.

Charles rode his horse into the big party going on and yelled, "We're here!"

"Who?" said his father.

"We!" said Sylvia, Millicent and Joe popping out of the armor.

"Eeeeeeeee! Dragons!" screamed the guests and six fainted.

Joe and Millicent gave the six mouth-to-mouth artificial respiration and the six woke up and said, "What wonderful dragons these are. We didn't know!"

Whurrr! Whurrr! (the sound of dragon wings)

The Dragon family flew through the window licking their lips. "Yipes!" screamed the guests leaping under the tables.

The Dragon family zoomed toward the guests. Suddenly they smelled the party food. They dived into the big bowls. "Mmmm-mmm," the dragons murmured.

The guests poked their heads up.

"Yum, yum," said Mother Dragon.

"Fun, fun," said the brother and sister dragons.

"Why, cooked noodles are better than raw people," exclaimed Father Dragon.

Charles' father said, "Please join us. We're having a party. Our children are already friends."

"Yes, yes," said Father Dragon. "Bring the noodles."

Everyone began to eat with such enthusiasm that noodles soon got on the table cloth. Then noodles got on the floor.

Noodles got on the window. Noodles got on the door. Some guests jumped into the serving bowls and got noodles in their hair. Noodles were tossed to the rafters and guests swang in the air. Noodles covered their faces and they shouted in little toots and when they fell on the silverware, they slipped it into their boots.

They rolled around on the table nibbling, chomping, and slurping, and those who gobbled their food too fast soon could be heard quietly, happily burping.

The dragons had never eaten a food so good. The guests had never felt so safe. So they vowed eternal friendship with hugging and singing.

Joe married Sylvia. Charles married Millicent. And with loving and laughter they gobbled up those noodles happily ever after.

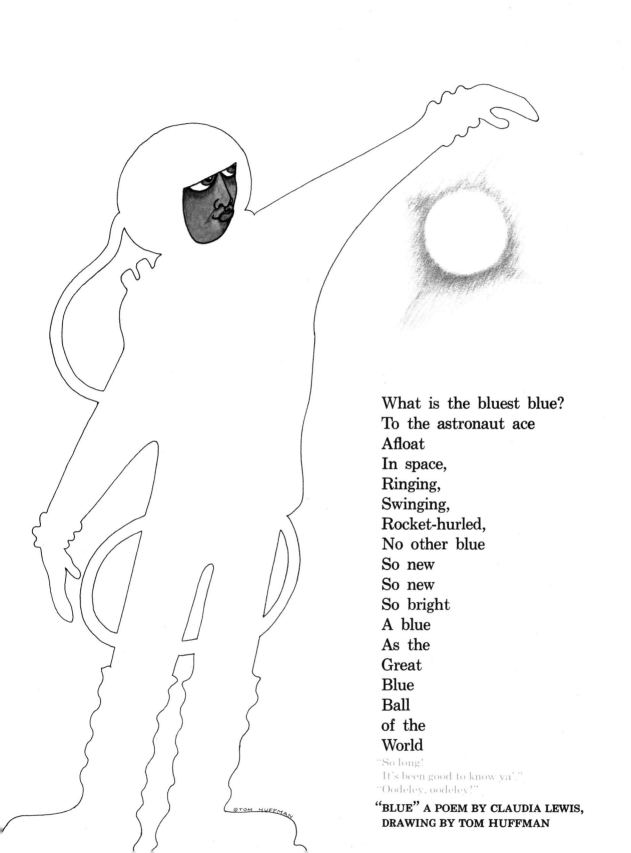

What is the bluest blue?
To the astronaut ace
Afloat
In space,
Ringing,
Swinging,
Rocket-hurled,
No other blue
So new
So new
So bright
A blue
As the
Great
Blue
Ball
of the
World
"So long!
It's been good to know ya'."
"Oodeley, oodeley!"

"BLUE" A POEM BY CLAUDIA LEWIS,
DRAWING BY TOM HUFFMAN

SOUNDS OF LANGUAGE

Part One

The Heart of the Program

The *Sounds of Language* reading program
is a fresh and enchanting collection
of poems, stories, articles, and pictures
that realistically prompt children to hear the spoken patterns
of the sentences they read.
As children gain skill in using their ears
to guide their eyes in reading,
they have a qualitatively different reading experience.

Consider the young chil
who has frequently heard his teacher rea
"Ten Little Indian
Once a child has these sound
clearly and solidly in his ea
he has little difficulty reading this old rhym
in its printed forn
Once his ears begin telling hi
what his eyes are seein
he approaches the reading with confidence and expectatio
And when he comes to his teacher and exultingly declare

I know that word, Miss Barber!
That word is "little!"

she has evidenc
that he is relating sight and sound in readin
And it is easy for her to take this child a step furthe
by asking him if he can find the number
or if he can find the word *India*
It should not surprise you to kno
that even at the first-grade leve
a child is already something of an exper
in analyzing languag
a fact overlooked in most reading program

1 little Indian boy. 1 little, 2 little, 3 little Indians, 4 little, 5 little, 6 litt

tle Indians, 4 little, 3 little, 2 little Indians,

2 TE

little, 6 little, 7 little Indians, 8 little 9 little 10 little, 10 little Indian boys.

Think of the three-year-old child on a bus
who says,

> *I rang the bell.*

A sentence sound he learned by listening.
At age four, he is apt to say,

> *I ringed the bell.*

A sentence sound that he never in his life heard.
Why then does he say it?
A child at four no longer simply imitates language sounds
that he hears in his environment.
He is beginning to figure out how language works
and how to make it work for him.
When he says, *I ringed the bell,*
he gives evidence that he is analyzing language
and that he knows how to change a verb
from present to past tense.

In similar ways in the *Sounds of Language* program,
a child is helped to become more and more expert in
using and analyzing language.
The aim is to help him become aware
of what he intuitively knows about language,
and to help him explore and verbalize
old and new learnings.

10 little Indian boys. ... little Indians, 10 little Indians, 9 little, 8 little, 9 little Indians, 10 ... Indians, 7 little, 8 little, 9 little Indians, 7 little, 8 little

—from *Sounds I Remember*

Language analysis emerges in abundance
at all levels in *Sounds of Language*
because the program is a total language and esthetic experience
which logically and comfortably connects a child
with his past experiences in using oral language
and with his intuitive knowledge of how language works.

Too many children in school have come to know reading
as word calling and drill,
with little or no opportunity
to claim language in its many dimensions.
The purposes of this teacher's edition, therefore,
are to help you join children and support them

1) in their growing appreciation of literature and language;

2) in a useful inquiry into how language works,
        both in its oral and written traditions;

3) in a useful inquiry into literary structure; and

4) in the development of esthetic awareness.

The pages of the pupil book (incorporated in this teacher's edition)
have been annotated for your convenience.
The annotations appear at the precise spot on the page
where they are needed to point up learning insights
and teaching strategies.

At no time is an annotation so prescriptive
that it precludes your insights from the teaching process.
To the contrary, the annotations are geared
to triggering all your insights and hunches
in helping children *latch on* to language and their humanity.

There is nothing complicated about this method of teaching.
Once you have read this informal dialogue
and the annotated pages,
you will feel comfortably at home with the program.
In fact, you may find yourself thinking:
Here, at last, is a program that helps me
use all of my knowledge and intuitions about language
—and about teaching.

Now, let's talk informally
about ways for using the *Sounds of Language* readers
to bring new dimensions
into your teaching of reading.
We have no choice but to help
all children learn to read.
They inherit the need to read
simply by living in our culture.
We, therefore, have the obligation to provide
wide-ranging ways for unlocking print.

What works for one child
doesn't necessarily work for another child.
What works for one kind of reading material
doesn't necessarily work for another.
Children are highly inventive and insightful
in ways of unlocking print—
until unimaginative reading instruction
tells them there is only one way to decode,
"*Sound out the words!*"
Actually, there are dozens of ways
to unlock the printed page.
And there are dozens of ways
that lead into the act of learning to read
before successfully pulling together
ear and eye and tongue and muscle
in the mature act of reading.

Some boys we have known
seemed at first to read more with their feet
than they did with their eyes.
You've had these kinds of boys
in your own classrooms.

Aren't they interesting
as they screw themselves up
into impossible positions
and keep perfect time to whatever is being read?
We should be saying to these boys:

> *Henry, you're so great at reading*
> *with your feet! How would you*
> *like to try reading with your eyes?*

And Henry wouldn't mind at all—
in fact he might be delighted to try—
knowing his comfortable way for responding to print
has been so respected.
But unfortunately,
we don't recognize Henry's rhythmical body response
as a reading behavior,
accustomed as we are to thinking about reading
as an eye exercise
and a "sounding-out" ritual.
Instead of praising Henry
and helping him include other parts of his body
in his response to the printed page,
we are likely to admonish:

> *Now, Henry, sit up straight*
> *and pay attention to your book.*

If Henry had the skill of self-analysis
and dared challenge the teacher's edict,
he might respond:

> *But I am paying attention.*
> *Rhythmical body response*
> *is part of reading a book.*

Only Henry doesn't have the language
for verbalizing his intuitive response to print.
And unless we have the awareness
to recognize what he is doing,
another potentially successful reader
will start the long and uncomfortable journey
of finding out that there is something wrong
with his way for learning to read;
and another potentially fine teacher
will be thrown into miscommunication with a child
simply because the definition of reading behavior
which has been made available to her
through teachers guides and college courses
is too narrow to accept and encourage
the many-faceted reading behaviors of real live children.

The *Sounds of Language* program makes it easy and enjoyable
for children and teachers to explore and perfect
multiple ways for unlocking print
and enjoying the miracle of language.
Children will learn to figure out the pattern
back of an author's way of putting a story
or poem or sentence together,
and to use this information for reading words
they didn't know they knew.
They will learn to figure out the different shapes of sentences
and to recognize unknown words
largely by where they fall in a sentence.
They will learn to figure out rhyme schemes and read new words
by recognizing where they fall in a certain rhyming slot.
They will learn to figure out underlying rhythmical patterns
and to use syllabic patterns
as one way to take hold of unknown words.

All of this, at first, may sound strange and complex
if you have not observed children using these natural ways
for making a go of reading.
But this essay will help you discover a multiplicity of ways
for using literature to bring new dimensions
into the teaching of reading.
The program is based on only a few practical teaching strategies.
These strategies work in kindergarten
as well as they work in eighth grade and all up and down the line.
The children themselves modify the strategies
by their individualized responses.

Once you own these strategies,
you can forget about the teacher's guide
and look forward to relaxed and creative reading sessions
where you are free to respond
to the children's individualized responses
and where you have a structural know-how
to help them learn to read.

The teaching strategies
explored in this essay are:

1) Recognizing That Language Works in Chunks of Meaning

2) Reading Aloud to Deposit Literary and Linguistic Structures
   in Children's Storehouses

3) Innovating on Literary Structure to Claim Basic Patterns

4) Figuring Out How Stories and Poems Work

5) Helping Children Verbalize Their Intuitive Literary Insights

6) Figuring Out How Sentences Work

7) Innovating on Sentence Patterns

8) Figuring Out How Words Work

9) Figuring Out How Print Works

10) Developing Skill in Comprehension

11) Linking Writing to Reading

12) Cultivating Literary and Esthetic Appreciation

13) Developing Sensitivity to the Three Levels of Language

14) Developing Sensitivity to Humanness

—drawings from "My Mother is the Most Beautiful Woman in the World,"
Sounds of a Young Hunter

Learning to read
is not something that happens
after a stereotyped readiness period
in first grade or kindergarten.
Learning to read
is the job of a lifetime.
Two-and-three-year-old children who are read to a lot
begin their reading careers early.
The day a child gets hold of a sentence pattern that works for him
and reads it into the telephone directory
or the Montgomery Ward catalog
or his daddy's newspaper at night,
he is launching himself on his reading career.
He is role-playing himself as a successful reader.
The day a child reads a book from memory,
he is furthering his reading career.

He, in truth, is finding joy and power
in the pages of a book,
a psychological posture that every successful reader
continuously brings to each reading encounter,
knowing, subconsciously if not consciously,
that he can make a go of print.
This is the first and foremost reading skill.

Part Two

The Teaching Strategies for Sounds of Language

Whether it be at home or at school,
when children are read to,
they begin their naturalistic ways
for latching on to print
and they continue to expand and refine these ways
throughout the course of a lifetime—
provided they are given helpful opportunities.
The *Sounds of Language* teaching strategies
will help you provide these opportunities
for children to respond to print
in naturalistic intuitive ways;
and they also will help you release children
to verbalizing their intuitive responses to language and print,
and develop them into word-unlocking skills.

1 RECOGNIZING THAT LANGUAGE WORKS IN CHUNKS OF MEANING

As each of us learned to speak the language,
simply by imitating the speech sounds that we heard,
we learned to cluster words into meaningful units within a sentence.
Even as babies using nonsense syllables,
we used intonation and clustering
to create a *sound of sense*.
Later as we learned vocabulary and sentence ways,
we made full use of sentence sounds (sometimes called melodies)
demonstrating that we intuitively understood
that language works in chunks of meaning.
Not once did we isolate the word sounds
from the sentence sound in which they were cast.
Not one of us said,

> "*I* (pause) *want* (pause) *my* (pause) *mommy!*".

Rather "*Iwanmymommy!*"
came out as a meaningful linguistic whole,
a fluid sentence sound with a cultural melody
that conveyed both feeling and thought.
Unfortunately, language instruction in schools
has ignored the natural workings of language
by such unnatural techniques as

A) focusing word recognition skills on individual words
rather than on the clustering of words within a sentence,

B) insisting on paragraph forms
with rigid right-left hand margins that ignore
the natural grouping of words within a sentence,

C) talking about word meaning as if a word
actually has a meaning outside the context of the
sentence in which it derived its meaning; and,

D) insisting that children in all of their school language activities
perpetuate these misconceptions.

The poets, more than anyone else in our society,
have tended to improve
the communication potential of their writing
by arranging their words into natural linguistic clusterings.

All of us are familiar with the ragged right hand margin of a poem
and may never have stopped to think
why the sentences are written this way.
Just observe how Margaret Wise Brown
accommodates the lines in "Four Fur Feet"
to the chunks of meaning within each sentence:

OH, he walked along the river

on his four fur feet,

his four fur feet,

his four fur feet.

He walked along the river

on his four fur feet

and heard the boats go toot—O.

—Sounds of a Powwow

How different this is from a page of prose in an ordinary book
where each line must move rigidly
from a left hand margin to a right hand margin
with only the paragraph breaks
to give a feeling of structure to the printed language.
This inflexible technique cruelly severs words in half
in order to accommodate the margins,
as well as ignoring the natural clustering of words
into chunks of meaning within each sentence.
Let's see what a prose sentence would look like
if it were separated into its chunks of meaning
to enhance the linguistic design of the sentence
rather than the arbitrary width of the page.

> *Sometimes the male lions*
>
> *may help ambush the game,*
>
> *but more often*
>
> *they take their rest*
>
> *under shady trees*
>
> *and watch*
>
> *while the lionesses stalk*
>
> *and kill the game*
>
> *that will become a feast*
>
> *for all of the lions.*

—"King of Beasts," *Sounds of Mystery*

As you observed, this is a complex sentence to read
but how much easier it becomes
when it is printed in its chunks of meaning.
Each of these groups of words has a meaning
that is more important than any single word within the group.
The words in each group, therefore, must be read together
as a subset of the more important set, the sentence.
Each subset leads into the next,
gradually amalgamating into the whole meaning of the sentence.
One of the miracles of our language
is its way of working in chunks of meaning.

An experienced reader does not move through a sentence
by reading each word separately.
Even though language is not ordinarily printed in chunks of meaning,
he learns to see—and sense—the groups of words
that best create meaning.
When a sentence is written from margin to margin across a column or
a page,with no special emphasis on the chunks of meaning, the reader
must do the work of seeing the words in clusters that release meaning.

This, at first, is not an easy task, but it is rewarding
because, soon, the reader finds himself
able to manage material that ordinarily would have stopped him.
Consider the problem of an inexperienced reader
who breaks a sentence into malfunctioning units, like this:

1) *"Where has*

2) *Sallie been*

3) *asked*

4) *to keep*

5) *Halloween?"*

6) *asked they.*

—from "Tomson's Halloween," *Sounds of a Young Hunter*

Such a child has a comprehension problem immediately
because he has violated the linguistic units within the sentence.
Just try reading the sentence orally as it is grouped here
and you will shudder at the absence of the sound of sense.
The only criterion for knowing a chunk of meaning when you see it
is to hear it.
A child's intuition about language,
once he has developed the concept of chunks of meaning,
will lead him through the sentence this way,
simply because this is the way he would speak it
and thereby exploit its sound of sense:

1) *"Where has Sallie been asked*

2) *to keep Halloween?"*

3) *asked they.*

Reading instruction that emphasizes single word recognition
above all else
actually creates reading problems for children
because units of meaning are torn rudely apart
and children are not freed
to use their accumulated linguistic insights.
The concept of chunks of meaning within a sentence
is not foreign to children,
because they naturally speak in chunks of meaning
as they frame their oral sentences.
They need only to be helped to see that they can recreate
these same chunks on the printed page,
even if books are not printed in this way.
Hopefully the day will come when books,
at least for elementary school children,
will have considerable material printed in spoken language patterns.

2 READING ALOUD TO DEPOSIT LITERARY AND LINGUISTIC STRUCTURES IN CHILDREN'S STOREHOUSES

Each of us has a linguistic storehouse
into which we deposit patterns
for stories and poems and sentences and words.
These patterns enter through the ear
and remain available throughout the course of a lifetime
for reading and writing and speaking.
The good reader is a person who looks at a page of print
and begins triggering patterns
that have been stored in his linguistic treasury.
These patterns range all the way
from the plot structure an author has used in a story
to the rhyme scheme that hangs a poem together,
to the placement of an adjective in front of a noun
as part of the shape of a sentence,
to the underlying rhythmical structure in a line of prose or poetry,
to the *ed* ending as part of the shape of a word.

As these various kinds of structures
are brought into play
as a result of encountering a new version
of the same old basic structure,
a child is able to figure out much of the new vocabulary
because he recognizes the similarity
between the new structure
and structures he has already claimed.
A poor reader is the person who looks at a page of print
and no patterns are triggered to help him unlock the page.
This can be because he has not been read or talked to very much
and therefore has not deposited
story and poem and sentence and word patterns
in his linguistic storehouse.
Or this lack of triggering can occur
even if he has been talked to a lot
if the oral language patterns are not the kind
he is encountering in print.
A Spanish-speaking child, for example,
has stored sentence patterns
where the adjective follows the noun.
This does not help him unlock English sentences
where the adjective precedes the noun.
He will first have to hear and store in his being
the typical shape of English sentences
before his linguistic storehouse can help him unlock English print.

Now you can see why reading aloud
the poems and stories in the *Sounds of Language* readers
is a continuing part of this reading program
for children of all ages throughout their school years.
Sometimes you are reading aloud and the children are listening,
sometimes you are reading aloud and the children are chiming in,
sometimes the children are reading in chorus,
sometimes the boys and girls are reading aloud in dialogue,
sometimes the children are chorusing a poem or story by memory,
sometimes you and the children are reading aloud together,
with the children following the print in their books
so their eyes can be seeing what their ears are hearing
what their tongues are saying.

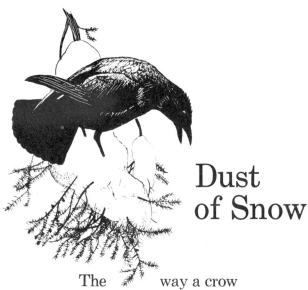

Dust
of Snow

The　　　way a crow
Shook down on me
The dust of snow
From a hemlock tree

Has given my heart
A change of mood
And saved some part
Of a day I had rued.

—"Dust of Snow" by Robert Frost, from *Sounds of a Young Hunter*

For example, a child who has heard frequently
and later read and chorused aloud "Dust of Snow,"
will have deposited within his linguistic treasury
a feeling for the sound and meaning of the word *rued*
that enhances his potential use of the word
in all kinds of communication—
reading, writing, speaking and listening.
He also will have a reservoir of potential
for shaping a sentence with the expertise
of this sentence shaped by a poet.
There is no better way for children to learn
to appreciate and use our language
than having broad and continuous experiences
that attune both the ear and the tongue—then later the eye—
to the rhythms, melodies and sounds of language.

Hopefully this reading aloud and language consolidation
will be accompanied by spontaneous body movement—
either the kind of swaying and clapping and shuffling
that children initiate on their own
or interesting movements suggested by you.
Whenever children engage their entire bodies
in their responses to print,
they have the best possible chance
to bring wholeness to the reading act
and intaking linguistic know-how.

3 INNOVATING ON LITERARY STRUCTURE TO CLAIM BASIC PATTERNS

One choice in deciding how to follow-up
your reading aloud of a story or poem
is to invite the children to utilize the author's pattern
for expressing their own thoughts.
By borrowing the underlying structure
of a poem or story or sentence that they have come to know,
they are involved in two linguistically sound learnings
as they hang their own ideas on that structure:

1) they are having intuitive experiences
   with the fact that stories and poems
   do have underlying structures,

2) they are building a bridge between
   the linguistic facts of their worlds
   and the linguistic facts of the printed page.

The invitation to "Write about anything you want to"
may fall heavily on the ears of a child
who doesn't own the basic language structures
to give wings to what he wants to say.

On the other hand, a child of seemingly meager vocabulary
can latch onto a structure that comes in through his ears
and deposits itself indelibly in his mind,
and suddenly find his vocabulary taking on new strength.

Christmas 1969

And lo it came to be
that she bore an infant
in the subway. Because
the apartment cost was
too high. She wrapped
him in paper towels
from a gas station. And
lay him on the cold walk-
way. The train rattled
by but no sound came
from him.

And it came to be
that friends heard of him
and came to see him.
They brought with them
gifts of grape drink, cigar-
ettes, and a few dollars.

—Kevin Clark, grade 6, Issaquah Valley School, Issaquah, Washington.

The *Sounds of Language* readers
make it possible for children of either rich or meager vocabulary
to find challenge in their new creations which come about
as they innovate on the dependable structures found in these books.
Your reading table may come alive
with fifteen new books (written by children)
each time you read a story or poem
and invite the children to borrow the structure
and to adorn it with their own thoughts and language.
What a wonderful source of material the reading table becomes
for the children's independent reading.
Since all of the innovative books
are built on structures which the children have already claimed
in read-aloud times with the *Sounds of Language* books,
the children will not only be able to read the new books more easily,
but they will be recognizing how useful

a person's knowledge about underlying structure
can be in helping him read.
Thus, children who have just finished reading:

Good night, Mr. Beetle,
Good night, Mr. Fly,
Good night, Mrs. Ladybug,
The moon's in the sky.

Good night, Miss Kitten,
Good night, Mr. Pup,
I'll see you in the morning
When the sun comes up.

—Sounds of Home

will tend to feel that they are meeting
an old friend when they come upon a child's innovated story:

Merry Christmas, Mr. Beetle,
Merry Christmas, Mr. Fly,
Merry Christmas, Mrs. Lady Bug,
Santa's in the sky.

Merry Christmas, Miss Kitten,
Merry Christmas, Mr. Pup,
I'll see you Christmas morning
When I open presents up.

Once the children have latched on to this notion
of borrowing a favorite literary structure for their own creations,
you will have many surprises in store.
Suddenly all of children's linguistic storehouse treasures
become available to them—
structures they have claimed both in and out of school—
and they begin to appear in the children's writing.
Imagine the surprise and delight of a fifth-grade teacher
who had asked his children to do a piece of writing
that would cause him to see pictures,
when a boy who had been considered an academic dropout
came up with this piece of writing:

The Frog

The frog in the pond a lony *(lonely)*
little fellow who lives with
the pussy wilow and the muss *(moss)*
who sits on a lilly like a bud wathing *(watching)*
the ixcitment of the day
when he sees a giant much bigger
than his size. He sits riady
coilled like a spring with bright
marrbled eys ready to dive
in the water and hid *(hide)* only to
disapear like mggic *(magic)* disgased *(disguised)*
with the polution of a once
lively and active pond.

—from Mr. Bredahl's sixth grade,
Roosevelt School, Minot, North Dakota

Where did the writing come from?
It has the ring of a poet,
yet the child obviously didn't copy it from print
for a poet would have grouped the words
into spoken speech units which this writing partially lacks.
Is this something this child heard
and deposited whole in his linguistic storehouse
and is now utilizing?
Or is it a combination of his own phrasing
and literary language he has stored?
The miracle is how beautifully and accurately
this boy has called upon his language storehouse
to fulfill his class assignment.
Luckily, this teacher did not feel
that it was *cheating* or *copying* or *uncreative*
to borrow literary lines and/or structure.
This is how a newcomer creates a language of depth and beauty.
Gradually he will transform and in other ways reshape
the language he has borrowed.
Meanwhile, in his borrowing,
he is role-playing himself as a distinguished user of language
and is tuning his ears to the beauty of speech.

Bruce's teacher experienced all of the wonder and surprise
of a genuine literary encounter
when she discovered these lines he had written:

Mystery of Bill Martin
True blue surprise rubbed over man's flat eyes
Truthful innocence scattered down Skinny's rectangular nose
—from Tucson Public Schools, class and grade unknown

Obviously Bruce has a well-stocked linguistic storehouse
and in self-selected ways he is experimenting
with combinations of words that please him,
albeit the sentence meanings are obtuse.

4 FIGURING OUT HOW STORIES AND POEMS WORK

Children like to figure out how things work.
From their earliest days
they are endlessly poking and pushing and pulling-apart
to find out what makes things go.
This is how they learned to talk.
They listened to the talk on all sides of them
and they began experimenting and figuring out how talk works.
Once they began to figure out what they needed to know,
they made talk work for them.

In a similar way,
when you read a highly structured story to children,
they will chime in with you long before you have finished the story:

Brown bear, brown bear,

what do you see?

I see a redbird

looking at me.

Redbird, redbird,

what do you see?

> **I see a yellow duck**
>
> **looking at me.** [1]

As you turn the page and the children burst out reading

Yellow duck, yellow duck,

what do you see?

knowing, without even looking at the print, how the story is working,
they are giving evidence
that they have not simply memorized the story.
They have figured out how the author put his story together
and they are using this information
to help them read pages you haven't even read to them yet.
Much of this kind of figuring-out is intuitive.
It goes on while you are reading aloud
and while the children are chiming the story along with you.
Your job is to help the children verbalize these intuitive insights
and to organize them into word-unlocking skills.
Knowing how stories and poems are put together
will therefore be a help both to you and the children.
To begin with, stories are a series of episodes
or happenings arranged in some kind of recognizable shape.
For our purposes we view an episode
as either an action within a series of actions
or a language pattern within a series of related language patterns.
In so far as possible, in designing the early *Sounds of Language* readers,
we have used the turning of the page to indicate a new episode.

---

[1] This story by Bill Martin appears
both in the *Kin/der Owls* and in the Level 1 *Instant Readers*.

A) Repetitive Sequence

In some stories, the episodes repeat one another.
We have called that kind of story structure *repetitive sequence*.

My name is Tommy.
I am not very big.

I am not as big as a goat. EPISODE 1
A goat is bigger than I am.

I am not as big as a horse. EPISODE 2
A horse is bigger than I am.

I am not as big as an elephant. EPISODE 3
An elephant is bigger than I am.

I am not as big as a whale. EPISODE 4
A whale is bigger than I am.

I am not as big as a dinosaur.

EPISODE 5

A dinosaur is the biggest thing I know.

—from "What Is Big?" *Sounds of Numbers*

Even on first acquaintance, a child will predict

1) that the pattern of phrasing will maintain,

2) that all of the creatures will be described as big/bigger,

3) that in each comparison, the last part of the first sentence becomes the first part of the second sentence.

When the children come to the last episode, numbered 5,
and the repetitive pattern breaks,
we have dramatically enlarged the new language pattern
to signal to the children that something has changed
and the repetition has stopped.
The enlarged type also is a semantic clue
that tends to trigger children
into use of the superlative form of the adjective *big,*
which in its own way
also signals the end of the comparative sequence.
These kinds of exaggerated clues help children learn to trust print,
knowing that an author will keep leaving visual clues
that help the reader decode.
Imagine a child's surprise, therefore,
to discover that the dinosaur is not *bigger than I am*
but is *the biggest thing I know.*
Couched as this variation is within so many dependable repetitions,
it does not cause a child to lose faith in structural repetitions,
but rather it invites him to develop another literary insight—
that when a repetitive pattern gets going,
the author will at some time break the pattern
in order to bring the story to an end.
His curiosity is, therefore, piqued
to predict ways the author can break a repetitive pattern.

Let's look at another example:

Round is a pancake,   EPISODE 1
Round is a plum,   EPISODE 2
Round is a doughnut,   EPISODE 3
Round is a drum.   EPISODE 4

Round is a puppy   EPISODE 5
    Curled up on a rug.
Round are the spots   EPISODE 6
    On a wee ladybug.

Here is the pattern break signalling that the story is ending.
Look all around,   EPISODE 7
On the ground, in the air,
You will find round things
Everywhere.

—from *Sounds of Home*

Although episodes 5 and 6 are patterned extensions
of the previous episodes,
the reliability of their beginning phrases
cues the children to predict
that they can make a go
of a somewhat different sentence.
And, when the children come to the last episode, number 7,
and it does not begin with the repeated phrase *Round is,*
they have a reliable clue for predicting
that this repetitive story is coming to an end.

And here's a repetitive pattern
that's worn smooth with a lifetime of continuations:

As wet as a [fish] — as dry as a bone;

As live as a bird — as dead as a stone;

As plump as a partridge — as poor as a rat;

As strong as a [horse] — as weak as a [cat];

As hard as a flint — as soft as a mole;

As white as a lily — as black as a coal;

As plain as a staff — as rough as a [bear];

As tight as a [drum] — as free as the air;

As heavy as lead — as light as a [feather];

As steady as time — as uncertain as weather;

As hot as an oven — as cold as a [frog];

As gay as a lark — as sick as a [dog];

As savage as tigers — as mild as a dove;

As stiff as a poker — as limp as a [glove];

As blind as a bat — as deaf as a post;

As cool as a [cucumber] — as warm as toast;

As blunt as a [hammer] — as sharp as an awl;

As flat as a flounder — as round as a [ball];

As brittle as glass — as tough as gristle;

As neat as a pin — as clean as a [whistle];

As red as a [rose] — as square as a box;

As bold as a thief — as sly as a [fox].

—from *Sounds of Mystery*

While most stories have more than one kind of pattern
in their make-up,
many of the *Sounds of Language* selections
have enough obvious repetitions in their underlying structures
that children are propelled into anticipating the next line or episode.
Naturally this is not an infallible method
of decoding print,
but it is highly useful in combination with
the many other decoding skills
which are developed in the *Sounds of Language* program.
Moreover, it releases children to a continuous flow of reading
without the traditional vocabulary breakdowns
that are engendered by word-by-word reading
and which rob the language of its melodies and structural rhythms.
Children enjoy the *aha!* feeling which comes
when they predict that the second and third billy goats[2]
will behave much the same as the first billy goat
and when they predict that much of the language (and action)
in the first episode will be repeated.
They feel that they have a successful hold on the story
in "The Three Little Pigs and the Ogre"[3]

when the first little pig outwits the ogre
and they predict that the other two pigs
will try to do the same.
When children make identification with a strong character,
such as Ol' Stormalong,[4] they will predict
that even when he turns into a cowboy and a farmer,
much of his talk and actions
will repeat the talk and actions of Ol' Stormalong, the sailor.
Once you are aware
that a repetitive sequence is one way
of arranging the happenings in a story,
you probably will think of many other stories
which are arranged in this style.
You probably will also remember
how easily the children were able
to take hold of those stories
when you read them aloud.
At the time, you may not have realized
that the children were not simply memorizing—
that they were responding to the reliable repetition
in the story structure.

"Blo-o-ows! Thar she blows!"

SWOOOsh!

"Hooray, a storm!" shouted Stormalong to the farmers.
"Now I can get the kinks out of my muscles.
Avast there, mateys! Storm ahead! All hands on deck!"

"Just sit down and rest yourselves,
me hearties," said Stormalong.
"I'll round 'em up,
just to get the kinks out of my muscles."

[2] "The Three Billy Goats Gruff," *Sounds of Laughter*

[3] *Sounds of Mystery*

[4] "How Ol' Stormalong Captured Mocha Dick," *Sounds of a Distant Drum*

Figuring Out How Stories and Poems Work TE 31

B) Cumulative Sequence

This is the house
    that Jack built.
This is the malt,
That lay in the house
    that Jack built.
This is the RAT
That ate the malt,
That lay in the house
    that Jack built.

—from *Sounds Around the Clock*

How pleasantly this old cumulative rhyme
falls into place.
Each new line (episode) adds a new thought
before repeating everything that went before.
Children who sense the cumulative nature of this story
have a lot going for them.
They know, for example, that all of each subsequent page
will be familiar to them
except for the one added thought.
They also know that each new page will have more type
than the preceding page
and that they will be able to easily read
this accumulating language because it is familiar.
Children, on the other hand,
who are taught to read word by word,
are often turned away from pages with a lot of type
because they do not have structural insights
to help them unravel the print.

Throughout *Sounds of Language* children will encounter
stories and poems and songs and jingles
put together with a cumulative structure.
Each new encounter will remind them
that their insight into new selections
is influenced by the fact
that the basic pattern of cumulative writing
has already been deposited in their linguistic storehouses
and is now available for a lifetime of use
in reading and writing and literary appreciation.

Just for fun, let's see at which point you sense
that "I Came to this Land"
is cumulative in structure.

> *When I first came to this land,*
> *I was not a wealthy man,*
> *Then I built myself a shack.*
> *I did what I could.*
> *I called my shack, Break-my-back.*
> *Still the land was sweet and good,*
> *I did what I could.*
>
> *When I first came to this land,*
> *I was not a wealthy man,*
> *Then I bought myself a cow.*
> *I did what I could.*
> *I called my cow, No-milk-now,*
> *I called my shack, Break-my-back.*
> *Still the land was sweet and good.*
> *I did what I could.*
>
> —from "I Came to this Land," *Sounds Jubilee*

Up until the line in the second verse,
"I called my shack, Break-my-back,"
this structure obviously is repetitive,
but the use of this particular line in sequence with the new episode
is evidence for predicting
that this is both a repetitive and cumulative sequence,
and that each new episode will include
an accumulation of the man's previously named possessions.

Thus, you can figure out all six verses of this story song
with just the following information:

> *I bought myself a horse,*
> *I called my horse, Lame-of-course.*
>
> *I bought myself a duck,*
> *I called my duck, Out-of-luck.*

Aha! Now you're sensing that each creature's given name
is rhyming with the categorical name of the creature—
another structural clue.
Now you have three kinds of literary structure
going for you—repetitive, cumulative and rhyme-rhythm.

> *I got myself a wife,*
> *I called my wife, Joy-of-life.*
>
> *I got myself a son,*
> *I told my son, "My work's done."*

Aha! The author now has broken the language repetition,
signalling that he has probably reached the conclusion of his story.
Observe the additional semantic shift
in the first word of the last chorus:

> ***For*** *the land was sweet and good,*
> *I did what I could.*

This indeed confirms the fact that the story is over.
Did you enjoy getting hold of the story
partly by recognizing how the author put it together?
That same *aha!* feeling of awareness
that came to you as you figured out the pattern
and then made the pattern help you read the story successfully
is the same feeling that children get
when they sense an author's plan.
At the end of this section on various types of literary structure,
you'll find suggestions
for helping children verbalize the *aha!* feeling
and developing it into a word-unlocking skill.

C) Interlocking Sequence

Sometimes the episodes in a story or poem or song
do not simply repeat or accumulate,
rather they interlock in an intriguing way.

The funny old man and the funny old woman
*   sat by the fire one night.*
"Funny old man," the old woman said,
*   "I don't know what to do.*
When I went to the barn to milk the cow,
*   the funny old cow wouldn't moo."*

The funny old man scratched his head,
*   "I know what to do," he said.*
"Take her to town to see Dr. Brown
*   and bring her home in the morning.*
That's what you do when the cow won't moo."

"But she's out in the woodshed lying down.
*   How will you take the cow to town*
and bring her home in the morning?"

"If she can't walk," said the funny old man,
*   "I'll push her in the wheelbarrow if I can*
and bring her home in the morning."

"But the goat's asleep in the wheelbarrow.
*   Where shall I put the goat?"*

"Put the goat on top of the garden gate.
*   The goat can sleep there very late*
till the cow comes home in the morning."

"But the rooster is roosting on the garden gate.
*   Where shall I put the rooster?"*

"Put the rooster in the butter churn,
*   so tight that he can't twist or turn*
till the cow comes home in the morning."

"But . . ."

—from "The Funny Old Man and the Funny Old Woman,"
Sounds of Laughter

Are you caught up in the intrigue
of this sequence, and ready to predict the

"But..." (says the old woman)

"Put..." (says the old man)

pattern on which this story is built?

Even if you had never learned
to sound out the word *butter*,
you are prepared to read this word in this story slot

"But my nice fresh butter is in the churn.

Where shall I put my butter?"

knowing how it interlocks with the preceding lines

"Put the rooster in the butter churn

so tight that he can't twist or turn

till the cow comes home in the morning."

Finally in this humorous story
when the old man says,

"Put the pig on a pillow in the feather bed,"

and the old woman says,

"No,"

instead of

"But,"

you know for sure that the interlocking pattern has been broken
and the story is coming to an end.

Now to exploit your structural know-how,
have a go at this:

I came to the river...

and I couldn't get across,

I jumped on a frog 'cause I thought it was a hoss,

The hoss wouldn't pull so I traded for a bull,

The bull wouldn't holler so I sold him for a dollar,

The dollar wouldn't pass so I threw it in the grass,

The grass wouldn't grow so I traded for a hoe,

The hoe wouldn't dig so I traded for a pig,

_ — — squeal _ _ — _ _ wheel,

_ — — run _ _ — _ _ gun,

_ — — shoot _ _ — _ _ boot,

_ — — fit _ _ thought I'd quit

And I did.

—an old rhyme, *Sounds of Mystery*

Think how much vocabulary is unlocked
simply by recognizing that these lines
interlock with one another
rather than simply follow one another.
You probably remember adult stories
where some happening triggered off
or brought together a chain of events,
such as in *The Bridge at San Luis Rey*
or Chaucer's *Canterbury Tales*.
Even the reading or viewing of Shakespearean plays
is both simplified and intensified
when you recognize the interlocking relationships
of characters.
The moment you con Lady Macbeth
or Claudius or Petruccio, for example,
you begin predicting events and language.
What a reading skill!

D) Familiar Cultural Sequences

Simply by living in our culture,
children have certain built-in structures going for them
that can be put to work in learning to read.
They know, for example, that the hours of the day,
the days of the week, the months and seasons,
the number system and the alphabet
have dependable sequences.
Sooner or later
children become familiar with and use these sequences
like another hand or foot or ear or eye
in dealing with the outside world.
The *Sounds of Language* program
exploits certain of these structures
as another way to help children appreciate the fact
that the recognition of underlying sequence
is an aid in decoding print:

In the first month of the year
I found one brown pony
and he followed me home.

In the second month of the year
I found two white kittens
and they followed me home.

—from "One, Two, Three, Four," *Sounds of Numbers*

Children are now prepared to read the words *third* and *three*
because they sense that along with the repetition
in this story
is a reliance on ordinal and cardinal numbers.
Similarly,

On Monday I make strong boxes . . .
　　On Tuesday
　　I make
　　narrow boxes . . .

—from "A Maker of Boxes," *Sounds of Laughter*

children who have never seen the word *Wednesday*
anticipate that it will be used in the next episode,
and will read the word in its appropriate slot,
confirming the fact that they recognize
the author's basic way of organizing his story.
It's a proud triumph for a reader.

Seventh graders can enjoy unlocking print
by using a familiar cultural sequence (the alphabet)
that has been with them since nursery school days:

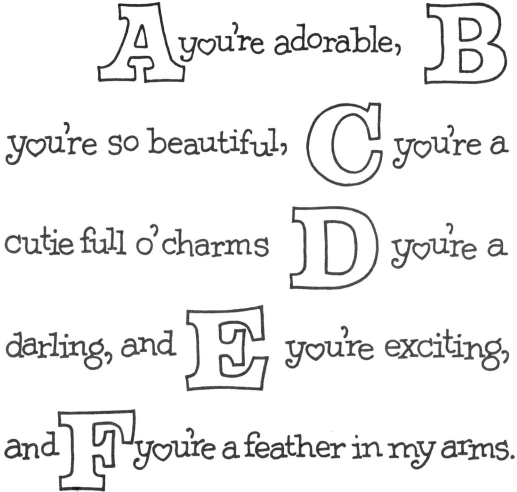

A you're adorable, B you're so beautiful, C you're a cutie full o' charms D you're a darling, and E you're exciting, and F you're a feather in my arms.

—from "A You're Adorable," *Sounds Jubilee*

Once you and the children recognize familiar cultural sequence
as the organizing factor in putting certain stories together,
you may wish to begin a bulletin-board collection
of such sequences.
And don't be surprised if the children list the count-down
as a sequence which is securely deposited
in their linguistic storehouses.

E) Chronological Sequence

Sometimes it is easy to hunch early in a story
that the episodes are arranged chronologically.
This kind of hunch gives the expectation
that the vocabulary will be influenced
by an ordering of events based on time.
Biographies and autobiographies
tend to work this way.
Very often detective stories
unfold in a time sequence.
Even in the old nursery rhyme when

> *Jack and Jill went **up** the hill*

you expect them to come tumbling *down*.

Children are in the mood
for spanning the events of a lifetime
when they read:

This is Johnny.

He is a baby.

He cannot walk.

He cannot talk.

But he can cry!

Johnny is 1 week old.

Now Johnny can walk.

He laughs and claps his hands.

He says "dada" and "mama"

and "baby."

Johnny is 1 year old.

Now Johnny is 4 years old. . . .

He is not a baby anymore. . . .

Johnny is 6 years old now

He is in the first grade. . . .

Now Johnny is 12.

He goes to junior high school. . . .

—from "Growing Up, Growing Older,"
Sounds of Laughter

As children follow Johnny's life
through to his happy grandfather days,
they anticipate and soon are comfortable with lifetime words
such as *junior high school, young man, college,*
home from the air force, wedding day.
Even as they study the art for clues,
children have strong notions of what they are looking for
(such as signs of physical aging, and signs of maturity)
because of their recognition
of the chronological sequence on which the story hangs.

In even wider ranging applications
of this particular literary know-how,
children will create useful expectations
based on other kinds of chronological sequencing:

1) the logical ordering of events in a story,
   particularly a mystery story where the solution
   usually comes at the end:
   such as "The Ghostly Hitchhiker,"
   Sounds Freedomring

2) the ordering of events on a trip,
   be it a spaceflight or a picnic,
   i.e. "Spaceship Bifrost," *Sounds Freedomring*

3) the shaping of events by weather patterns,
i.e. "Snowbound," *Sounds of a Distant Drum*

4) explanatory sequences such as giving directions,
i.e. "How to Brush Your Teeth," *Sounds of a Young Hunter*

F) Problem-Centered Sequence

The minute Mother Meadowlark awakens
with a snake curled about her nest,
there is no doubting that she has a problem.[5]
Whenever a main character in a story
is confronted with a crucial problem,
the person reading the story can predict
that one episode after another will occur
until the problem is solved.
Once the problem is solved
the reader does not expect the story to go on
for fifty more pages.
He knows that the story is finished.
There isn't that much more to talk about.
The episodes which occur in solving the problem
can be repetitive, cumulative,
interlocking or chronological.
They can also be arranged
around familiar cultural sequences.
In other words,
a story does not have only a basic shape.
It can also have shapes within shapes.
Children reading "The Billy Goats Gruff"[6]
soon recognize that the episodes which occur as the three goats
solve their problem with the troll
are repetitive.

[5] "Mother Meadowlark and Brother Snake," *Sounds of the Storyteller*
[6] *Sounds of Laughter*

The bridge goes,

"Trip, Trap! Trip, Trap! Trip, Trap!"

each time a goat crosses over.
The troll threatens each time.
The goats respond.
When the third goat breaks the repetitive pattern
and solves the problem,
the story comes to an end.
In their reading of the story,
children have two kinds of structural insight going for them:

1) the problem of the troll and its solution;

2) the repetition of action
   and vocabulary from episode to episode.

In "The Web of Winter"[7]
the main character encounters a problem
when he discovers a young duck unable to fly
because it is frozen in the ice.
From that point on, the episodes move chronologically.
As Bill frantically tries to free the bird
and the day moves toward night,
the children reading the story
are reaching out toward a solution.
And while the problem-centered, chronological structure
does not predict the exact language,
it does prepare the children to expect vocabulary
related to the efforts to save the duck,
to the actual saving of the duck,
to the passing time of day,
to the vocabulary associated with the passing time of day,
such as *suppertime, darkness, headlights*, etc.
and to certain character traits.
All of these linguistic insights
are germane to unlocking the print.

[7] *Sounds of Mystery*

Some poems and stories
are put together with a dependable rhyme-rhythm scheme.

The Owl and the Pussy-cat went to sea
In a beautiful pea-green boat:
They took some honey, and plenty of money
Wrapped up in a five-pound note.

—from "The Owl and the Pussy Cat," *Sounds After Dark*

You may have been taught
that this is an A-B-C-B rhyme-rhythm scheme,
meaning that the second and fourth lines rhyme
and the rhythm is predictable.
Heaven forbid that we lecture children
about the A-B-C-B rhyme-rhythm scheme!
But we can help them verbalize the fact
that when you have figured out
the author's rhyming-meter plan,
it is easier to read the rhyming words
and to syllabicate certain words
used in the rhyme-rhythm slots.

Slowly ticks the big clock;

Tick-tock, Tick-tock!

But Cuckoo clock ticks double quick;

Tick-a-tock-a, tick-a-tock-a,
Tick-a-tock-a,☐ [8]

Do you find yourself supplying the word *tick*
to keep the rhyme scheme going?
This is how it is with response to rhyme scheme.

[8] "The Big Clock," *Sounds Around the Clock*

One way to help children verbalize
how useful a rhyme scheme can be
in recognizing vocabulary
is to read them a regularly patterned verse
and ask them to supply words you leave out.

Boys and girls, supposing you keep your books closed
while I read you an old rhyme.
I'm going to leave out some of the words
and you see if you can say those words
even though you've never heard the poem:

This is the story

Of Susie Moriar.

It started one night

As she sat by the [   ]

The fire was so hot,

Susie jumped in a [   ]

The pot was so black,

Susie dropped in a [   ]

The crack was so narrow,

Susie climbed on a wheel[   ]

The wheelbarrow was so low,

Susie fell in the [   ]

The snow was so white,

Susie stayed there all [   ]

The night was so long,

Susie sang a [   ]

—from "Susie Moriar," *Sounds of Laughter*

As the children supply the missing words,
they are responding to both the rhythmical and rhyming patterns
of this old jingle.
It is important to help them verbalize
their ways of figuring out the missing words
and to discuss the fact that
in their independent reading,
they can use this kind of structural insight
to figure out certain unknown vocabulary.
At some point in the discussion,
it can be useful to suggest:

> *Children, supposing you wanted*
> *to change the poem about Susie Moriar.*
> *Let's see where we can go with*

> *"This is the story of Jennie McGoo.*
> *It started one night as she . . ."*

As the children pick up the aa-bb-cc, etc. scheme
of the original jingle
they may be suggesting:

> *This is the story of Jennie McGoo.*
> *It started one night as she went to the zoo.*
> *The zoo was so bright,*
> *Jennie stayed there all night . . .*

Some children, however, may not respond
to the rhythm-rhyme scheme of the original jingle
and may come up with something like

> *This is the story of Jennie McGoo.*
> *It started one night as she went to sleep.*

When such a suggestion is made,
your role is to accept it positively
and help the children see the difference
between this and the original pattern.

Isn't this interesting, boys and girls?
Chuck has suggested a pattern
that doesn't rhyme the way the original poem did.
Let's follow Chuck's lead for awhile
and see where we go.

"This is the story of Jennie McGoo.
It started one night as she fell asleep.
Next thing she knew she was floating on a cloud . . ."

And so develops an innovation
that is patterned on story ideas
rather than the original rhyme scheme.
Both kinds of innovating are important.
As the children discuss differences
between rhyming and non-rhyming patterns,
they will further appreciate how recognition
of a rhythm-rhyme scheme
helps a person unlock unknown vocabulary.

Obviously there are other and more subtle literary structures
such as a story like "Old Lucy Lindy"[9]
and "Yallery Brown"[10]
in which the episodes hang on character development
but for purposes of this discussion
we have confined ourselves to those story patterns
which are most productive
in helping children predict language
and thereby unlock vocabulary.

In all of this discussion
of ways for putting stories and poems together,
we have been faced with the interesting fact
that whenever many of anything come together,
be they objects or events or words or people,
they either fall together helter-skelter
or they fall into an arrangement of some kind.
An earthquake produces hit-and-miss.
Language, whatever else, creates order.

[9] *Sounds of the Storyteller*
[10] *Sounds Freedomring*

When children are helped to verbalize
their recognition of the various ways
authors can arrange episodes in a story or poem,
they develop a reading skill
that forever lifts them out of the
little-steps-for-little-feet way of viewing a book.
A book or story or poem, whatever else it is,
is not a succession of isolated words
to be sounded out
or an unmanageable succession
of disassociated thoughts and events.
Traditional "basic" reading and language instructions
are not "basic" in the least
unless they include opportunities
for children to develop their naturalistic and intuitive skills
in unlocking the flow of language
in its basic cultural patterns.
It's as important for a child to know
how a piece of writing is unfolding
as it is for him to know
how a word unlocks.
The joyful fact is
that as a child takes root and strength
in his abilities to anticipate literary structure,
he, simultaneously, is developing word-unlocking skills
that save him from being stranded
with "sounding out" as the only way
to manage unknown words.

5 HELPING CHILDREN VERBALIZE THEIR INTUITIVE LITERARY INSIGHTS

You may be wondering
how to help children
verbalize their structural insights.
Actually, your discussion with the children
occurs all along the line.

If the children quickly chime in
during your first reading of a story,
you may wish to engage them in easy conversation
about their ease in chiming in.

> *How come you children were able to read*
> *so much of that story*
> *without hearing it first?*

Their homely explanations will tell you
whether or not they are using
the structure of the story
as one of their ways for unlocking print.

> *When he said, "I'm not as big as a goat"*
> *and "I'm not as big as a horse,"*
> *I knew he was going to keep on saying*
> *"I'm not as big as a . . . . ."*

This is a young child's natural way for telling you
that he is beginning to recognize repetitive sequence.

> *How does it happen you children*
> *read that word* Wednesday *so easily?*

> *"Well, when the author said*
> *'On Monday I build . . .' and*
> *then when he said, 'On Tuesday*
> *I build . . .' I knew he was going*
> *to say, 'On Wednesday . . .' "*

Here a child is verbalizing his awareness
of structure built on familiar cultural sequences.

> *Isn't it interesting, children,*
> *when you figure out how an*
> *author put his story together,*
> *it helps you in your reading.*

This kind of remark will help children
generalize their experience in the use of literary structure
to unlock print.
It also helps give them the vocabulary
for verbalizing what they have experienced.
A word of caution:
generalizing statements of this kind do not come
before the children have had the experience
of successfully using story or poem structure
to make their reading easier.
If the generalizations are to be the children's—
and they must be the children's
if they are to become part
of their personal collection
of word-unlocking skills—
they must grow out of first-hand experiences.
When they do grow out of first-hand experiences,
the children will claim the generalizations as their own,
depositing them in their linguistic storehouses
for future reference.
If the children are reading independently
and can recognize words
with or without help from literary structure,
you may wish to come at your questioning
from a different angle.

> *Children, supposing you had never seen*
> *the word Wednesday (or any other word*
> *that can be anticipated*
> *by knowing the structural sequence of the story).*
> *Is there anything in this story*
> *that gives you a hint*
> *that could help you read the word?*

This kind of questioning may lead
to a full-blown inquiry
into the various ways stories and poems are put together.
The children may wish to collect and categorize
favorite stories and poems they have read in the past:
repetitive, cumulative, interlocking, familiar cultural sequences,
problem-centered, rhythm-rhyme scheme.
All of this activity should have the zestful spirit
of scientific inquiry.
The children's satisfaction will come
from really figuring out
how something in their world works.

If you are teaching older boys and girls
who have never had experiences
with this approach to word-unlocking,
you may wish to get hold of a set of *Instant Readers*.[11]
These Bill Martin books are written
around the basic literary structures
and the books are discussed from this point of view
in the Teachers Guide.
Because the books are short and the structures are exaggerated,
the children can analyze them more easily
than they can longer stories.
You can also use the earlier *Sounds of Language* readers
with older boys and girls
if you reassure them
that you are doing grown-up things with the books.
Once you get into analyzing the author's plan
for putting his story together,
the children will respect the use of the younger books.

[11] Holt, Rinehart and Winston Inc.

And don't forget to browse through
the *Sounds of Language* books provided
for your particular class.
In even the seventh and eighth grade anthologies
you will find numerous short selections
that lend themselves to obvious literary analysis.

You may have to remind yourself
that these books do not have to be read
page-by-page from cover to cover
as most other readers do.
You can pick and choose from anywhere in the book,
depending on the interests and purposes
of the children and yourself.
Neither do the selections have to be exploited
in a single lesson and then left as "finished."
You can return to favorite selections
dozens of times throughout the year
for different purposes.

> *Boys and girls, do you remember*
> *the story "Ming and Ling"* [12]
> *that we enjoyed so much?*
> *Let's take another look at it. This time . . .*

Who knows how many useful excursions
children can conduct
through a story or poem that has been deposited
in their linguistic storehouses.
This is the reason for depositing the literature—
to make it available for a lifetime
of analysis and pleasure.

[12] *Sounds Freedomring*

Some of the best opportunities
for analyzing literary structure will come
when the children are borrowing the author's pattern
and hanging their thoughts and vocabulary on it.

Boys and girls, let's take a look
at this rather simple story:

"I am not as big as a goat.
A goat is bigger than I am.

I am not as big as a horse.
A horse is bigger than I am.

I am not as big as an elephant.
An elephant is bigger than I am.

I am not as big as a whale.
A whale is bigger than I am.

I am not as big as a dinosaur.
A dinosaur is the biggest thing I know."

—from "What Is Big?" *Sounds of Numbers*

If you were to borrow
the author's exact pattern
and make your own story out of it,
what would be important to remember?
Do you think you can make
even a simple pattern like this
interesting to fourth graders?

The children will probably verbalize
that the author has a plan for repeating.
They will probably notice that the describing word *big*
is central to the language pattern.
They may comment on his way for breaking the pattern
to bring the story to a close.
They may comment that the creatures
keep growing larger.
Fourth graders have been known
to come up with innovations
on even simple structures
that give them pleasure.

I am not as bony as my sister.
My sister is bonier than I am.

I am not as bony as a fish.
A fish is bonier than I am.

I am not as bony as spareribs.
Spareribs are bonier than I am.

I am not as bony as a skeleton.
A skeleton is the boniest thing I know.

—from a fourth grader, Corbett School, Tucson, Arizona

A sixth grader chooses the pattern from "A Turkey Speaks"
in *Sounds of a Distant Drum* for his innovation.

Taco Speaks

I have never understood
why anyone would
 roast the shell
 buy the meat
 chip the pickles
 chop the lettuce
when they could
sit back
and call. . . . .

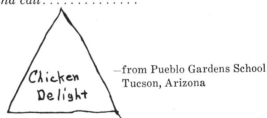

—from Pueblo Gardens School
Tucson, Arizona

Gradually you can help the children generalize
that when they are reading on their own
it is a good idea to be curious
about how the author put his story together
and that once they get the *aha!* feeling,
meaning that they have caught on to his plan,
they will be partly prepared for the vocabulary
they will encounter,
and that their structural insight
is both a writing and a reading skill.

6 FIGURING OUT HOW SENTENCES WORK

In the same sense
that a story has a shape
and a poem has a shape,
so does a sentence have a shape.
A speaker pauses, intones, gestures
to show how the words group together
and thereby reveal his meanings.
A writer uses punctuation
to help the reader see
how the words group together.

The concept of *shapes of sentences*
is somewhat implied
in our earlier discussion of *chunks of meaning*.
In speaking and writing,
words do not simply follow one another
in unrelated separateness.
They cluster together to form a chunk of meaning
and these chunks of meaning
are basic to the shape of a sentence.
Not only that.
These chunks of meaning within a sentence
do not simply follow one another in random style.
They form a pattern as they fall next to one another
and recognizing the pattern is helpful in decoding.
One additional facet in the shaping of a sentence
is the fact that there is a definite order
in which many individual words fall in English sentences.
A chunk of meaning about a pretty girl
will not reverse this culturally established order
and call her a *girl pretty*.

Let's take a closer look
at these three characteristics
that influence the shapes of sentences
and see what the implications are
for developing reading skills
that are not provided for in most reading programs.

A) Sentences Work in Chunks of Meaning

One useful way to help children understand
that chunks of meaning
are basic to the shape of a sentence,
is to read aloud a sentence from a familiar story
and ask the children to keep their books closed
and raise their hands each time
they hear a chunk of meaning:

So the little squeegy bug
followed Creepy the Caterpillar
to his home under the cattail leaf,
and soon was safe and warm,
away from the storm,
and he slept soundly
until morning.

—from "Little Squeegy Bug," *Sounds After Dark*

Remind the children that different people may hear
different chunks of meaning
so they will not be worried about right and wrong answers
when they enter into a later discussion
of where the various chunks begin and end.

At no time should a child feel embarrassed
over his selection of a chunk of meaning.
Even if he errs,
he will self-correct (the hallmark of an educated person)
when he becomes comfortable with this concept.
And by the way, if you should find yourself
selecting different chunks of meaning
from the ones we have indicated
in the sentence from "The Little Squeegy Bug,"
don't become alarmed.
Frequently more than one choice is possible.
The test is: *Does the selection of a particular chunk of meaning*
have integrity in and of itself,
and does it leave a complete chunk on either side of it?

Another useful way to help children latch on
to the chunks-of-meaning concept
is to compare the line-by-line text of a story
which is arranged in chunks of meaning
in a *Sounds of Language* reader
with a chapter in their social studies book or other textbook
where traditional paragraphing style is used
to shape sentences to rigid right-left hand margins
regardless of chunks of meaning.
On the opposite page is a pictorial comparison
of language in paragraph form
with language in chunks of meaning.
Which more readily invites your reading interest?
Since a chunk of meaning is a unit of sense,
the children may profit from discussing
whether or not breaking the sentences into units of sense
makes for more reader ease and understanding.
Accept any observations the children care to make.
Some children may be so accustomed
to the rigid right-left hand margins
that they actually find this newer page design more difficult at first.
Whatever their reactions,
this kind of comparing and free discussion
will further their understanding of the fact
that sentences work in chunks of meaning.

BLIZZARD HITS
WESTERN STATES

AIR FORCE'S "OPERATION FEEDLIFT" BALKED BY CONTINUING BLIZZARD

CHICAGO, Jan. 20—One of the worst storms in memory hit Montana, eastern Washington, Utah, Nevada, Wyoming, Colorado and the Dakotas today in the form of blizzards, floods and bitter Arctic cold.

Some areas were buried under as much as 80 inches of snow, which forced the closing of schools and blocked highways. Freezing winds blew roofs off buildings, smashed windows and ripped down power and telephone lines. Brief gusts of the blizzard winds reached speeds as high as 95 miles an hour in parts of Montana and the Dakotas.

CHICAGO, Jan. 20—
One of the worst storms in memory
hit Montana,
eastern Washington,
Utah,
Nevada,
Wyoming,
Colorado
and the Dakotas today
in the form of blizzards,
floods
and bitter Arctic cold.

Some areas were buried
under as much as
80 inches of snow,
which forced
the closing of schools
and blocked highways.
Freezing winds
blew roofs off buildings,
smashed windows
and ripped down
power and telephone lines.
Brief gusts of the blizzard winds
reached speeds
as high as
95 miles an hour
in parts of Montana
and the Dakotas.

—from *Sounds of a Distant Drum*

At some point in your figuring out how sentences work,
you will want to invite the children
to take a paragraph from a story or article
that is printed with the traditional right-hand margin
and break the sentences into chunks of meaning.
The markings may vary from child to child
but no marking should violate a unit of sense.
When variations do occur,
be sure to discuss the children's reasoning
back of their choices
to determine whether or not
a child is sensing the meaning
back of the clustering of words he has selected.

Somewhere during your discussion of ways
for breaking the rigid right-hand material
into chunks of meaning,
you will want to help the children verbalize the fact
that once they are able to break unbroken sentences
into chunks of meaning,
they are developing a skill
that will stand them in good stead
in their independent reading.
Gradually they will build the habit
of seeing chunks of meaning
whether or not the text has been printed that way.
This is germane to dealing
with the meaning encased in print.

You may wish to consider punctuation
while you are discussing chunks of meaning.
As a matter of fact,
this may be the first time
some of your children see the actual sense to punctuation.
They may have seen commas and periods
and all the rest
primarily as items to get right or wrong
as they fill in blanks in workbooks.
Now with this new look at the ways sentences work,
they may enjoy discussing
how punctuation came to be in the first place.

When man invented the code
that we call written language,
he immediately found the need
for additional inventions besides the letters
to make writing work.
He therefore invented periods and commas
and other signals
to help the reader hear
what the code was saying.
Won't it be interesting
if the children decide
that printing sentences
in chunks of meaning
can make
certain punctuation
unnecessary!

The pickety fence

The pickety fence
Give it a lick it's
The pickety fence
Give it a lick it's
A clickety fence
Give it a lick it's
A lickety fence
Give it a lick
Give it a lick
Give it a lick
With a rickety stick
Pickety
Pickety
Pickety
Pick

—by David McCord,
from *Sounds of a Young Hunter*

SOX SONG
RED SOX
BLUE SOX
WHITE SOX
GREEN SOX
BROWN SOX
BLACK SOX
COLORS·IN·BETWEEN SOX

—from *Sounds After Dark*

B) Sentences Work Because of WORD ORDER

One other characteristic of English sentences,
is the *order* in which individual words
are placed next to one another.
A three-year-old knows this.
He will say:

> *Me hit you.*

It is true he is using
the incorrect form of the pronoun,
but he will not ruin the basic shape
of the sentence and say:

> *Hit me you.*

He will not rearrange the usual word-order
and put the verb in front of the subject pronoun.
He will say

> *big boy*

He will not say

> *boy big*

He will not deny the fact
that in the English language
the adjective usually comes in front of the noun.
As a school child,
if he is helped to experiment with sentences
and to verbalize his intuitive knowledge
about word-order in English sentences,
he will partially unlock words
because of where they fall
and what function they perform in the sentence.
That child coming to this sentence, for example,

I found six spotted puppies.

will not sit and endlessly spit and sputter
over the *sp* sound in *spotted*
and then give up in despair if he can't sound out the word.

He will first of all recognize
that *spotted* is a describing word,
falling as it does, in front of *puppies*.
With this dependable structural clue,
he finds it useful to know that the word begins
with the *sp* sounds.
Knowing that the word describes *puppies*
narrows the range, as it were,
to the short array of culturally anticipated words
such as:

> *little puppies*
> *white puppies*
> *black puppies*
> *tiny puppies*
> *collie puppies*
> *friendly puppies*
> *hungry puppies*
> *spotted puppies*

Instead of being confronted with the whole wide world
of words at random
he now is seeking only an *sp* word that can appropriately
describe *puppies*,

> *spotted puppies.*

What a difference in psychological posture!
What a cultural reliability
that supports a child's best efforts!

In a different context,
a writer sometimes distorts natural *word order*
for emphasis on rhythm or dramatic effect
as Walter de la Mare does in this amazing sentence:

> All but blind
> > In his chambered hole
> Gropes for worms
> > The four-clawed Mole.

> —from "All But Blind," *Sounds of Mystery*

Figuring Out How Sentences Work TE 63

C) Sentences Work in Sequence Patterns

Another characteristic of English sentences
is the way in which
the various chunks of meaning
are connected with one another.
Interestingly enough,
these clusters of words
pattern in much the same way
that the episodes in a story pattern.

1) Repetitive Sequence

Over in the meadow

in the sand

in the sun

Lived an old mother turtle and her little turtle one.

—from "Over in the Meadow," *Sounds of a Powwow*

Repetition of chunks of meaning
is central to the shape
of this sentence.
Leave out *in the sand* and *in the sun*
and the basic design of the sentence
has been altered.
Once the basic designs for arranging sentences
have been deposited in the children's linguistic storehouses,
they own them for a lifetime of transforming
in their speaking and reading and writing.

2) Cumulative Sequence

Sometimes the chunks of meaning in a sentence
just keep adding on to one another
to give the sentence its shape.

> Then, each monkey pulled off his cap ...
>
> and all the yellow caps ...
>
> and all the blue caps ...
>
> and all the red caps ...
>
> and all the polkadot caps ...
>
> came flying d o w n o u t of the tree.

—from "Caps for Sale," *Sounds of a Powwow*

Young children are great at writing cumulative sentences
once they discover the power in the little word *and*.
You've seen these sentences:

> *I went home from school*
> *and then I ...*
> *and then I ...*
> *and then I ...*
> *and then I ...*

Instead of criticizing the children
in our well-intentioned effort
to get them to write more interesting sentences,
we should praise them for their discovery.

*Julie, that's just about the longest sentence
I ever saw.
Did you know that all of your life
you'll be seeing and hearing sentences that are put
together that way? Let's take a look at your long sentence
and see if we can figure out how it goes together.
How did it get to be so long?*

Accept any homely observations
the children care to make.

> *Well, I just kept saying*
> "and then, and then, and then . . ."

is a beginning verbalization
of the shape of a cumulative sentence.

If the children made observations
about the cumulative sequencing
from episode to episode in "The House that Jack Built,"
they may enjoy going back to the story now:

This is the COCK that crowed in the morn,

That waked the priest all shaven and shorn,

That married the man all tattered and torn,

That kissed the maiden all forlorn,

That milked the cow

    with the crumpled horn,

That tossed the dog, that worried the cat,

That killed the rat, That ate the malt,

That lay in the house that Jack built.

—from Sounds Around the Clock

Imagine what fun it will be to discover
that each new episode is actually a cumulative sentence.

In your discussion of the various ways
chunks of meaning are laid next to one another
in a sentence,
don't press for exact terminology.
Older boys and girls may enjoy some terminology
after they have explored the shapes of sentences (and stories)
but the most important part of the explorations
is their homely verbalizing of their self-selected observations
about the ways in which sentences work.

3) Interlocking Sequence

> "Oh!" said Sallie,
>   and this time it was so low,
>   one could scarcely hear it,
>   for she was remembering
>   the cabbage stalk
>   and that she had seen Diccon
>   over her left shoulder.
>
> —from "Tomson's Halloween," *Sounds of a Young Hunter*

Sometimes the chunks of meaning in sentences
do not simply repeat or add on.
They interlock with one another
(as the chunks do in the sample sentence here)
in ways that create the sentence form and meaning.
For the most part,
an interlocked sentence does not reveal its full meaning
until the last segment in the chain of interlocking.

Consider, for example,
how incomplete the meaning of the following sentence is
until the last segment hinges in:

> To the Sun
> Who has shone
>   All day,
> To the Moon
> Who has gone
>   Away,
> To the milk-white,
> Lily-white Star
> A fond goodnight
> Wherever you are.

—"Last Song," by James Guthrie,
Sounds of a Distant Drum

Did you notice the repetitive sequence of this sentence?
And also that the sentence maintains a simultaneous
repetitive and interlocking sequence.
Interestingly enough,
as you will observe in the two sample sentences given here,
the chunks of meaning in one
can be reordered (re-arranged) without destroying the meaning,
while in the other
the various chunks of meaning cannot be rearranged
without destroying both the shape and meaning of the sentence.
It is as if a cyclone came along
and stripped the sentence of its sense.
Of all the sentence patterns,
the interlocking sequence is perhaps the one
that best helps children understand
that sentences are not simply long strings of isolated words
hung together with a capital letter and a period.

Sentences, like stories,
are shapes within a shape.
They are chunks of meaning
which are laid next to one another
according to a design.
Recognizing the design
helps to unlock the meaning.

4) Chronological Sequence

Chronological sentences are probably the easiest
to figure out
in terms of recognizing their basic shape.
Everything moves ahead so orderly:

First, the

outside surface of your upper teeth; second, the

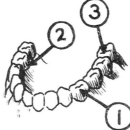

The same three areas of the lower teeth
need careful cleaning: 1) outside, 2)
inside, 3) biting edge.

inside surface of   these teeth; third,

the grinding surfaces of the upper teeth.

—from "How to Brush Your Teeth," *Sounds of a Young Hunter*

Here's another sample:

> Then he reached up
>
> to make sure that they were straight—
>
> first his own striped cap,
>
> then the four yellow caps,
>
> then the four blue caps,
>
> then the four red caps,
>
> then on the very top the four polkadot caps.

—from "Caps for Sale," *Sounds of a Powwow*

And still another which is nonetheless chronological
because the time sequence is less obvious.

> So she (the Grandmarina)
> took it (the Magic Fishbone)
> from the hand of Princess Alicia
> and waved her magic fan over it,
> and it instantly flew
> down the throat
> of the dreadful little
> snapping pug dog next door
> and nearly choked him,
> and that was good!

—from "The Magic Fishbone," *Sounds Jubilee*

Once children sense that a sentence is moving forward
in chronological sequence,
they join right in with the author (anticipate)
in planning how the chunks of meaning will be arranged.

This kind of feeling that it is possible
to work one's way through a complicated looking sentence
because of recognizing its structure,
develops into a highly useful work-unlocking skill.

5) Rhyme-Rhythm Sequence

You can take a tub with a rub and a scrub

in a two-foot tank of TIN,

You can stand and look at the whirling brook

and think about jumping IN;

You can chatter and shake in the cold black lake,

but the kind of bath for ME,

Is to take a dip from the side of a ship,

in the trough of the rolling SEA.

—from "The Kind of a Bath for Me,"
Sounds of the Storyteller

This sentence moves forward
with a rhyme-rhythm sequence that helps give it its shape.
Children will readily recognize
that the intrigue and charm of the sentence
stem equally from the rhyme—
both internal and terminal— and from the rhythm.

In the following example, however,
it is the anticipation of rhyme, not rhythm,
that focuses the sentence sequence
and the unlocking of the word *precisely.*

. . . putting it my way, but nicely,

You are precisely my cup of tea!

—from "Getting to Know You," *Sounds of the Storyteller*

Here again, it's rhythm, not rhyme, that shapes a sentence:

Now, pray, where are you going?"
said Meet-on-the-Road.
"To school, sir, to school, sir,"
said Child-as-it-Stood.

—from "Meet on the Road," *Sounds After Dark*

Here is another sentence
so rhythmically shaped
that it stands alone like a poem:

ONCE IN THE GOLDEN TIME
when an Irish king sat in every province
and plenty covered the land,
there lived in Connaught
a grand old king with one daughter.

—from "The Princess and the Vagabond,"
Sounds of a Distant Drum

By clapping the rhythm of these sentences
and others that appeal,
children can develop sensitivity
to the rhythm of language,
a skill absolutely essential to anyone
who is to make a go of writing and reading.
You can, for example, invite someone to clap out a page of print
that all of the class has read frequently
to see if the selection can be recognized
solely by the linguistic rhythm.
At the same time
the children will be developing syllabication skills
in a far more functional setting
than looking a word up in a dictionary
for its stressed and unstressed patterns.

By clapping (and dancing) the rhythm of a sentence:

> I hoe and I plow
> I plow and I hoe
> And the wind drives over the main.
>
> I mow and I plant
> I plant and I mow
> While the sun burns hot on the plain.

—from "Farmer" by Liberty Hyde Bailey,
Sounds After Dark

the children will be getting the language
into their muscles as well as their minds,
a childhod naturality that makes language learning
pleasant and easy
until the pedants take over and deny children the use
of their basic language learning equipment.

Obviously there are other basic shapes to sentences
than the ones suggested in this essay,
but our purpose in this discussion is simply to alert you
that the clusters of words within a sentence
do fall together in various patterns
and that recognition of the pattern
is an aid in word-unlocking.
You may wish to jot down a few sentences from a favorite story
and see what observations you can make
about the patterns into which
the clusters of words fall.
First divide the sentences into their chunks of meaning
as we have done on these pages.
Then you are on your own.
Far more important than labeling the various shapes
is the recognition that sentences are not strings of words
which happen to fall together.

7 INNOVATING ON SENTENCE PATTERNS

By now you know
that when you read aloud to children
you are depositing various sentence patterns
in the children's linguistic storehouses
for a lifetime of use.
You probably are also aware
that when the children chime in on the reading,
especially in alive and dramatic ways
that include bodily movement,
they are themselves claiming and depositing these patterns.
One further activity
to help make these basic sentence structures
easily available to children for word-unlocking
in their reading and for writing and speaking,
is to invite them into systematic
and at the same time creative and lively experimenting
with the various patterns.
Here are four sentence manipulations
which have proved especially useful
for this kind of experimentation.

A) Transforming Sentences

Transforming a sentence
is the act of using the exact structure of a sentence
as the basis for creating a semantically new sentence
through either word-by-word substitution
or substitution of whole clusters of words.

I   never   saw   a   purple   cow.

—from *Sounds of Numbers*

Your first step in helping children transform this sentence,
after all of you have enjoyed reading the whole poem
from which it came,
is to copy the model sentence on the chalkboard,
leaving space between each word.
Then your conversation goes something like this:

Children, I'm going to draw a line
to the word cow.
Now, supposing we didn't want
to use the word cow.
What other words could we use
instead of cow?

Suggestions will begin to flow.

I   never   saw   a   purple   cow.

> horse
> pig
> rabbit

Children, all of our naming words are animals.
Supposing we wanted another kind of naming word—
one that would make a spooky sentence.

I   never   saw   a   purple   cow.

> horse
> pig
> rabbit
> spook
> vampire

Now, children, supposing we didn't want
to use the word purple?
Who else has a describing word?

Again the suggestions will flow.

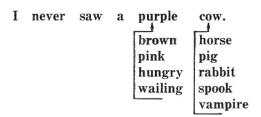

I never saw a purple cow.

brown	horse
pink	pig
hungry	rabbit
wailing	spook
	vampire

And so it goes until the children have suggested
vocabulary substitutions for all of the words.
You may wish to enter the game,
especially if the children are not having fun
with the substitutions they suggest.

Children, does anyone in this class
like silly sentences?
Well, I'm going to give you a new action word
that will really make a silly sentence.

I never saw a purple cow.

kissed
loved
hugged
milked
married

Now the lid is off and the children's merriment
knows no bounds as they contemplate kissing purple vampires
and marrying pink spooks.
You may wish to invite the children

to go back to their tables
to write sentences of their choice.
At some point you may wish
to begin gentle conversation
about the word order in the sentence.

> *Isn't it interesting, children,*
> *that we don't say:*
>
> **I never saw a cow purple.**
>
> *I wonder why not.*

The children will probably suggest
that it just doesn't sound good—
meaning that their ears have already picked up
the usual word order in English sentences.
Gradually these kinds of conversations
help children add information
to their growing notions about how sentences work.
The *Sounds of Language* readers abound
in useful sentence patterns for the children to transform.
We have annotated a few of these sentences
to get you and the children started.
No attempt has been made to annotate every sentence
that lend itself to this kind of language analysis.
The peak value of the activity will come
when you and the children learn to go over a story
after enjoying it in its wholeness,
perusing it for *model sentences* rich in analysis potential.
It is your and the children's own selection
and manipulation of *model sentences*
that firmly connects the language learnings
with a child's personal use of language.
This is a qualitatively different learning experience
from that of filling in little blanks
in typical language workbooks.

Imagine what fun you and the children will have
when you select an intriguing sentence like this one
from E. B. White's *Charlotte's Web*
as a model to transform:

Soon the children will be far-ranging in their choices
of serious and silly sentences offered by the framework:

> They hated the incessant dripping of the rain

> The witch dreamed of a heady ride on her broomstick

> The motor made a suspicious wheezing during the night

From time to time, you yourself will want
to suggest a vocabulary substitution
such as *skeleton, ghost, ferocious, monotonous,*
knowing that one strong, colorful word
will result in a flurry of additional substitutions.
When children become deeply involved
in transforming activities,
there's never time for each of them to read aloud
all of their self-selected sentences.

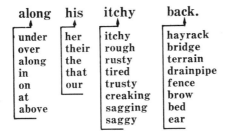

along	his	itchy	back.
under	her	itchy	hayrack
over	their	rough	bridge
along	the	rusty	terrain
in	that	tired	drainpipe
on	our	trusty	fence
at		creaking	brow
above		sagging	bed
		saggy	ear

through   the   sagging   roof.

with her irritable cat.

of our scary escape.

This offers an opportunity for them to write sentences
that eventually they can read to one another.
You can also suggest to the children
that they keep in their notebooks
a list of model sentences that especially appeal to them
for later transforming in their personal writing.
Awarenesses of this kind
are a sound linguistic base for both reading and writing.

B) Expanding Sentences

Expanding sentences is another technique
for helping children become aware
of the shape of sentences
and for helping them develop this awareness
into reading and writing and speaking skill.
This sentence manipulation is exactly
what the term *expanding* connotes.
Any simple sentence can be expanded
by adding phrases, clauses or describing words.

Children, let's take a sentence
from our old jingle, "Susie Moriar."

This   is   the   story   of   Susie   Moriar.

Let's see if we can think of some describing words
to put in front of Susie.

This   is   the   story   of   Susie   Moriar.

                                       funny
                                       kind
                                       nice

Now let's think of some describing words
to put in front of **story**.

This   is   the   story   of   Susie   Moriar.

                   rhyming   funny
                   silly   kind
                   impossible   nice

Now who would like to try reading a sentence
using any of the words on the board?
Have you noticed, boys and girls,
how our sentence is getting longer and longer?
There is one other way we can expand this sentence
and make it even longer.
We can add a whole collection of words
that belong together.

This	is	the	story	of	Susie	Moriar.
		rhyming		funny		who lost her teeth
		silly		kind		who likes to bake cakes
		impossible		nice		who stands on her head

It's easy to see
that in writing the following sentence,
Anthony could have started with the simple statement:

The   king   was   old.

and then expanded it:

The King was so old
he could not dance the
twist so he said to
one of his girls to hold
him and do the twist
in slow motion.

—1st Grade, J. J. Ingalls School
Kansas City, Kansas

Older boys and girls search their linguistic storehouses
for single words and clusters of words
to make their sentence expanding worthwhile:

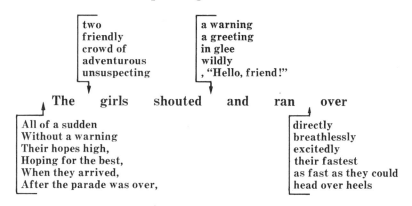

An expanded sentence can be more dramatic,
"paint more pictures,"
or produce a more interesting array of sounds,
but it is not necessarily a better sentence.
In the process of expanding sentences, however,
children become keenly aware of the placement and function
of phrases and clauses and individual words
within a sentence.
And as they read their expanded sentences aloud,
they overtly are making judgments
about the kinds of sentences they do and do not like,
thus taking another step in the development of
and appreciation for a personal style
in writing and speaking.
It is this aware development
of a personal style
that helps children appreciate the fact
that authors of stories and poems
also have preferred styles.

```
            ┌ new
            │ old
            │ big
            │ open
            │ dilapidated
            │ comfortable
            │ air-conditioned
            └ well-lighted
                    ↓
to    Hippy Hippo's    cage  ↑ .
                    ┌ nearby
                    │ in the arena
                    │ beyond the bridge
                    └ under the tree
```

—from "Hippy Hippo," *Sounds of Mystery*

A child with this kind of awareness
can browse through the first few pages
of a book he has selected from the library shelf
and make beginning judgments about the kinds of words
he will be unlocking simply by conning the author's sentence style.
If the sentences are involved
and packed with adjectives and adverbs,
this child will be sending signals to his linguistic storehouse,
as it were,
to trigger stored patterns to help with the reading ahead.

C) Transforming and Expanding Sentences

As children gain skill in sentence manipulations,
they will undoubtedly want to combine
two or more of the methods suggested here.
For example, colorful sentence possibilities emerge
when a model sentence is both transformed and expanded.
Consider the wide range of sentences
that is inherent in this diagram:

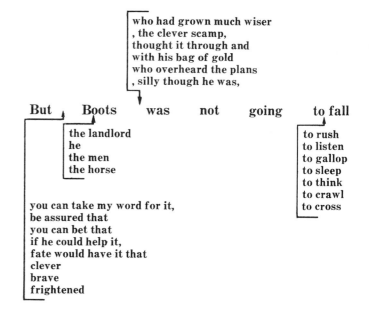

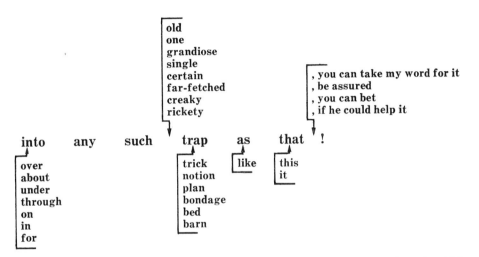

old
one
grandiose
single
certain
far-fetched
creaky
rickety

, you can take my word for it
, be assured
, you can bet
, if he could help it

into   any   such   trap   as   that   !

over
about
under
through
on
in
for

trick   like   this
notion   it
plan
bondage
bed
barn

—from "How Boots Befooled the King," *Sounds of Mystery*

D) Reducing Sentences

Another sentence manipulation
that is highly useful in helping children
figure out how sentences work
is reducing sentences.
When a person reduces a sentence,
he eliminates all unnecessary words, phrases and clauses.
The danger in reducing a sentence is that one is apt
to alter or destroy the sentence meaning
or to tamper with the author's style of writing.
As you and the children go through your *Sounds of Language* readers
in search of sentences to reduce,
you may have the same difficulty we had
when we searched for sentences to annotate for you.
The sentences are generally too well written for reducing.
However, in terms of children's learning,
the search is what is important.
As they consider which words or phrases or clauses
can or can't be eliminated,
they will be experimenting with the shapes of sentences
and will be storing their learnings for later use.
Now let's reduce a few sentences and analyze the results.

A bird ~~also~~ has another way to ~~help~~ keep ~~himself~~ warm in winter.

By seeing to it that ~~the~~ birds ~~near your home~~ have plenty to eat,
you can help "keep ~~their furnaces roaring"~~ ~~and~~
their bodies warm in winter.

The bird's outer feathers
~~are staggered like shingles on a roof~~
~~to~~ keep out the rain and snow.

—from "How Birds Keep Warm in Winter," Sounds of Mystery

In the first sentence, the reducing sharpened the sentence.
The eliminated words are truly unnecessary.

In the second sentence,
the meaning is definitely altered by the deletions.
In the third sentence,
the question is not so much whether meaning has been altered
but whether the author's style has been tampered with.
As the children read Bernard Martin's article,
they will discover that here is an author
who paints pictures in the sentences he writes.
By eliminating such a vivid picture as
(feathers) *staggered like shingles on a roof,*
the sentence is rendered unimaginative,
albeit the sentence still makes its point
that the bird's feathers keep out the rain and snow.
One useful question to ask the children
after they have reduced an author's sentence is:

> *What do you think Bernard Martin*
> *would think about his sentence now?*

If they are referring to the third sentence above,
some children will probably conclude:

> *Well, he probably wouldn't like it very much.*

Then it can be profitable to look at other sentences
that suffer from being reduced.
The children may wish to turn
to a discussion of their own preferred sentence styles:

> *Jerry, would you say that you like best*
> *to write reduced or expanded sentences?*

More than one Jerry has been known to respond:

> *Well, I really like to write reduced sentences*
> *but you're always trying to get me*
> *to write expanded sentences.*

There are no right or wrong answers to these kinds
of linguistic inquiries.
Hopefully, the children will become versatile enough
to write and read many sentence styles.

Of one thing we are certain
from our observations in research classrooms
around the country:
children who have opportunities
to experiment with the shapes of sentences
will never again view reading as a matter
of sounding out isolated words.
They will not easily bog down or stop dead in their tracks
when they come to unknown words
because they will feel the strength of the language know-how
deposited in their linguistic storehouses
both in the form of literary and linguistic patterns
and in the form of worthwhile generalizations
about how language works
which they formulate in experimentation and discussion.

E)   Rearranging Sentences

As we have already discussed,
ours is a word-order language.
The function of a word is highly dependent
on its position in the sentence.

> *I never saw a purple cow.*

A person who has listened to English sentences
all of his life, be he seven or seventy,
will hunch that the word *purple*
describes the word *cow*,
falling as it does directly in front of *cow*.
To change the word *the*
from first to second position in this sentence

> *The day is gone.*

destroys the meaning of the sentence
because the structure has been destroyed.
On the other hand,
the structure of some sentences
is not inflexible.

Jan came crying with her broken doll in hand.

can be significantly rearranged within the limitations
of our language system without a loss of meaning:

With her broken doll in hand, Jan came crying.
Jan came, with her broken doll in hand, crying.
Crying, with her broken doll in hand, came Jan.

Let's consider the sentence patterned on internal rhyme
which we enjoyed earlier in this discussion:

1) You can take a tub

2) with a rub

3) and a scrub

4) in a two-foot tank of tin.

This sentence can be easily rearranged 2– 3– 1– 4
without destroying the structure or meaning.
You probably see other possibilities for rearranging,
while retaining the structure and meaning.
Consider the following sentence in the same light.
You readily can see multiple possibilities
for rearranging this sentence:

A truck came bumping
along the shore road,
its headlights shining
through the weeds.

—from "The Web of Winter," *Sounds of Mystery*

When you work with sentences this way on the chalkboard,
be sure to invite the children to make judgments
as to which arrangement they prefer.
This is germane to developing a personal style in writing,
for it is only by putting words together
in ways that are consistent with personality
that a person develops a *style* of writing.

Rearranging sentences is one of the many structural activities
that mark *Sounds of Language* as a comprehensive linguistic program.
Unlike some linguistic programs
that focus primarily on the shape of words,
Sounds of Language accepts realistically the fact
that the sentence is the basic unit of meaning in our language
and that an understanding of sentence structure
is basic to intaking sentence meaning.

Rearranging sentences best begins
with a recognition of the clusters of words
which are arranged in a particular way
to create the basic shape of the sentence.
Once a sentence has been divided into chunks of meaning,
a useful question is:

> *Children, do you see any clusters of words in this sentence*
> *which could be moved around?*

This awareness of movable parts in a sentence
helps children in reading long and difficult sentences.
Not only do they learn to read through it one chunk at a time,
but they also learn,
if a sentence has a difficult beginning,
to start reading the sentence at an easier point
and later pick up the more difficult chunks
when they have some sentence context to help them.
In unlocking this sentence, for example,
a child who has gained skill in rearranging sentences
will not bog down on the introductory chunk of meaning
if the words are unfamiliar to him.

Pressing his lithe body

against the plastered wall,

he listened

and heard Nag and Nagaina

whispering together

outside in the moonlight.

—"Rikki Tikki Tavi," *Sounds of Mystery*

Rather, he will skip down to the third chunk,
he listened,
which offers a more direct entry into the sentence.
Certain children have intuitively done this
as the natural way for making a go of a book,
until narrow reading instruction cuts them off
from this sensible, linguistically sound way
for handling complex print,
and instead teaches them to stop dead in their tracks
while they try to sound out each word
in that complicated first chunk of meaning.

Throughout *Sounds of Language* you will find
type arranged in unique and intriguing patterns—
part of our scheme to invite children
to use chunks of meaning to unlock
the linguistic puzzle.

I LOVE YOU, BIG WORLD. I wish I could call you And tell you a secret: That I love you, World... I love you, World...

by *Paul Wollner*

AGE 7

UNITED STATES

—from *Sounds of a Powwow*

8 FIGURING OUT
HOW WORDS WORK

In basal reading programs and phonics programs
children spend their waking hours
considering the various ways in which words work.
In fact, in most of these programs
the word seems to be the only unit of language
worth studying.
Children learn about beginnings of words
and ends of words and middles of words.
They learn about special endings such as inflected endings.
They learn how the various letters behave in words.
And all of this they learn (or try to learn)
in line with prescriptive lesson plans
laid out in the teacher's guide.
When it is beginning consonant season,
heaven help the child who is good at looking at ends of words.
In some programs, children have to wait to beginning second grade
to even know that words have middles,
because that is when the teacher's guide
presents medial vowels.
Moreover, the methods used in teaching about words
are largely prescriptive.
Children are not invited to experiment with words
and come up with their own generalizations.
They are asked to memorize other people's generalizations
about what happens when two vowels go walking,
even though we all know that the first one does the talking
only when it feels in the mood.

You may or may not be using one of these programs
in your classroom.
Whether you do or not,
you and your children still need
the kind of spontaneous word analysis time
that is made possible with the *Sounds of Language* program.

In the same way that the children figure out
how stories and poems and sentences work
by experimenting with structures and verbalizing their discoveries,
children need to use their self-selected ways
for figuring out how words work.

Sometimes your open-ended questioning after reading a story or poem
will trigger discussions
which help children figure out how words pattern.
Supposing you have read:

One Misty, Moisty Morning

When cloudy was the weather,

I chanced to meet an old man

Clothed all in leather.

He began to compliment

And I began to grin:

"How do you do?"

And "How do you do?"

And "How do you do?" again.

—from *Sounds of Numbers*

After you and the children have thoroughly enjoyed the poem
through oral and various arrangements of choral reading
and after the children are using books
so their eyes are seeing the same patterns that their ears are hearing,
you might ask:

> *Children, what do you see interesting*
> *about those two words* misty *and* moisty?

Accept any observations the children care to make.

Misty, Moisty

If Henry tells you that they both
have *y* at the end,
don't become ill at ease
if you are only studying beginning consonants
in your other reading program.
Some children are better at observing the ends of words
than they are at observing the beginnings of words
when they first start looking at print.
If these children learn
that nice boys don't look at the ends of words
simply because a prescriptive phonics program
is insisting on beginning sounds,
they begin to feel that there is something wrong
about them and reading
and they learn not to focus on the patterns of words
and certainly not to report their observations
if they do take a look.
How much better to praise Henry
for his accurate observation.

> *Henry, you're so great*
> *at looking at the ends of words.*
> *Perhaps you can find something else interesting*
> *about the way* misty *and* moisty *end.*

By now Henry is with you full force.
And on the heels of his success
in looking at the ends of words,
he can probably also be invited
to take a look at the beginnings of the two words.
By now some child will probably report to you,

> *Look.* Moisty *is bigger in the middle.*

Now the children have come face-to-face
with an interesting generalization about the ways words work.
They have beginnings and endings and middles.

nggallopinggallopinggallopinggallopinggallopinggallopinggal
ggallopinggallopinggallopinggallopinggallopinggallopinggallo
allopinggallopinggallopinggallopinggallopinggallopinggallopi

The generalization has meaning
because in the first place,
they were scrutinizing the printed form
of two words that entered their linguistic storehouses
through the heat and drama of read-aloud.
They are not just cold words on a workbook page.
They are words the children truly own.
The generalization also has meaning
because the children were able to sneak up on it,
as it were,
knowing it intuitively from their experiences
with oral language
and gradually verbalizing this facet
of the shape of words they are seeing in print.

One useful question
for getting this kind of discussion going is simply:

> *Children, what do you see interesting*
> *about the words on this page?*

As the children report observations
about how letters fall next to one another in words
you will have an interesting diagnostic
of who the individual children are as word-unlockers.
The child who reports seeing three words
that "all have two t's in the middle"
is telling you that he sees letter patterns in words.
The child who reports a word
"that looks just like a fish,"
may be telling you that he is one of those children
who goes into reading by seeing pictures in words
rather than spelling patterns.
How exciting!

from a word design from *Sounds of a Distant Drum*

ggallopinggallopinggallopinggallopinggallopinggallopinggallo
gallopinggallopinggallopinggallopinggallopingg allopinggallop
llopinggallopinggallopinggallopinggallopinggallopinggallopin

One productive activity
in helping primary children figure out how words work
(as well as how sentences work),
is to invite them to collect word cards
that they especially want.
This is markedly different from handing out
the same word cards to all children
with the requirement that they learn the word
as part of their basal reading program.
In this latter approach, it is the teacher who is reaching out,
trying to capture the child
and get him to learn the word selected by the teacher's guide.
When children ask for word cards of their own choosing,
they are the ones doing the reaching-out
and consequently the motivation comes from within themselves
rather than from the pressures of the outside world.
Children the nation over
demonstrated to us what they can be like
when they are invited to claim interesting words as their own.
The culture offered children the word

Supercalifragilisticexpialidocious

on the wings of a song.
We didn't tell the children they had to learn the word
before they were allowed to sing the song.
We didn't tell them that
if they were in the low reading group
we would give them a small, uninteresting word
to take the place of this complex, exciting word.
And the children responded to our freely given invitation.
It was so exciting going around the country
while "Mary Poppins" was in full swing.
The children demonstrated how they can behave
when their love of words is rewarded
by a truly worthwhile offering.
Not only could they read supercalifragilisticexpialidocious.
They could count the syllables and spell it backwards!

Words in the *Sounds of Language* reading program
are thought of as the personal possessions of each child.
At the end of reading a story or poem
you need only ask:

> *Did anyone hear a word*
> *you would like as your own?*

Once you give a child a word card
for each of his favorite words or phrases,
the fun begins!
Children will compare words.
They will swap with one another.
They will ask you for a blank card
to copy a friend's word.
They will arrange their word cards in patterns that

1) begin alike,
2) sound alike,
3) end alike.

They will create sentences on their desks.
Their favorite words are apt to appear
in their drawings and in their speech.

And you—think of the possibilities
for your involvement!
One bright, sunshiny morning you might announce:

> *Boys and girls,*
> *you'll never guess what I did last night.*
> *I sat up writing parts of sentences.*
> *When I hold one of these parts*
> *up in the air, if you have a word*
> *that will finish the sentence,*
> *hold it up.*

Suddenly your room will come alive
with thirty different sentences
as children hold up word cards to complete
a provocative sentence starter such as:

> *Someday I am going to kiss a* _____.

Cinderella

astronaut

skinny

afternoon

dinosaur

wago

dragon

magician

musician

piccolo player

scientific

horse face

Figuring Out How Words Work TE 97

Another day you might suggest:

Children, do you know what let's do today?
Let's put one rubber band
around the word cards you do recognize
and one around the words you don't.
Then supposing you choose
one unknown word each day
to work on and change over to your known words.

On other days the children can arrange their words alphabetically,
can group them with rubber bands
as naming words, action words, and describing words.
You can tell from this discussion,
that giving children word cards
is not the end,
but rather the beginning of a whole host
of language encounters
that help children claim the glory and workings of words.
Although it is true that filling out word cards
demands effort on your part,
you will find yourself basking in the rich rewards.
How exciting to have children ask for and value new words,
and through innate curiosity about things they value,
to analyze these words down to their most unique characteristic.
By the way, if you think alphabetizing
is the preferred way for arranging and filing word cards,
you may want to listen to your children.
Children have been known to make arrangements of

exciting words,
    letter writing words,
story writing words,
    hard words,
easy words,
    and even last week's words.

Interestingly enough, when children themselves
decide on methods of categorizing and filing,
they know exactly where to look for the word they need.

Those of you who teach older boys and girls
may be wondering how you can offer
the joy and productivity of word cards.
Actually, older boys and girls
have been known to do this same kind
of self-selected word collecting
with various kinds of word lists in their notebooks.
A boy who keeps a list of describing words worth using
when you want to indicate whether you're for or against a team,
is more highly motivated
than the boy who is idly writing sentences
using a list of *today's new words.*
Throughout the *Sounds of Language* program,
children are helped to analyze
the printed characteristics of words.
Surprisingly enough,
the most useful investigation
does not necessarily focus on beginnings and endings and middles.
In terms of a child's natural way for moving into print,
the first step in word analysis
is to hear and say the word orally
and count the number of syllables.
The sound of a word is its most unique characteristic
and it tends to be reflected in the printed symbol.
Let's pronounce and take a look at the word *station:*

The workmen
are going to build
a new police station here.

sta/tion

Ear and eye work comfortably together
in the word *station.*
It is easy to hear that there are two parts.
What are the useful steps to take in word analysis?

First: *"Let's listen to the word station, Chuck.*
              How many sounds do you hear?"

Second: *"Look at the word, Chuck. (sta/tion)*
              I am writing it on the chalkboard the way you say it."

Third: *"Now read the sentence in which you found the word, Chuck.*
              Do you hear two sounds in station?"

Fourth: *You move from here to any next sensible step.*
              It might be to look
              at that intriguing tion syllable

          "Let's look at some other two-syllable words
           that look something like the word station.

sta	**tion**
na	**tion**
no	**tion**

Who knows where you go from here?
It might be to other two-syllable words
in the story, "The House Biter."
It might be to the wonderful
four-syllable word *education*
or to the intriguing *stationary*
that carries the original word *station.*

But whatever sequence you take,
you must be secure in the fact
that you can follow your own hunches
and your own common sense
in response to clues given by the children.
Children love to analyze a word they have discovered
in the context of a meaningful language pattern.
Let's not fool ourselves into believing
that there is only one sequence in word analysis.
Individual children and teachers have their own continuities
and this program invites you to respect these differences.

Then along came ALITTLEFISH

9 FIGURING OUT HOW PRINT WORKS

When a child looks at a page of print,
something dynamic must happen if we hope for him to become
an intelligent, self-motivated reader.
Oh, we can force him to read as we do in many programs,
but unless he himself elects to explore the page of print
in an effort to make sense out of it,
we can safely assume
that he is not learning much about reading.
The traditional answer to this
has been simply to write stories with scaled vocabulary
so that a child's eyes will immediately see familiar words,
but there is much more
that can encourage a child to explore a page of print
than the sighting of familiar words.

You will discover that on many pages of *Sounds of Language* readers
the type swells, lurches, screams, whispers,
undulates, turns somersaults,
and even subsides in pictorial and narrative context.

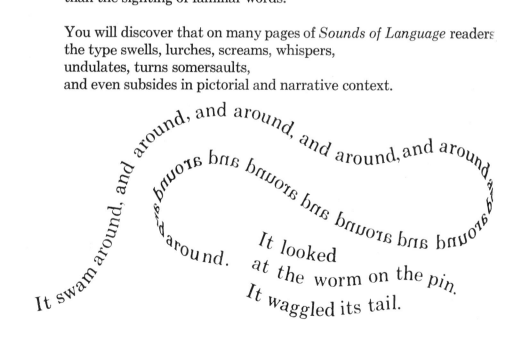

It swam around, and around, and around, and around, and around, and around, and around, and around, and around. It looked at the worm on the pin. It waggled its tail.

FOOD, GLORIOUS' FOOD! HOT SAUSAGE & MUSTARD!

—from *Sounds of a Distant Drum*

Having type behave in intriguing ways is not foreign to children.
We adults have grown accustomed to schoolbooks
where the same size and style of type
move relentlessly from left to right, page after page,
and it is easy to forget that today's children are encountering
imaginative and flamboyant uses of type on TV,
in magazine advertising
and even on their cereal boxes.

Watch children's faces as they follow the dancing type
in "*Ten Little Indians*" from *Sounds I Remember.*
Notice how intently their eyes move with the type
and how their spirits buoy with the playful design.
In impressive ways these young children are learning
the most basic characteristic of type—
it moves from one place to another.

The sad fact is,
most of the early reading programs,
with their insistence on a rigid left-to-right
non-varying pattern of print,
actually cut children off from a fundamental cultural experience
which tells children that print is
a very versatile and exciting human invention
which to a large degree bends itself to the desires of the user.
Rules about beginning on the left and moving to the right
are not impressive invitations into the world of print.
It is a child's recognition that type moves,
a recognition that most easily comes
from pages where the movement is exaggerated,
and his determination to figure out the plan
back of the typographical puzzle
that motivate a child to make a go of reading.
Once he is caught up in the excitement
of following the movement of type as he reads,
he will himself come to the generalization
that for the most part in the English language,
type does move from left to right.

As you leaf through the *Sounds of Language* books,
you will discover that in addition to other
exciting typographical innovations,
the type generally is set in the pattern of spoken language,
just as the type in this essay
has been printed in facsimiles of oral language patterns.
Various methods have been used
to cause the reader to focus attention on selected words,

i   t relationships.
  m   n
    p   e
      o   r
        r   e
          t   h
            a   n
              n   n
                t ideas, and i

And now for a moment of frankness . . .
When you first looked at this series of books,
did you realize that it was for purposes
of helping children figure out how print works
that the books were designed as they are?
Children are curious about how print works,
just as they were curious about how spoken language works.
The *Sounds of Language* readers reward this curiosity
by helping children relate all that they know about spoken language
as they unravel the secrets of print
and make these secrets work for them.
You will want to help the children verbalize
their adventures with print in the *Sounds of Language* readers.

*Children, can you see the shapes of those words
slurpy and glurpy? Take a close look.*

—from *Sounds Around the Clock*

and I, Trotting to market with cheeses and pie, Trotting to
market with cheeses and pie, Hey la la, Ho la, My donkey
and I. Hey la la, Ho la, Oh Donkey take care, If you should
stumble, we'll never get there, Hey la la, Ho la, My donkey
never get there, Hey la la, Ho la, Oh Donkey take care. Hey la
la, Ho la, If no one should buy, we'll eat those cheeses, And we'll
eat that pie, Hey la la, Ho la, If you should stumble, we'll
My donkey and I, We'll eat those cheeses, If no one should buy.

An old song, author unknown. painting by Vic Herman

—from *Sounds After Dark*

As the children pore over this especially designed page,
they are role-playing in exaggerated fashion
the fact that if a person studies the puzzle of a page of print
he will discover signals and patterns
that help him decode what he is encountering.

In a similar way
when a child looks at the printed page of the old song above
and says, "I know where that song begins,"
he is showing that he has found enough clues
to get a start on unravelling the puzzle.
Which clues worked for him?
Was it the capital letter? Starting on the left?
The space in the lower left-hand corner?
The actual clues he found do not matter as much as the fact
that he expects his search to be rewarded.

Figuring Out How Print Works TE 105

One indication that the children are beginning
to make typographical arrangements work for them
is their experimentation with intriguing arrangements
of words and letters and numbers in their own writing.
The more children can get the notion that written language
is an exciting and dependable puzzle
with multiple clues for the person who is reading,
the more confident and successful they will be
in their independent reading.

For the psychological advantages as well as for pure enjoyment,
from time to time write on the board
familiar sentences in reverse direction,
in scattered fields of letters,
in upright rocketing,
in straight downward plunges,
in crisscross fashion.
And even upside down and backwards.

Then watch the children delight
as they put all of their linguistic skills
into the decoding of the language.
It is dramatic experiences like these
that stand children in good stead
as they engage in the routine aspects of decoding.
Children will work at identifying initial consonants
or medial vowels or moving from left to right
with more personal determination and pleasure
when they see such activities
as part of the larger and more exciting process
of figuring out the puzzle of print.

10 DEVELOPING SKILL IN COMPREHENSION

Contrary to the view of many reading programs,
comprehension is not merely a matter
of the reader's proving that he has "read" the selection.

All too often this kind of proving simply means
listing main events, main characters, key words,
character traits, and snatches of figurative language.
Comprehension activities takes on true character
when they involve the reader or listener in such ways
that he comes to grips
with his and his colleagues' personal interpretations
in relation to the author's intended meanings.
If you care about this kind of comprehension,
much depends on the kind of questions you ask children.
For example, a question like

How far did John walk?

has only one possible answer to children
who have just read that John walked six miles.
Even if a child gives the "correct" answer,
what has he actually gained from this "educative process"?
As a matter of fact, the first child who gives the answer
closes the discussion.
The "educative process" comes to a close.
There is nowhere else the discussion could possibly go.
And how smart some children are in knowing
which children in the group will give the *correct answers* first!
Many simply do not expect to participate
in unimaginative rituals of this kind,
and gladly play the role of passive observers
because the situation structures such roles.

Think, on the other hand, what happens to children
if the teacher accepts the fact
that she doesn't have to make the children prove
that they have read the story threadbare,
and, therefore, can ask intriguing comprehension questions,
such as,

> *Children, the story says John walked six miles.*
> *How far is six miles?*

Every child now—even those who read less well than others—
views himself as an active participant in the discussion
and will gladly contribute his thoughts and feelings,
knowing that the purpose is to examine and probe personal meanings.

You may want to ask yourself if your questions
are the kind that stimulate thoughtful discussions
by which each reader can evaluate the meanings
he gleaned from and brought to the story.
Nothing is more exciting, more conducive to learning,
than to participate in a cross-fire of opinions and ideas
generated by a common experience, such as story meanings.
Here are some examples of questions
that will trigger off lively discussions
that will contribute to children's comprehension of the world
in which they live:

> *How long is a person young?*

The story "Growing Up, Growing Older" says,

> *John is now a young man.*
> *He is eighteen years old.*

How easy and unrewarding it would be to ask:

> *How old was John when he was a young man?*

A child could answer *18 years old* and be correct,
but what kind of thinking,
what kind of language usage,
what kind of mental and emotional involvements
does his answer promote?

The openness of a true comprehension question invites children
to put everything they know about life
(in this case, what constitutes being young or old)
into their answer.
It also invites all children to participate in the discussion,
not only he who happens to speak first.
And make no mistake!
When you ask children how long a person is young,
you are going to get an array of life-related answers.
Many a child feels old at six,
and anyone old enough to go to college is positively antiquated.

Your comprehension questions about a story
will trigger off a whole hierarchy of meanings
ranging from gross understanding to precise verbalizing,
from a simple restatement of story meanings
to a complex conjecture about the whole realm of living.

Annotated in *Sounds of Laughter* for the consideration of both you
and the children is the question:

> *Is it hard not to speak in anger*
> *when your heart is filled with anger?*

The children have just been reading
the story of an Indian boy and his grandfather
and they have heard the grandfather advise the boy
not to speak in anger.
But the concern of the moment is not the grandfather's advice.
The concern is the feelings of the alive children in your classroom
who are encountering this advice.
We must not assume that comprehension can be measured
only in terms of "correct" answers to tight little questions.
The important thing is,
each child is pitting his own meanings against the author's
and gradually coming to know what the story means to him.
The cross-pollenation that occurs
in such discussions
also invites children to question their own meanings
and even to organize new meanings.

Here are some examples of questions
that should trigger lively discussions
that will both focus the literary experience
and contribute to children's comprehension of human behavior.

A) *Why does the author suggest that on Halloween night*
it is "just as well" to answer civilly
when one is asked a question?
"Tomson's Halloween," *Sounds of a Young Hunter*

B) *If Bill held an after-school job for which he was paid a salary,*
would he, after finding the trapped duck, have
ignored the reporting-in time, just as he did
when it was time to report in to his mother at dark?
Would you? "The Web of Winter," *Sounds of Mystery*

C) *Do you like Mr. Lincoln better with or without a beard?*
Why? "A Vote for a Beard," *Sounds of a Young Hunter*

D) *Well, children, what do you think*
of a free-wheeling literary-artistic-dramatic-boisterous
story like this?
"How Old Stormalong Captured Mocha Dick," *Sounds of a Distant Drum*

Another insightful way of getting into
a full-blown discussion of story meanings
is to ask questions that relate to the author or artist's techniques
of putting a story or a picture together.

A) *A comparison of the descriptive line in "Facts About*
Angry Bears"
with the dramatic story line in "Little Balser and the
Big Bear"
(or any other comparison of a factual article
with a story with a strong plot), for example,
will reveal much of children's understanding of the
selections,
although, ostensibly, they are discussing literary
structure. —from *Sounds of a Young Hunter*

B) *What has the artist done in this picture to convey to you that this is a make-believe story?*
"Proud Peacock," *Sounds Jubilee*

C) *What clues do you get from the title and the illustrations as to what kind of reading you will find in this selection?*
"The Birth and Growth of a Tree," *Sounds of a Distant Drum*

Enough comprehension questions have been annotated
throughout this program
to give you the feel of framing open-ended questions
that promote a depth of comprehension and feelings of self-respect.
Once you have experienced
the dynamics of a vital group discussion,
in contrast to a boring kind of question-answer ritual,
you will be well on your way to becoming that kind of teacher
whom children remember and revere.
The art of good teaching has deep roots
in the ability to motivate meaningful discussions.
Of course, post reading discussions are not the only way
for children to organize their reading meanings.
When the fourth grade teacher reads

Giant Thunder striding home

wonders if his supper's done.

'*Hag wife, Hag wife, bring me my bones!*'

'*They are not done,*' the old hag moans.

'*Not done? not done?*' the giant roars

and heaves his old wife out of doors.

and Bill blurts out "*Sounds just like my father!*"
it is not necessary to ask a lot of tight little questions
about who came striding home and what wasn't done.
Bill's comprehension is proved in his spontaneous response
and the laughter of his classmates
is ample proof that Bill's comprehension is shared.

When the kindergarten teacher opens to the title page
of an honest-to-goodness spooky book
and Therese promptly gets up from her place
at the teacher's feet
and moves as far away from the book as possible
while still remaining in hearing range,
there is little doubt but that Therese understands
the mood of the story.
And as the story progresses
and Therese keeps moving back and forth—
now near the book, now far away—
she is using her entire body
to express her comprehension of the story.
Six-year-old Brenda's spontaneous response to A. A. Milne's line

So I think I'll be six now for ever and ever.

—from *Sounds Around the Clock*

needs no explanation.

I do not want to be six
for ever because I want to be
a nurse because I want to help
people and a whole gob of
people will say thank you. Brenda

—1st Grade, J. J. Ingalls School, Kansas City, Kansas

Children are bubbling with spontaneous responses
to stories and poems until they learn
that there is only one thing that happens
after reading a story:
the teacher asks questions.
If your children do not seem to respond spontaneously
and you have a notion it is because
they are in this other habit of thinking about story response,
you may have to be the one in your class who responds
spontaneously to a story
in order to get the whole spontaneous,
personalized reaction-thing going.
After reading about John and his six mile walk,
for example, if you slap yourself on the thigh
and exclaim

WOW! What an idiot!

and in other ways role-play the fact
that this kind of responding is a legitimate way
for showing comprehension,
the children will soon pick up the invitation
and reading time will take on more life.

And of course you are aware
that painting and dancing and creative dramatics
are also productive ways
for organizing personal meanings
brought into play by a story or poem or article.

One last thought about comprehension.
You may be interested to reread our discussion
FIGURING OUT HOW STORIES AND POEMS WORK, page 24.
And **FIGURING OUT HOW SENTENCES WORK,** page 56.
In both of these teaching strategies
are numerous suggestions
of times when the structure of a story or poem or sentence
deeply influences the meaning.
Those of us who study language in human affairs
can only conclude that structure is itself
one expression of meaning.

The post-reading discussions in *Sounds of Language*
that are triggered off by the open-ended comprehension questions
and by certain language-analysis questions

A) put each child in touch with his own thoughts and
feelings that have been generated by the reading,

B) put him in touch with the feelings and thoughts
of other children who supposedly shared an "identical"
reading experience, and

C) help him verbalize his growing insights
into the workings of language, both in oral and written
form.

The child's self-expressions, therefore, have a rare dynamic quality
as he searches for verbal ways to express the inner growth
that his reading occasioned.
Every speaking skill he employs,
everything from sentence patterns to figures of speech,
is influenced by the integrity of his speaking situation.
His *preciseness* in self-expression, therefore,
actually is preciseness in making language work to express
and thereby validate his own personality.

11 LINKING WRITING TO READING

In *Sounds of Language* children are helped
to develop writing skills
in the same naturalistic, linguistically sound ways
that they learn to read.
Just as kindergarteners and young first graders
latch on to highly structured rhymes and stories
and role-play themselves as readers,
these same young children begin innovating
on the author's pattern and role-play themselves as writers.

Hello! My name is Pamela, K.
I am a maker of costumes.
I make funny costumes and scary
costumes. These are the
costumes I make.

—2nd Grade, J. J. Ingalls School
Kansas City, Kansas

Gradually they learn to use their *Sounds of Language* books
as resource books for personal writing.
They know that these books are crammed
with story patterns and rhyme schemes and sentence patterns
that are theirs for the asking.
They also know that they have the practical know-how,
transforming sentences, for example,
for taking an author's structure
and hanging their own thoughts on it.

As one young child exultantly declared
after borrowing the literary structure
and sentence patterns of "The Billy Goats Gruff"
to successfully write his own story about three skunks
who encountered a troll on their way to eat garbage:

I only needed three new words

for my whole story—

skunk

and garbage

and smelly.

I almost needed the word stinked

so I could say

the skunk stinked the troll,

but I remembered

you gave me the word skunk

and I could use that to say

the skunk skunked *him.*

—from Mueller School, second grade, Wichita, Kansas

Once children become accustomed to using their reader this way,
you will be amazed by both the quality and quantity
of their writing.
Moreover, you will have a solution to the nagging problem
of what kinds of "seat work" to provide the rest of the class
while you are busy with a few children.

12 CULTIVATING LITERARY AND ESTHETIC APPRECIATION

The content of the *Sounds of Language* readers
is specifically planned to place literary appreciation
at the heart of the reading program.
From the very first day of first grade
throughout the entire elementary school experience,
children using *Sounds of Language* readers
will be living in the midst of a gallery of contemporary art
and in a climate of literary appreciation
that sensitize their responses and imprint their memories
with high idealism and soul-stirring emotions.

Esthetic response can only be nurtured.
It cannot be taught.
By a wide and continuing exposure
to stories, poems, art, photos, and language
that possess some pretension to taste,
children will begin to know what they do and do not like.
Knowing what one does not like
is equally important as knowing what one enjoys.
Whatever else, a child's response must be self-selected,
and it must be sincere.
We teachers need to learn how to live with children's responses
which move against the grain of our own preferences
and which reveal pleasure in the mundane.
Many children, for example, will necessarily go
through a long period of literary exposure
before they are apt to sense the worthwhileness
of Emily Dickinson's poem "Autumn"
as compared to the joy they found in their favorite comics.

Be assured that those pleasurable times of the day
when you read aloud to children
are all a part of a program in literary and esthetic appreciation,
as well as a part of the reading program.

One especially productive technique
for helping children make these kinds of value judgments
comes about through an adaptation of Sidney Simon's value line
suggested in the drawing on the opposite page.
Simply list a few of the stories and/or poems and/or articles
the children have been reading
and suggest that they rate each one
by placing it in a self-selected spot
on their own copy of the value line.
In order to help the children understand
that the value line is not an instrument
for placing one selection at the low end of the line,
another at the high end,
and the rest at equal intervals along the line,
you might want to engage them in conversation
about their use of the line.
Help them understand that the value line
does not only apply to the seven stories
they are rating at this time.
The value line has places for all the stories
they have or ever will read.
The seven stories they are rating today
might all fall at the middle or top of the line.
Or they might scatter up and down the line.
You see, the value line is actually part of each of us.
It is man's way
for placing a value on things he encounters in life.
The value line might be used to rate happenings
or foods or school subjects or teachers or movies, etc.
The important thing to remember is—
there is no special ruler to measure the experiences of such stories, etc.
and to place them on the value line.
It is a person's response from his value
that places them one place or another on the value line.

Don't try to tell the children all about the line
at one sitting.
Put the line on the board
and start using it informally,

asking the children for suggestions
as to where some of the stories might fall.
As you talk together and the children differ
about certain ratings,
they will come to understand how the line works.
After a few minutes, suggest that they draw their own lines
and place the seven stories where they want them.

1) *Magic Fishbone*

2) *The Power of Eye*

3) *The Grandmother Story*

4) *The Buck and the Old Man*

5) *How the Camel Got His Hump*

6) *The First Schlmiel*

7) *Every Man Heart Lay Down*

—selections from *Sounds Jubilee*

LOW   MID   HIGH

Once the children have placed the stories somewhere on the line,
the fun begins.
Invite the children to meet as a group
to discuss their various placements.
How your classroom will ring with developing values
as the children explain and even defend
their various designations on the line!
And what a basic learning for the children
when they discover that three people can read the very same story
and come up with highly different evaluations—
all of which can be defended.
They might even deduce that if three different teachers
rather than just one gave them report card grades,
they would come up with differing marks.
What a nice blow to the righteousness of report card grades!

13 DEVELOPING SENSITIVITY TO THE THREE LEVELS OF LANGUAGE

Sounds of Language rejects the notion of "right" and "wrong"
in judging a child's language performance.
We recognize, instead, that there are three levels of language
that every child has a right
to experiment with, enjoy, and claim as his own.

A) Home-Rooted Language

The first level of language,
indigenous to the child's life itself,
is his *home-rooted (in-group) language.*
This language may or may not be grammatically correct.
It is the language he inherited from his family,
the language that is native to his soul
and sounds best to his ear.
This language may or may not feed comfortably
into the classroom,
but if we want our classrooms to be language laboratories
where a child feels free to experiment
with new linguistic patterns,
we must first of all respect the language he brings to school.
Both you and the children may be surprised to see
the number of selections in *Sounds of Language*
that are written in *home-rooted language.*
This can help both you and the children
better respect vernacular for its beauty
and for its direct communicative impact.
Isn't it fortunate that folklore
has helped us keep the richness of home-rooted language
in the bloodstream of our language heritage!

A copperhead snake made for me
one day when I was hoein' my corn.
Happened I saw him in time,
and I lit into him with the hoe.

He thrashed around,
bit the hoe-handle a couple of times,
but I fin'lly killed him.
Hung him on the fence.
Went on back to work,

—from "The Snakebit Hoe-handle," *Sounds of a Young Hunter*

For a picture of what linguistic heights
young children can reach
when their home-rooted language is respected,
see the dictated story from a young primary child
on the next page.
Obviously someone had read "The Billy Goats Gruff"
to this child, and just as obviously,
the child stored the basic structure of the story
in his linguistic storehouse.
Notice how faithful he is to the fact
that this is a story organized around a problem.
How faithful he is to the repetition in the episodes!
How faithful he is to the solving of the problem!
If the school had *made* him feel uncomfortable about his language,
he would have "dried up" and looked like one of those "children
without language"
we hear so much about.
We ourselves wonder if it is so much a matter
of "children without language"
as it is a matter of children who have been asked in effect
to check their home-rooted language outside the classroom door.

Them all going up to the grass where you eat and the mean old troll said "Who walkin' on my bridge?" I comin' up to eat you and little Billy Goat said "Don't eat me. Wait for my next brother to come.

So da troll said O.K. I will wait. So he waited and the next brother comed and the big old troll said who walkin on my bridge. Me, next billy goat Gruff. Wait don't eat me wait.

Then boomp boomp I comin up to eat you. So he did. He tossed the mean old troll up to the sky and eat him all up.

B) Public Language

The second level of language is *public language*.
This is the corps of language ways
that society uses to carry on its organized life.
It is the grammatically correct language that facilitates
broad and precise communication with the English-speaking community.
When standards of "right" and "wrong" are used
to evaluate language (heaven forbid!)
public language is the form that is said to be "right."
Public language should not be made available to children,
on the basis of "right" and "wrong,"
but rather as one of three ways to express themselves.

Different situations call for different kinds of language.
Just as public language works best in some situations,
so does home-rooted language in others.
When a child knows that he has a choice in language usage,
public language for him gains intrigue and respect.
Many articles and essays in *Sounds of Language* are written
in public language
to help children appreciate its direct, uncluttered, and practical
effectiveness.

Most of the Indian tribes
of the early American frontier
lived by hunting buffalo
and other animals.
These tribes were wanderers.
They were good hunters
and fierce warriors.

—from *Sounds of a Distant Drum*

Westfield, Chautauque Co NY
Oct 15,1860
Hon A B Lincoln
Dear Sir
My father has just come from
the fair and brought home
your picture and mr Hamlin's.

—from *Sounds of a Young Hunter*

The children may be interested in discussing
why Grace Bedell chose public language
when writing her letter to Abraham Lincoln.
This can lead to a discussion
of whether certain home-rooted expressions
might be appropriate in a letter to a best friend, to a stranger.
These discussions of language choices
give children feelings of power and pleasure
about themselves as language users.

C) Life-Lifting Language

Sing hey! Sing hey!
For Christmas Day
Twine mistletoe and holly
For friendship glows
In winter snows,
And so let's all be jolly.

— an old rhyme from *Sounds of a Young Hunter*

The third level of language is *life-lifting (literary) language.*
It is any bit or unit of language,
such as a story or poem or expression,
that is so memorable that it tends
to impress itself indelibly on the mind
and thereby become part of the culture's cherished language ways.

In
December   *"Get*
autumn   *ready*
calls   *for a*
its   *winter*
warning,   *morning!"*

It has been our experience
that many children whose home-rooted language
does not open-end comfortably into the public language
take on the public forms more easily
through poetry and other literature
than they do in lessons on public language.

Peck

    peck

      peck

on the warm brown egg.

OUT comes a neck.

OUT comes a leg.

    How

      does

        a chick,

who's not been about,

discover the trick

of how to get out?

—"Baby Chick" by Aileen Fisher,
Sounds of Numbers

Consider the language thrust that any child will receive
if, throughout his elementary school years,
he has such broad and continuous exposure to memorable language
that he intakes into his mind's treasury
twenty or more poems a year.
This experience in and of itself
provides a major bridge for any child
into the culture's language storehouse,
and, at the same time, fills his mind
with high idealism and humanistic feelings.
The pervasive use of choral reading and choral speaking
in *Sounds of Language* is geared to this end.

Speak gently, Spring, and make no sudden sound;

For in my windy valley, yesterday I found

New-born foxes squirming on the ground—

    Speak gently.

—from "Four Little Foxes" by Lew Sarett,
Sounds of a Storyteller

Developing Sensitivity to the Three Levels of Language TE 125

All: We sing of thee, America,
         Land we love, America,
         Hear our song of Liberty,
         Our country 'tis of thee.

Narrator: Our country 'tis of thee we sing,
         land of New England meadows and southern cottonfields,
         of county fairs, and ticker-tape parades,
         barefoot boys with fishing rods
         and Ladies' Day at the baseball park.
           A land of steel,
         and industry,
         and invention
         with a heart as big as Texas
         and dreams as tall as the great Northwest.

All: But where did it all begin?
         Who made it possible?

Narrator: Well, to start with
         There was a man . . .

—from "Our Country 'Tis of Thee,"
Sounds of a Distant Drum

Moreover, the choral speaking and choral reading
that children continuously do as part of this reading program
help them develop an appetite for the life-lifting language of literature.
As children's ears begin to know the pleasures
of this kind of language and this kind of reading,
their whole disposition toward life as well as toward literature
is affected.

In developing attitudes of literary discrimination,
each child should be encouraged to keep a running list
of his five favorite stories and poems.
Whenever he wants to add a new favorite to his list,
he necessarily must decide which of his former favorites
must be removed.
Only by exercising his own judgment in these matters,
without interference by an over-anxious adult,
will he gradually refine his sensitivities to literary ways.

Paul Bunyan

A poem by Arthur S. Bourinot

Solo: HE CAME,
STRIDING
OVER THE MOUNTAIN,
THE MOON SLUNG ON HIS BACK,

All: LIKE A PACK,

Solo: A GREAT PINE
STUCK ON HIS SHOULDER
SWAYED AS HE WALKED,
AS HE TALKED
TO HIS BLUE OX
BABE;
A HUGE, LOOMING SHADOW
OF A MAN,

All: CLAD
IN A MACKINAW COAT,
HIS LOGGER'S SHIRT
OPEN AT THE THROAT

Solo: AND THE GREAT MANE OF HAIR

All: MATCHING,
MEETING

Solo: THE LOCKS OF NIGHT,
THE SMOKE FROM HIS CAULDRON PIPE
A CLOUD ON THE MOON,

All: AND HIS LAUGH
ROLLED THROUGH THE MOUNTAINS
LIKE THUNDER
ON A SUMMER NIGHT

Solo: WHILE THE LIGHTNING OF HIS SMILE

All: *Split* THE HEAVENS
ASUNDER.

Sounds of a Distant Drum

14 DEVELOPING SENSITIVITY TO HUMANNESS

Often in classroom teaching
we become so preoccupied with "skill development"
that we tend to forget that the primary purpose of teaching
is to help children claim kinship with man's humanity.
As you use the *Sounds of Language* selections
to create a spiritual setting in your classroom
that inculcates and fosters feelings of individual worth
and high idealism,
you can be assured that you are engaging
in humanly-useful language teaching and "skill development."

For it is *on the wings of words*
that man claims his identity with his culture.
We must help children find access to those words.

Can you imagine, without giving yourself over
to a feeling of great joy and accomplishment,
what will happen to children who for six years
during their elementary school reading experiences
feel the flow and depth of life-lifting language in their daily lives?

And if the *Sounds of Language* program
fulfills all of its expectations,
you and I and every concerned human being
who has dedicated himself to helping children learn
will have developed a camaraderie
that will change the course of language instruction in our schools
and make language truly available to children
in terms of their emerging human needs.